THE LAWYER'S GUIDE

TO BUYING, SELLING, MERGING, AND CLOSING A LAW PRACTICE

SARINA A. BUTLER
RICHARD G. PASZKIET,
EDITORS

GENERAL PRACTICE,
SOLO AND SMALL FIRM DIVISION
SENIOR LAWYERS DIVISION

Cover design by ABA Publishing.

The materials contained herein represent the opinions and views of the authors and/or the editors, and should not be construed to be the views or opinions of the law firms or companies with whom such persons are in partnership with, associated with, or employed by, nor of the American Bar Association or the General Practice, Solo and Small Firm Division, unless adopted pursuant to the bylaws of the Association.

Nothing contained in this book is to be considered as the rendering of legal advice, either generally or in connection with any specific issue or case; nor do these materials purport to explain or interpret any specific bond or policy, or any provisions thereof, issued by any particular franchise company, or to render franchise or other professional advice. Readers are responsible for obtaining advice from their own lawyers or other professionals. This book and any forms and agreements herein are intended for educational and informational purposes only.

© 2008 American Bar Association. All rights reserved.

No part of this publication may be reproduced, stored in a retrieval system, or transmitted in any form or by any means, electronic, mechanical, photocopying, recording, or otherwise, without the prior written permission of the publisher. For permission, contact the ABA Copyrights & Contracts Department at copyright@abanet.org or via fax at 312-988-6030.

Printed in the United States of America.

12 11 10 09 08   5 4 3 2 1

Library of Congress Cataloging-in-Publication Data

The lawyer's guide to buying, selling, merging, and closing a law practice / edited by Sarina Butler.—1st ed.
   p. cm.
   Includes index.
   ISBN 978-1-59031-932-1
   1. Law firms—Economic aspects—United States. 2. Practice of law—United States. 3. Law offices—United States. 4. Consolidation and merger of corporations—Law and legislation—United States. I. Butler, Sarina.

KF315.L38 2007
340.068—dc22

2007037575

Discounts are available for books ordered in bulk. Special consideration is given to state bars, CLE programs, and other bar-related organizations. Inquire at Book Publishing, ABA Publishing, American Bar Association, 321 North Clark Street, Chicago, Illinois 60610-4714. www.ababooks.org

Contents

Preface	xi
About the Editors	xiii
About the Contributors	xv

Chapter 1
Overview of the Sale and Purchase of a Law Practice   1
by Robert Ostertag

I. Introduction	1
Key Points	1
II. History of the Concept: Why We Can Now Sell	1
A. Discussion	3
III. Who May Sell a Law Practice?	3
IV. Who May Purchase a Law Firm?	4
A. What Is a Personal Representative?	4
V. What May Be Sold?	5
A. Covenants Not to Compete	5
VI. Client Issues	6
A. Client's Confidences and Secrets	6
B. Conflicts of Interest	7
VII. Valuation	7
VIII. Payment Plans	8
IX. Other Concerns	8
A. Non-Responsive Clients	8
B. Management of a Deceased Lawyer's Clients	9
C. Malpractice Communication	9
X. Conclusion	10
Further Reading	10

Chapter 2
The Ethical Aspects of Acquiring a Law Practice   11
by Peter Geraghty

I. Introduction	11
Key Points	11

Hypothetical A: Sale of a Law Practice	12
Hypothetical B: Law Firm Merger	12
Hypothetical C: Duties of a Lawyer Who Acquires the Practice of a Deceased Solo Practitioner	12
II. Sale of a Law Practice	13
A. Fees Charged to Clients after Sale of the Law Practice	13
B. What's in a Name?	14
C. Competence	15
D. Avoidance of Conflicts of Interest	15
III. Law Firm Mergers	16
A. The "Hot Potato" Doctrine	16
B. Screening	18
C. ABA Ethics Opinions	19
D. State Bar Opinions	20
IV. Duties of a Lawyer Who Acquires the Practice of a Deceased Sole Practitioner	21
V. Conclusion	23
Forms, Guidelines, and Checklists	23
A. Informal Opinion 1384: Guidelines to the Disposition of Closed or Dormant Client Files	23
Further Reading	24

Chapter 3
Valuation of a Law Practice   25
by James Cotterman

I. Introduction	25
Key Points	25
II. What Is Being Valued—What Is Being Transferred?	25
A. Valuing the Business	26
B. Valuing the Practice	26
III. The Special Problem of a Law Practice	27
A. ABA Guidelines	27
IV. Valuing Partner/Shareholder Interests (The Internal Transfer)	28
V. The Earnings Multiple	28
A. Developing the Standard Multiple	29
B. Adjusting the Multiple	29
C. Structure of Payments	30
D. Insurance	31
VI. Valuing the External Transfer	31
VII. Value the Business	31
VIII. Value the Practice	32
A. Internal Transfers and Past Transactions	32
B. Multiple of Income Approach	32
C. Capitalized Cash Flows	33

D. Capitalized Excess Earnings		33
IX. Structuring the Deal		34
X. The Seller's Perspective		34
XI. Conclusion		34
Forms, Guidelines, and Checklists		35
A. Checklist: Items to Consider When Valuing the Business		35
B. Revenue Multipliers for Law Firms		36
C. Earnings Multipliers for Law Firms		36
D. Revenue Multiplier—Adjusted Profit Margin/Adjusted Earnings Equivalents		36
Further Reading		36

Chapter 4

Setting a Price on a Law Practice: Checklist for Valuation — 37
by Shannon Pratt

I. Introduction	37
II. Checklist for Valuing a Law Practice	37
A. The Assignment	37
B. Appraiser(s)	38
C. Documents and Information	38
D. Normalizing the Financial Statements	39
E. Evaluation of Buyer	39
F. Valuation Methods	39
G. Questions to Ask	40

Chapter 5

Tax Consequences of "Retiring" a General Partner's Interest in a Law Partnership — 41
by John Clynch

I. Introduction	41
Key Points	41
II. Description of a Partnership	42
III. Retirement of a Partner: Section 736	43
IV. Brief History of Section 736	45
V. Section 736 and Self-Employment Tax, Covenants Not to Compete, Installment Payments, and Passive Activity Losses	48
A. Self-Employment Tax	48
B. Covenants Not to Compete	48
C. Installment Payments	49
D. Passive Activity Losses	51
VI. Retiring Partner Scenarios	52
A. Scenario #1	52

B. Scenario #2	53
C. Scenario #3	53
D. Scenario #4	53
E. Scenario #5	54
VII. Anti-Abuse Provisions and Purchase of Partnership that Falls under Section 736	54
VIII. Conclusion	55
Further Reading	55

Chapter 6

Merging Law Firms — 57
by Ward Bower

I. Introduction	57
Key Points	57
II. The Consolidation of the Industry	57
A. Prospects for Success	58
B. Why Do Law Firms Merge?	59
C. Law Firm Mergers vs. Corporate Mergers	59
D. External Drivers of the Consolidation	61
III. Steps in Preparing for a Merger	62
A. The Business Case	62
B. Compatibility Factors	63
C. Negotiation Items	64
D. Due Diligence	64
E. Term Sheet	65
F. Integration Plans	65
IV. Conclusion	65
Forms, Guidelines, and Checklists	66
A. Scope Merger Checklist	66
B. Integration Plan Guide	66
Further Reading	66

Chapter 7

Selling a Niche Practice — 69
by John Ventura

I. Introduction	69
Key Points	69
II. What Is a Niche Practice?	69
A. What Is Unique to Selling a Niche Practice?	70
III. Why Do You Want to Sell Your Practice?	71
A. Do You Really Want to Sell Your Practice?	71
B. What Are You Going to Do after You Sell Your Practice?	71

IV.	How Long Will It Take You to Sell Your Practice?	72
V.	Who Do You Need to Help You Sell Your Practice?	72
	A. Certified Public Accountant	72
	B. Law Firm Management Consultant	73
	C. Business Evaluator	73
	D. Business Transaction Attorney	73
VI.	How Do You Value Your Practice and Price It for Sale?	74
	A. How Do You Develop a Prospectus for Potential Buyers?	74
	B. How Do You Think about the Best Interests of Your Clients?	75
	C. Finding a Buyer	75
	D. Negotiating the Sale	76
VII.	Make Sure You Follow the Rules of Professional Conduct	77
VIII.	Conclusion	77
Forms, Guidelines, and Checklists	78
	A. Checklist for the Sale of a Niche Practice: Matters to Be Considered When Drafting the Agreement	78
Further Reading	79

Chapter 8

Checklist for Closing or Preparing for the Closing of a Law Practice   81

by Jay G Foonberg

I.	Introduction	81
	Key Points	81
II.	When Is It Necessary to Close a Law Practice?	82
III.	Who Is Going to Do the Work of Winding Down or Closing the Practice?	82
IV.	Specifically, What Has to Be Done?	83
	A. Occupancy	83
	B. Tracking Down Information	83
	C. Computers & Electronic Information	84
	D. Client Lists: Active and Closed Files	86
	E. Disposal of Office Furnishings and Books	88
	F. Trust Accounts	88
	G. Notices & Forwarding	88
	H. Files & Accounts	89
	I. Protection of Staff	90

Chapter 9

Business Responsibilities in Closing a Law Practice   93

by Constance K. Putzel

I.	Introduction	93
	Key Points	93

II. Closing Another Lawyer's Law Office	94
III. Closing Your Own Law Office	96
IV. Closing Any Law Office	96
A. Settle Accounts	96
B. Close Bank Accounts	97
C. Safekeeping Property	97
D. Review All Leases, Equipment Leases, and Service Contracts	98
E. Contact All Vendors	98
F. Notify Licensing Authority	98
G. Identify Insurance Policies	99
H. Determine Tail Insurance	99
V. Conclusion	100
Further Reading	100
Appendix 9-1 Client-Lawyer Relationship: Rule 1.17 *Sale of Law Practice*	103
Appendix 9-2 Law Office Expense Checklist	107
Appendix 9-3 Client-Lawyer Relationship: Rule 1.15 *Safekeeping Property*	109
Appendix 9-4 The Maryland Lawyers' Rules of Professional Conduct: Rule 1.15 *Safekeeping Property*	111
Appendix 9-5 Equipment Lease or Service Contract List	113
Appendix 9-6 "Why Attorneys Need Tail Insurance"	115
Appendix 9-7 Law Office List of Contacts Inventory	123

Chapter 10

The Ethical Aspects of Winding Down a Law Practice   135
by Peter Geraghty

I. Introduction: The Scenario	135
Key Points	136
II. Sale of a Law Practice	136
A. State Versions of Rule 1.17	139
B. Law Review Articles, Treatises	141
III. Winding Down the Practice	141
A. Client Confidences	142
B. Client Files	143
C. What Should a Lawyer Do with Client Files for Clients the Lawyer Cannot Locate?	145
IV. Preparation for the Protection of Client Interests When a Lawyer Dies or Becomes Disabled	147
V. Conclusion	149
Appendix 10-1 Client-Lawyer Relationship: Rule 1.17 *Sale of Law Practice*	153
Appendix 10-2 Report 8(a)	157

Appendix 10-3	ABA Committee on Ethics and Professional Responsibility Op. 1384 American Bar Association	163
Appendix 10-4	American Bar Association Standing Committee on Ethics and Professional Responsibility: Formal Opinion 92-369, *Disposition of Deceased Sole Practitioners' Client Files and Property*	165

Chapter 11

Preservation of Files: To Destroy or Not to Destroy — 171
by Jay G Foonberg

I. Introduction	171
Key Points	171
II. File Maintenance, Preservation, and Destruction	171
A. Why Destroy the File?	172
B. Old Files, New Lawyers	172
III. Defining "The File"	173
IV. Closing the File	173
A. Implied Consent to Destruction	173
B. Disposal of Files of Unlocatable Clients	174
V. General Observations Concerning File Destruction	175
VI. Destroying the File	175
A. Non-Client Files	176
VII. Conclusion	176
Forms, Guidelines, and Checklists	177
A. Implied Consent to Destruction Letter	177
Further Reading	178

Chapter 12

Ending Client and Employee Relationships — 179
by Harold G. Wren and James H. Wren, II

I. Introduction	179
Key Points	179
II. Ending Relationships with Employees	180
A. The Long-Time Secretary	180
B. The Older Employee	180
C. The High-Tech Employee	181
D. The Paralegal	181
E. The Bookkeeper	181
F. The Associate	181
G. The Investigator	182
H. Problems Common to All Your Employees	182

III.	Ending Relationships with Clients	182
	A. Using an Assisting Lawyer	182
	B. Notifying Your Clients	182
IV.	Other Specific Client Communication Issues: Real Life Examples	183
	A. Relocating Your Practice	183
	B. Representing a Deceased or Disabled Lawyer	183
	C. Moving from the Bar to the Bench	184
V.	Closing Your Practice	186
	A. Physical Assets	186
	B. Intangibles	186
	C. Insurance	186
	D. Communications	186
	E. Bar Relations	187
VI.	Conclusion	187
Further Reading		187

Appendix 12-1	Agreement to Close Law Practice	191
Appendix 12-2	Sample "Office Closing" Letter	199
Appendix 12-3	Sample Transfer of Client File Form	201
Appendix 12-4	Sample Acknowledgment of Receipt of File	203

Index 205

Preface

Nearly three decades ago, lawyers began floating the idea that a law firm could be sold. For solo and small firm practitioners and their families, this novel concept was crucial to their financial future. Up until then, the only assets of a law practice which could be sold were the office building or leasehold interest, a law library, and office equipment. All the rest—a client base, good will, client files—were simply vapor. They were less transferable than the air in a deflated balloon.

It didn't really matter that large law firms, such as the founding partners of the country's oldest law firm, Cadwalader, Wickersham & Taft LLP, in existence since George Washington's time, had been accomplishing those goals for years through complex partnership agreements. Those options just weren't available to solo and small firm lawyers.

For solo and small firm practitioners, the only option was the old workaround of bringing in an associate and, after a decent interval, selling the building and fixtures at an inflated price. For some, the practice was worth more to a spouse in a divorce than after the death of the lawyer. All of that just reeked of subterfuge, and moreover, it just wasn't fair.

Death and old age aren't the only reasons precipitating the sale of a law practice. Solo and small firm lawyers depart the practice for many reasons—retirement, disability, job changes, cross-country moves, other prospects, and health and lifestyle changes and choices. It's not just an issue for octogenarians. For every lawyer selling a law practice, there's another interested in buying a practice, as a way of opening a new practice or expanding an existing one. And sometimes even solo and small firms merge practices.

In 1989, the Supreme Court of California became the first court in the nation to permit the sale of a law practice, sparking the attention of the American Bar Association's to develop a Model Rule. The ABA General Practice Section, as the General Practice, Solo and Small Firm Division was known back then, took the lead in the movement. John A. Krsul, then chair of the Section, recruited solo and small firm lawyers Alan DeWoskin, Don Rikli, and Robert Ostertag to research and craft what would become ABA Model Rule 1.17, paving the way for solo and small firm lawyers to reap the benefits from the sale of their law practices.

Now, we all know that a Model Rule is just that—a model. It's little more than a guideline with the ABA seal of approval until adopted by each state and territory regulating the practice of law in its own jurisdiction. This team, under the banner of the General Practice, Solo and Small Firm Division, created a network to rally the adoption of Model Rule 1.17. And the tides turned.

More work remained to define the rules under which Model Rule 1.17 would operate. How would a law practice be valued? What were the ethical considerations in selling, transferring, merging, and closing a law practice? Could only part of a practice be sold? What were the tax ramifications of the transaction? How would clients' interests be protected?

This book, the product of years' worth of experience, is the primer and the roadmap for solo and small firm lawyers. Each of the contributors is an expert in the field, with solid experience in selling, buying, valuing, merging, and closing a law practice. Special thanks to the efforts of the ABA's Senior Lawyers Division, in particular, Malinda Allen, former SLD Book Publishing Committee chair, for her dedication to the Division and her efforts in developing this book.

Our heartfelt thanks go to pioneers and trailblazers Alan DeWoskin, Robert Ostertag, and Don Rikli for their tireless and relentless efforts in making the law practices of solo and small firm lawyers across the country the valuable assets they deserve to be.

John P. Macy
Immediate Past Chair
General Practice, Solo & Small Firm Division

About the Editors

SARINA BUTLER, American Bar Association Associate Executive Director, Communication Group, directs many of the Association's member communication programs, including ABA Publishing. She has worked extensively with the GPSolo Division, especially in conceiving publisher products, including this book. In a 30-year career, her work in strategic communication, marketing, public affairs, and investor relations has earned her numerous awards and recognitions. She believes that at the ABA the most important result of her work is a satisfied member.

RICHARD G. PASZKIET, ABA Deputy Director of Book Publishing, works with numerous ABA member entities in developing their book programs. He has served as executive editor for the GPSolo Division book program, focusing on issues that confront the solo practitioner. He has more than 20 years of publishing and communications experience, and is an instructor in business writing at DePaul University in Chicago.

About the Contributors

WARD BOWER is a principal of Altman Weil, Inc. He heads consulting assignments in law firm organization, strategic and partnership planning, mergers, and compensation-related issues. He has consulted to leading law firms throughout the world. Mr. Bower has authored articles for numerous publications, including *The American Lawyer*, *The National Law Journal*, *ABA Journal*, *International Financial Law Review* and *Legal Business*. His comments on the legal scene have appeared in legal, business and general publications ranging from *Of Counsel* to the *New York Times*, the *Times of London*, *Wall Street Journal*, *Time* and *U.S. News & World Report*. Mr. Bower is a frequent speaker on law office management-related topics, and has made presentations for legal groups throughout the world. Mr. Bower is a former Council member and Division Chair of the Law Practice Management Section of the American Bar Association, and he also has served as a Committee Chair and as a Council member of the Section on Legal Practice of the International Bar Association. He is a Fellow of both the American Bar Foundation and the College of Law Practice Management. He has chaired the IBA's Working Group on MDPs since its inception in 1996

JOHN CLYNCH was recently hired as a tax associate at Deloitte Tax LLP in Seattle. He has four credits remaining to earn his LL.M. in Tax at the University of Washington School of Law, where he earned his J.D. Mr. Clynch was named the Deloitte and Touche Scholar by the University of Washington Law School Foundation in 2006. While in the LL.M. Tax Program, he worked as Dean Emeritus Roland Hjorth's research assistant, focusing on cancellation of indebtedness issues regarding loan repayment assistance programs. Mr. Clynch also worked as an assistant attorney for the University of Washington School of Law's Federal Tax Clinic. He received funding for his chapter on partnership tax from the University of Washington School of Law.

JAMES D. COTTERMAN is a principal with Altman Weil, Inc. He advises clients on compensation, capital structure and other economic issues, governance, management, and law firm merger assessments. Before joining Altman Weil in 1988, Mr. Cotterman was manager of acquisitions for a public company in the health care industry, where he developed, evaluated, negotiated and integrated merger opportunities. Mr. Cotterman is a regular contributor to *The Altman Weil Report to Legal Management*, and is the lead author of the ABA's monograph, *Compensation Plans for Law Firms*. He has been the supervising author for Matthew Bender's loose-leaf text *How to Manage*

Your Law Office and is currently a member of the Board of Editors of *Accounting and Financial Planning for Law Firms*. His writings have appeared in *The American Lawyer, The National Law Journal, Law Practice Management, International Law Firm Management* and many other publications. Mr. Cotterman is a frequent speaker and lecturer including presentations for annual and regional conferences of the American Bar Association and the Association of Legal Administrators, as well as numerous state and local Bar and ALA meetings.

JAY G FOONBERG is the Law Practice Management Section Council Liaison to the GP/Solo Division Council, and the Senior Lawyers Division Liaison to the Law Practice Management Section. His contributions in this book are based on 17 years of doing CLE on these topics. He is the author of the ABA best-selling book, *How to Start & Build a Law Practice*, now in its 5th edition, and has been writing for the ABA for more than 30 years. He has been honored with the GP/Solo Division Donald Rikli Award for lifetime services to the solo and small firm lawyers of America. He holds his B.S. and J.D. from UCLA. He may be contacted through www.Foonberglaw.com.

PETER GERAGHTY has been the Director of ETHICSearch (http://www.abanet.org/cpr/ethicsearch/home.html), the ABA Ethics Research Service for the ABA Center for Professional Responsibility, since 1990. He has written widely on legal ethics issues in such publications as the *Professional Lawyer*, and is also the author of the "EYE on ETHICS" column for the *Your ABA* electronic newsletter. Mr. Geraghty received his B.A. from Connecticut College in 1978 and his J.D. from Northwestern University School of Law in 1984. Prior to attending law school, he was a Peace Corps Volunteer in Togo, West Africa.

ROBERT OSTERTAG, a veteran small firm practitioner from Poughkeepsie, New York, has devoted many years of his career to the organized bar at all levels. He is a past president of the Dutchess County, NY, and the New York State Bar Associations and is a longtime active member of the ABA's House of Delegates, its General Practice, Solo & Small Firms Division, and now its Senior Lawyers Division. He has written and spoken frequently on subjects involving professional ethics and the sale of law practices. Mr. Ostertag is the 2004 recipient of the ABA's then GP/Solo & Small Firms Section's Lifetime Achievement Award.

SHANNON PRATT is Chairman and CEO of Shannon Pratt Valuations, a national business and professional practice valuation firm headquartered in Portland, Oregon. He is also the author of *Valuing a Business, Valuing Small Businesses and Professional Practices, The Lawyer's Business Valuation Handbook, The Cost of Capital, The Market Approach to Valuing Businesses, Business Valuation and Taxes* (with Judge David Laro), and *Standards of Value* (with Jay Fishman and William Morrison).

CONSTANCE K. PUTZEL received her B.S. Degree from Goucher College and her J.D. from the University of Maryland School of Law. Mrs. Putzel has been in the private practice of law in Maryland for more than 50 years, concentrating on Family Law and Elder Law, and is now of counsel to the law firm of Eleanor C. Naiman,

Esq. in Baltimore County. Mrs. Putzel has served on the Section Council of the Senior Lawyers Division of the American Bar Association and on the Editorial Board of *Experience*. She is the author of *Representing the Older Client in Divorce*, published by the ABA's General Practice Section.

JOHN VENTURA is the Director of the Texas Consumer Complaint Center, which is part of the Center for Consumer Law at the University of Houston Law School. Before this he owned a consumer bankruptcy firm in the Rio Grande Valley of South Texas with offices in Brownsville, McAllen, Harlingen, and Corpus Christi that he sold in 2004. Mr. Ventura is also the author of 13 books including *The Bankruptcy Kit, The Credit Repair Kit, Good Advice for a Bad Economy, The Business Turnaround and Bankruptcy Kit, Fresh Start, Beating the Paycheck to Paycheck Blues, The Small Business Survival Kit, The Will Kit, Everything Your Heirs Need to Know, Law For Dummies, Divorce For Dummies, The Everyday Law Kit for Dummies*, and *Managing Debt for Dummies*.

HAROLD G. WREN has been of counsel to James R. Voyles, Attorney, Louisville, Kentucky, since 1991. He holds his A.B. and LL.B. from Columbia, and his J.S.D. from Yale. Mr. Wren first practiced with Willkie Farr & Gallagher of New York, and then entered the academic world, where he was Dean of three law schools and a teacher at four others. His books include *Creative Estate Planning* (1970) and *Tax Aspects of Marital Dissolution* (with Leon Gabinet) (2d ed. 1997). He is a past chair of the Senior Lawyers Division of the American Bar Association.

JAMES H. WREN, II received his B.A. from the University of Richmond and his J.D. from the University of Virginia Law School. He is a commander in the United States Army and a member of the Kentucky Bar Association. Mr. Wren currently works as an assistant public advocate for the Commonwealth of Kentucky.

Chapter 1

Overview of the Sale and Purchase of a Law Practice

by Robert Ostertag

I. Introduction

The purpose of this initial chapter is to introduce the reader to some of the issues often confronted in the transfer of a law practice. Particular attention will be given to the purchase/sale of solo practices, which, unlike the merger of law practices, is a relatively new concept of particular potential benefit to the solo sector of our profession. Done correctly, it is not a simple transaction, but it is one that can achieve substantial benefits. Many of the issues touched upon here will be discussed later in more substantive chapters. This chapter addresses how the concept of selling a law practice came about and the basic issues to be addressed.

Key Points

- The primary purpose of the various buy/sell rules is to place solo practitioners on a more equal footing with their large firm colleagues.
- Some 43 state-wide jurisdictions allow the sale of law practices, primarily by rule (many by Rule 1.17), but in a few instances by ethics opinions or otherwise.
- State laws define who may buy and sell practices as well as what materials may legitimately be sold. Sales of goodwill are complicated by variable definitions.
- The need to protect client confidences and secrets while communicating potential issues is one of the largest ethical and logistical considerations in selling a practice.
- Valuing or appraising a practice is generally achieved by three methods: use of comparables, use of multipliers, and consideration of past revenues.

II. History of the Concept: Why We Can Now Sell

Once upon a not-so-distant time ago, back in what for some might be considered "the good old days," life was simpler, work days were shorter, and the practice of law was less trying and competitive. Solo practice was a common and almost exclusive feature of so many American communities, but few of us ever really considered passing anything of particular value from our practices to our surviving spouses or next of kin. Death would normally close the office with nothing of value there but our desks, our chairs and books, and whatever other tangible property we might own. Nothing in the form of goodwill would pass. In point of fact, we had no goodwill, or so they told us. So why even think about it?

But one day someone, somewhere, concluded that if those outside the law profession could turn their financial risks, efforts, and entrepreneurial achievements into comfortable retirement, spendable wealth, and death benefits, so could we lawyers.

We don't really know who that first someone was, or just what he or she undertook to modify our thinking, but we do know of someone who did think about it and who considered it important enough to address. His name was Donald Rikli, and he was a solo practitioner from Highland, Illinois, a community of about 8,000 just across the Mississippi from St. Louis and up the road a piece. Don was an energetic, enterprising, thoughtful, and successful lawyer with a booming practice, at least when measured by community standards. While he employed substantial assistance, he remained a solo equity owner of his practice. He considered himself no less an entrepreneur than the insurance broker across the street, the independent banker next door, or the department store owner the next block over. More to the point, he asked why the local physicians, dentists, and civil engineers could sell their professional practices and retire while he could not. After all, he practiced law to make a living, not for fun (although to him, at least, it was fun). But if other professionals could secure their retirements and support their heirs as a fruit of their labors, why couldn't he?

The answer, of course, was that those who controlled our professional lives believed—and convinced us as well—that the practice of law, although a business in the sense that it provided a living, was distinct from other professions in being one with rules of ethical conduct that could not accommodate the sale of clients and their files. Clients, after all, were not saleable commodities, and their files were full of their confidences and secrets that could not be imparted to others, including prospective purchasers. Indeed, the maintenance of a client's confidences and secrets was a core ethical value upon which our profession was created and nurtured, and one upon which it has endured. However, Don wondered why physicians and other professionals, constrained by similar obligations to their patients and clients, could dispose of their practices without similar concerns. He thus set out to correct the problem as he saw it.

It was in 1989 when the State Bar of California, having by then also considered the problem, invited a representative of the General Practice Section to speak with its Board of Governors. Alan DeWoskin of St. Louis, who then was engaged in the project with Donald Rikli, took on the responsibility. To a significant extent, it was the force and logic of Alan's presentation that resulted in California's adoption that year of the first judicial rule in the nation permitting lawyers to sell the goodwill aspects of their law practices, a revolutionary concept at the time. A year later, the American Bar Association, at the urging of Donald Rikli and others, adopted its own model rule (Rule 1.17) permitting lawyers to sell the goodwill aspects of their law practices. However, the ABA's model codes of professional conduct have never had the force of law or regulation but have always been merely aspirational, intended primarily to encourage state authorities to adopt them. Don Rikli and a small group of his colleagues went to work. Don created contacts in virtually every state whose efforts were directed toward encouraging the promulgation of similar rules permitting lawyers to sell the goodwill aspects of their practices.

Don Rikli died unexpectedly in 1991. By that time, however, he had contacts working on the project in virtually every state-wide jurisdiction. Also, at that time, primarily through his own and their efforts, some nine states had already adopted rules similar to the ABA's Model Rule. Unfortunately, however, Don's own state of Illinois was not among them. It had considered and had rejected the concept, the only state to have done so. Ironically, therefore, when Don died, his solo practice, other than its furnishings and equipment, was basically valueless and could not be converted into future financial security for his widow.

Today, based largely upon Donald Rikli's groundwork, forty-three state-wide jurisdictions allow the sale of law practices, primarily by rule, but in a few instances by ethics, opinions, or otherwise.

A. Discussion

The primary purpose of these various buy/sell rules is to place solo practitioners on a somewhat equal footing with their large firm colleagues. As earlier suggested, the sale of a solo practitioner's goodwill implicates ethical considerations involving the release of clients' confidences and secrets to prospective purchasers, some or many of whom, having obtained such information, might decline to complete the transaction. Since large firm retirement and other similar plans do not involve the release of client confidences or secrets beyond the firm's boundaries, no potential violation of such rules of professional conduct is implicated. So while the floor is not fully leveled, the means for a solo's egress from the profession have been provided. Let us, therefore, briefly introduce some of them. Be aware, however, that since many of the rules differ from others in one small way or another, the following comments are introductory only and generalizations at best.

> Practitioners should carefully apply whatever rules of their respective jurisdictions may govern the sale of law practices.

III. Who May Sell a Law Practice?

Prospective sellers fall into three primary categories: retiring solos; law firms from which one, some, or all members are retiring or otherwise abandoning the practice; and the "personal representatives" of deceased, disabled, or missing lawyers.

The term "retirement" generally is meant to include a cessation of private practice within a geographic area as, for example, the county or city wherein the selling lawyer has practiced. Sometimes it includes a contiguous city, county, or other geographic area as well. In Delaware and Rhode Island, for example, the rules understandably require the cessation of practice throughout the entire jurisdiction. Some rules prohibit the selling of the attorney's renewal of practice altogether; others set conditions for some form of continuing or reemerging legal activities sometime, somewhere. For example, a selling lawyer may retire from private practice to ascend to the bench, to enter into government service, or to perform pro bono service for the poor, assuming—albeit without initial intent to do so—that such activity will not conflict with, limit, or otherwise interfere with what has been purchased by the purchasing lawyer. In another example, a selling lawyer in Westchester County, New York, might wish to open or continue a satellite practice far away in Rochester, New York.

A law firm may also sell its practice when all its members are retiring from or leaving private practice or have become disabled by age or infirmity such that they elect to terminate their professional activities. The same or similar rules of transfer generally apply to them.

The rules also generally permit a "personal representative" of a deceased, disabled, or missing lawyer to sell the lawyer's practice. That arrangement may unsatisfactorily implicate confidentiality issues that will transcend the ability of committees on professional conduct or similar lawyer regulatory agencies to control them, as will be mentioned later in this chapter.

IV. Who May Purchase a Law Firm?

The rules generally provide that one or more other lawyers or law firms may purchase part or all of a selling lawyers's practice, but this raises many questions. Who are "other lawyers?" Are they only lawyers or the firms of lawyers licensed to practice law in the selling lawyer's jurisdiction? May they be lawyers from other jurisdictions who are as-yet unlicensed to practice in the selling lawyer's jurisdiction but who intend to apply for admission? May the firms of such lawyers purchase? What about multi-jurisdictional firms with just one or more lawyers licensed to practice in the selling lawyer's jurisdiction? What about multi-jurisdictional firms with no equity partners at all who are licensed or entitled to practice law in the selling lawyer's jurisdiction? Currently, the answers are unclear. These types of issues may eventually bring varied results under specific state rules when ultimately tested. Multi-jurisdictional rules of practice have recently been adopted in at least some states and they, too, diverge in various ways. Care, therefore, must be taken.

A. What Is a Personal Representative?

Many questions also arise over the issue of a personal representative. The term "personal representative" certainly includes an estate executor or administrator. It probably would include most court-appointed guardians, committees, and conservators, but sometimes with prescribed limitations of authorized activity. But for purposes of practice transfer, does it include a surviving spouse or other close relative of a deceased lawyer? Frequently, that person is not a lawyer to whom codes of professional conduct apply. That again implicates issues involving the confidences and secrets of clients. What about the personal representative of a disabled or missing lawyer? Are spouses and other family members included in that class? And what about the disabled or missing lawyer's attorney-in-fact, particularly if unlicensed to practice law? Will a missing lawyer's attorney-in-fact be deemed under state law to be able to act on behalf of the missing lawyer who may be deemed not yet to have died, but who ultimately may be found in fact to have died even before the attorney-in-fact shall have acted? These are issues to be considered and resolved.

V. What May Be Sold?

Generally, everything from a law practice may be sold including cash, furniture, equipment, fixtures, supplies, software, the law library, the real property if the selling lawyer or firm owns it, leasehold interests, telephone numbers, accounts receivable (usually less the cost of collection), outstanding client disbursement advances, and all other forms of tangible property owned by the selling lawyer or the firm. But such property could always have been sold without the new rules. What about the one intangible item of property at issue: the selling lawyer's or firm's goodwill? That can now be sold in almost all states.

Some transfer rules provide for the sale of parts of practices, meaning particular areas of practice that a lawyer may wish to terminate without discontinuing the rest. That implicates special considerations of its own in terms, for example, of defining what is a specific area of the law that a selling lawyer wishes to convey, and that a purchasing lawyer may wish to purchase, and under what conditions and where may the selling attorney continue to practice, if at all.

A. Covenants Not to Compete

Given that the rules generally prohibit the selling lawyer from privately practicing within certain geographic areas extending, upon occasions, to the entire state jurisdiction, what about covenants not to compete? We refer here to partially retiring or temporarily disabled selling lawyers. The general inclusion in the rules of geographical limits within which a selling lawyer may not thereafter practice in competition with a purchasing lawyer suggests that a selling lawyer may reopen somewhere beyond those geographic limits. That, in turn, suggests the acceptability of—and perhaps the need for—covenants not to compete as part of the transaction. Covenants not to compete generally may be geographic in nature and/or temporal, and may involve what is and is not to be sold (e.g., one's entire practice or part of it). Courts in most jurisdictions look carefully at covenants not to compete and frequently view them with disfavor unless reasonable in their terms.

> As for covenants not to compete in the practice of law, courts generally look even more closely at them and generally disfavor them on the ground that they impose limitations upon a client's right to select his or her own lawyer.

If the rule involved creates a geographic limitation upon the selling lawyer's right to practice following the disposal of all or part of his or her practice, one would presume that a covenant not to compete with a buying lawyer within that geographical limit, whatever it is, would be deemed reasonable and acceptable, all other provisions aside. But perhaps it would be considered unnecessary. What about a greater covenanted geographic area than that provided by rule? We probably would be dealing with an issue of reasonableness of terms. The lesson to be learned, however, is the need for extreme care in the inclusion within the transaction of a covenant not to compete, with necessary reference not only to the agreement, but also to the law in one's own jurisdiction.

VI. Client Issues

A. Client's Confidences and Secrets

Among the most serious problems relating to the transaction between a selling lawyer and a purchasing lawyer, and to the merger of firms, is that of the preservation of clients' confidences and secrets. The preservation of clients' confidences and secrets is one of our profession's core values. A decade or so ago when the then "Big 5" accounting firms attempted to impose upon us a takeover of our profession that they euphemistically called multidisciplinary practice, the major stumbling block to its acceptance by the American Bar Association's House of Delegates was the anticipated breach of those canons of our ethical rules that relate to confidences and secrets. Accountants have no such rules, at least as to their attest function. In point of fact, they have been held by the Supreme Court to be the "nation's watchdogs."

> A confidence is generally defined in our codes of ethics as information protected by the attorney-client privilege under applicable law. A secret is generally defined as other information gained in the professional relationship between a lawyer and his or her client that the client has requested to be held inviolate, or the disclosure of which would be embarrassing or would likely be detrimental to the client.

Clearly, very many files in virtually every lawyer's office contain client confidences and/or secrets that are protected by these definitions. Within those terms, therefore, what is it that a selling lawyer may disclose to a purchasing lawyer about his or her clients and their files?

The rules seem to indicate rather uniformly that a prospective selling lawyer may provide a prospective purchaser with as much information about clients and their files as will disclose the existence of conflicts of interest, or their absence, that is not protected as client confidences or secrets under applicable ethical code provisions. Among such items of information that must be disclosed is each client's very identity unless identity itself is a secret (although it usually is not). But the disclosure of even that basic information may be limited by rule to situations wherein clients are advised of the purchasing lawyer's identity and consent to the disclosure to him or her of their own identities. Obviously, that can make a determination as to whether the purchasing lawyer has a conflicting interest with a particular client difficult. What to do?

The rules also generally tell us that the selling lawyer may disclose information concerning the status and general nature of his or her clients' matters and any information already available in public court files except, of course, client secrets, together with information concerning the financial terms of the attorney-client relationship in each instance and the payment status of each file. Obviously, this area of the transaction, along with the problem of valuation, is most difficult.

The rules also usually provide that if the prospective purchaser has learned any of the selling lawyer's clients' confidences or secrets in the process, he or she must maintain those confidences and secrets just as if he or she represented those clients and was their lawyer.

This subject will be covered more completely in subsequent chapters of this book.

> The material should be read carefully, particularly since a refusal on the part of a client to allow his or her confidences and secrets to be disclosed to a prospective purchaser may very well include grievance considerations and the likelihood of an aborted transaction if violated.

B. Conflicts of Interest

Another major issue involves the possible existence of conflicting interests between one or more of a selling lawyer's clients and the prospective purchaser. The rules generally provide that, prior to the disclosure of any clients' confidences and secrets, the selling lawyer must provide the purchaser with information sufficient to enable him or her to determine whether any conflict exists between the prospective purchaser and the seller's clients or prospective new clients.

Before such issues may be addressed, of course, each and every selling or merging lawyer's clients must be notified of the proposed transaction. The rules generally tell us that written notice of a seller's intent to sell to a specific buyer must be given to each of the seller's clients, and that the notice must include such reasonable information as there is about the purchasing lawyer, the client's right to retain other counsel instead, the client's right to just pick up his or her file and do with it as he or she wishes, and the fact that, if the client takes no action within a stated period of time to object to his or her file being transferred to the purchaser as proposed, his or her consent to the transfer will be presumed, subject to any conflicting court rule or statute. Moreover, and again usually subject to conflicting statute or rule, the original fee arrangement with the seller must be honored by the purchaser unless the client agrees to a new fee arrangement.

VII. Valuation

> The economic value of one's practice depends to a great extent upon the likelihood of future receipts no matter who the clientele may be or what valuation method is used.

A frequently asked question is, "If I am a solo practitioner with no institutional clients, but whose clientele consists primarily of people seeking wills, real estate contracts, and my handling of estates, what can my practice really be worth?" The valuation process will be discussed in depth in later chapters. Suffice it to say, however, that one should not assume total lack of value from the absence of institutional clients.

If you happen to be the reputed best in your community at what you do, there is potential value there. Factors normally considered relate to the quality of the selling lawyer's practice, its work product in addition to its location, its general nature, the length of time it has existed, its operational discipline and reputation, its number of clients, its fee structure, its profitability, and the experience and expertise of its staff, among others. These are very subjective tests for which there are no regulated testing standards. Some appraisers work solely as appraisers and some as accountants or

> **Planning Ahead.** Aside from the mechanics of the sale or merger of a law practice, is the need to plan ahead for the unknown. While a lawyer is alive and healthy, it is incumbent upon him or her to plan for disability and death, not merely for retirement, especially if he or she is a solo practitioner. Such arrangement should obviously be in writing. There should be agreement on the basic rules of takeover and on the responsibilities and authority to be assumed. Such an agreement should include financial details, such as the method for determining fees, access to bank accounts (including the clients' trust accounts), and the future for office staff, including their continued employment, if at all, and their likely future areas of responsibility and authority.

otherwise. The choice of a good appraiser is vital to the transaction.

There are basically three frequently used appraisal methods. The first involves the use of comparables in the community, if any. This is a method frequently used to evaluate real property but may be difficult to use here if there is a lack of existing comparables in the community. A second method uses multipliers (frequently 1 or 1.5 times a firm's previous year's gross revenues, depending upon the extent of repeat business that may be expected). A third method also involves consideration of past revenue, but with other factors included as well. All of these methods will be discussed in subsequent chapters.

VIII. Payment Plans

What professional and financial arrangements are to exist? How is one to plan financially? What steps are to be taken, and when? Suffice it to say that among the planning essentials is the selection of a lawyer to handle the practice. As for payments of the purchase price, there is an old adage that if the purchaser has cash, he need not negotiate over terms. But if the buyer has limited resources, terms become very important. A critical ingredient in the payment plan is the purchaser's need to provide collateral to the seller that is separate and apart from the law practice itself.

A lawyer's Last Will and Testament should provide what responsibility the executor (either lawyer or layperson—it matters) should and should not have with regard to the practice, its finances, the clients and their files, and the office in general, with particular reference to who is to have the authority to dispose of the practice or operate it during a period of disability.

Various state bar associations have recently sought to address the planning problem. Oregon, Virginia, and now New York have produced written materials and forms. New York's is available free of charge on the Internet.

IX. Other Concerns

A. Non-Responsive Clients

Many practice transfer rules provide in substance that if a client, once notified of his or her lawyer's plan to sell the law practice, does not object to the transfer of his or her file within a stated period of time, he or she is presumed to have consented to it.

Some of those clients may have moved away or died. Among the questions to consider in that situation are:

- Who is counsel of record upon the passage of such time?
- When does the seller relinquish and the purchaser assume responsibility for the file?
- Will the purchaser even want to assume responsibility for a file under those circumstances?
- Will the client be willing to pay future fees to the prospective purchaser?
- How does one know?
- Whose malpractice carrier will cover whom, and when?

B. Management of a Deceased Lawyer's Clients

A number of questions arise over the management of a deceased lawyer's clients. If a deceased lawyer's estate neglects to promptly protect the decedent's clients' interests, is there potential liability for damages resulting therefrom? Clearly there is none in malpractice unless the decedent's personal representative is a lawyer subject to malpractice litigation. But what about the exposure of others, if any?

What about the breach of clients' confidences and secrets? Someone must enter the deceased lawyer's files if only to determine the need for immediate representation, and then perhaps for purposes of valuation. Does that constitute a breach of confidentiality? It would seem so. Who is to assume responsibility for the deceased lawyer's trust account? And what about client fees advanced to the deceased lawyer but that are not yet earned? Who is to determine what has been earned? Who is responsible for those funds?

Another conundrum involves closed files. They, too, probably contain confidences and secrets and should not be transferred to purchasing lawyers without the clients' or former clients' informed consent. Can clients be found? Will the purchasing lawyer even want such files? If not, what is to become of them? Many lawyers maintain closed files for years and years; this is not a good idea, but those files must be dealt with.

What about a deceased lawyer's staff? Their responsibility to maintain confidences and secrets, as required by codes of professional responsibility, derives from their employer, the deceased lawyer. Obviously the deceased lawyer is no longer subject to his or her code of professional responsibility. Is there a remaining derivative employee responsibility or exposure to liability?

Selling lawyers have the responsibility of selling to competent counsel. Upon a lawyer's disability or death, what responsibility has his or her personal representative or family to do so? What about liability and damage issues?

C. Malpractice Communication

Does a purchasing lawyer have the duty to a client to disclose the selling lawyer's malpractice or incompetence in connection with his or her matters? What exposure will the purchaser have, if any, with respect to the file if he or she does not disclose? In many jurisdictions, hold harmless agreements involving lawyers' malpractice are ineffectual, or ineffectual under certain circumstances. Would that rule apply to a purchaser's possible exposure regarding the seller's malpractice and the purchaser's possible failure to disclose it?

What about a temporary lawyer's own malpractice during a disabled attorney's period of disability? What liability would flow, and to whom? And what if the temporary lawyer walks off with the disabled lawyer's best clients?

X. Conclusion

Aside from these, there are multiple other issues to be considered in preparing for retirement, disability, or death. Solo practitioners and their clients are particularly exposed to danger. As earlier stated, the transaction is not easy and there are a host of hidden traps. The moral of the story, and of this book, is to plan ahead, in writing, with competent help and with a well-thought-out awareness of as many potential problems as may occur.

Further Reading

Continuing Education of the Bar—California. *Law Firm Transitions: Buying, Selling, Merging or Closing a Law Practice: Program Handbook*. Oakland, California: Continuing Education of the Bar, 2004.

DeWoskin, Alan E. "The Sale of a Law Practice." *The Compleat Lawyer* v. 14, no. 4 (Fall 1997): p. 48.

Frederick, Paula. "Want to Sell Your Law Practice? Now You Can!" *Georgia Bar Journal* v. 10 no. 6 (April 2005): p. 50.

Maville, John H. "Sale of a Law Practice: Out of the Shadows and into the Rules—A Look at the ISBA's Proposed Transfer-of-Practice Rule." *Illinois Bar Journal* v. 91, Part 6 (2003): pp. 292–297.

Poll, Edward. *Selling Your Law Practice: The Profitable Exit Strategy*. Venice, California: LawBiz Management Co., 2005.

"Rule 1.17 Sale of Law Practice." *Brandeis Law Journal* v. 44 no. 1 (Fall 2005): pp. 164–171.

Chapter 2

The Ethical Aspects of Acquiring a Law Practice

by Peter Geraghty

I. Introduction

This chapter will address the ethical issues involved when a lawyer acquires a law practice either through the purchase of a practice under Rule 1.17 *Sale of a Law Practice* of the *ABA Model Rules of Professional Conduct* or through merger of the lawyer's existing practice with another practice. It will also address the obligations of a lawyer who steps in to manage the practice of a deceased solo practitioner.

Key Points

- Significant variations in the state versions of ABA Model Rule 1.17 *Sale of a Law Practice* render it crucial for the practitioner who is contemplating buying a law practice to check the rules of professional conduct that have been adopted in the individual jurisdiction.
- Under ABA Model Rule 1.17, the purchaser of a law practice is not allowed to increase the fees charged to clients by reason of the sale.
- When law firms A and B merge, they may not drop certain of firm A's clients that may have conflicts with firm B's more lucrative clients so that they can continue to represent them.
- Under the ABA Model Rules, screening is not permitted as a means of resolving conflicts of interest that would result from the merger where one or more lawyers from firm A has confidential client information that would otherwise disqualify the merged firm from representing one of firm B's major clients.
- Lawyers who assume responsibility for a deceased solo practitioner's practice have ethical obligations to promptly review the client files, to protect client confidences, and to contact the deceased lawyer's clients for instructions.

The following hypotheticals illustrate the ethical issues implicated in each of these different factual settings:

Hypothetical A: Sale of a Law Practice

You are a solo practitioner with a concentration in family law in a medium-sized jurisdiction. Another solo practitioner in your jurisdiction is retiring and wants to sell his practice that has a concentration in estate planning. You would like to develop your estate planning practice and are very interested in purchasing the practice.

What, if any, ethical issues should you be aware of if you should decide to go forward with the purchase?

- Can you charge the clients at different rates than those charged by the seller's firm?
- What can you call the practice once you have acquired it?
- What should you do if you do not have the expertise you feel is necessary to handle certain ongoing matters that are currently being handled by the seller's practice?

Hypothetical B: Law Firm Merger

Your firm (firm X) has a concentration in the representation of hospitals and nursing homes and is located in a medium-sized metropolitan area. You are considering merging with another firm (firm Y) that has a concentration in elder law and estate planning. You believe this practice will complement your firm's practice, but you are concerned about potential conflicts that may surface between your firm's clients and clients of the other firm.

- In the event that you discover that there are conflicts between client A of firm X and client B of firm Y, can you withdraw from the representation of client A so that the merged firm can continue to represent client B?
- In the event that lawyers in firm X possess confidential information about one of their clients that would otherwise disqualify the merged firm from continuing to represent client C, one of firm Y's major clients, can the merged firm avoid disqualification by screening firm X's lawyers from any participation in matters involving client C?

Hypothetical C: Duties of a Lawyer Who Acquires the Practice of a Deceased Solo Practitioner

You have a solo practice in metropolitan area. From time-to-time you have collaborated with another solo practitioner in the area on a variety of matters. You have also entered into an agreement with this practitioner that you will step in and manage his practice in the event of his death or disability. You have just learned that this lawyer has passed away unexpectedly. What are your obligations with respect to this lawyer's practice?

II. Sale of a Law Practice

Rule 1.17 *Sale of a Law Practice* of the *ABA Model Rules of Professional Conduct* addresses the ethics issues that attend to the sale of a law practice. For a brief history of the development of Rule 1.17, a copy of the full text of the Rule, a discussion of the ethics issues that can arise from the seller's perspective, and a list of scholarly articles and treatises that discuss the Rule, see Chapter 10. As noted in that chapter, there are significant variations in the state versions of Rule 1.17. It is therefore crucial for the practitioner who is contemplating buying a law practice to check the rules of professional conduct that have been adopted in the individual jurisdiction.

From the purchaser's perspective, ethics issues pertinent to the sale of a law practice include Rule 1.17's requirement that the fees charged may not be increased by reason of the sale, the importance of checking for conflicts of interest, and the purchaser's obligation to undertake to represent the clients of the purchased firm competently.

At the ABA Mid-Year Meeting in 2003, nearly every Model Rule was amended pursuant to the ABA Ethics 2000 Commission's (E2K) recommendations. A redlined version of the Model Rules that shows the E2K-inspired amendments along with the Reporter's explanation of changes memoranda for each Rule is located on the ABA Center for Professional Responsibility's website at http://www.abanet.org/cpr/e2k/home.html.

> Note that the full text of most of the state bar opinions cited in this chapter is available on the respective state bar websites, links to which are available on the ABA Center for Professional Responsibility's website (www.abanet.org/cpr). Digests of these opinions are also available in the *ABA/BNA Lawyers' Manual on Professional Conduct*.

A. Fees Charged to Clients after Sale of the Law Practice

Subpart (d) of Rule 1.17 states that the purchaser is not allowed to increase the fees charged clients by reason of the sale. The rationale behind this part of the Rule is that the purchaser should not be able to selectively discourage certain clients from continuing on with the firm after the purchase. An E2K amendment clarified this part of the Rule in that the pre-E2K version permitted the purchasing lawyer to charge a higher fee if the amount charged did not exceed the amount the purchasing lawyer customarily charged other clients for similar services. Subpart (d) of the Rule now states:

> (d) The fees charged clients shall not be increased by reason of the sale.

Paragraph 10 of the Comment to Rule 1.17 states:

> **Fee Arrangements Between Client and Purchaser**
>
> [10] The sale may not be financed by increases in fees charged the clients of the practice. Existing arrangements between the seller and the client as to fees and the scope of the work must be honored by the purchaser.

The E2K Reporter's memorandum gives the following explanation for the amendment:

> Paragraph (d) of the current Rule states that the fees charged clients shall not be increased by reason of the sale. However, it also allows the buyer of a

practice to tell the seller's clients that the buyer will not work on their cases unless they agree to pay a greater fee than they had agreed to pay the seller. The only limit is that the buyer may not charge the seller's clients more than the buyer charges the buyer's other clients for "substantially similar services." This is problematic because the seller could not unilaterally abrogate the fee agreement as a matter of contract law. The seller could have withdrawn as permitted under Rule 1.16, but the seller certainly could not have refused to continue the representation unless the client agreed to a modification of the fee contract. In this regard, the Commission thinks the buyer should stand in the shoes of the seller and has modified paragraph (d) accordingly. This proposal is in accord with the rules of California, Colorado (written contracts only), Florida, Iowa, Minnesota (must honor for one year), New Jersey, New York, North Dakota, Oregon, Tennessee (proposed rule), Virginia and Wisconsin.

The Commission proposes to delete paragraph (c)(2) in light of the modification in paragraph (d). Its only purpose was to require that notice be given to the seller's clients of the buyer's right to require increased fees under paragraph (d), which right has now been eliminated.

B. What's in a Name?

If you purchase the Jones law practice, what can you call it? Can you continue to practice under the name Jones Law Firm or must you change the name? What if younger associates acquire the practice from the older named partners in the firm Smith, Jones and Baker? Can they continue to call the firm Smith, Jones and Baker?

In general, for a law firm to continue with a firm name once the named partners are no longer a part of the firm, there must be a "continuing succession in the firm's identity." See paragraph 1 of the Comment to Rule 7.5 *Firm Names and Letterhead* of the *ABA Model Rules of Professional Conduct*. For example, it has long been accepted practice that listing deceased lawyers in firm names is generally acceptable if the firm is the same firm or a successor firm to the one in which the deceased lawyer practiced. See Connecticut Informal Ethics Op. 99-37 (1999); Michigan Informal Ethics Op. RI-45 (1990); Missouri Informal Ethics Op. 940056 (1994); New York State Ethics Op. 45 (1967); and South Carolina Ethics Op. 96-01 (1996). If the lawyer or lawyers acquiring the practice are already associated with the firm, they also may be able to use the firm name because there is a continuing line of succession. See, e.g., North Dakota Opinion 98-6 (1998) (younger lawyers in law firm who acquire shares of the firm in exchange for capital contributions to the firm are not subject to the sale of a law practice rule and may continue to use the old firm's name because there is a continuing succession in the firm's identity); see also Pennsylvania Informal Ethics Op. 97-79 (1997) (lawyer-employee of deceased solo practitioner may form professional corporation using deceased's name since technical relationship of employee, associate, or partner is not relevant to status as successor firm).

However, where the firm has been sold to a new lawyer or group of lawyers, there is no such continuing identity, and the continued use of the firm name may be considered to be misleading under Rules 7.1 *Communications Concerning a Lawyer's Services* and 7.5 of the ABA Model Rules.

C. Competence

Continuing on with Hypothetical A, you have just purchased a law firm that has a concentration in estate planning. Your practice is concentrated in family law matters. Once you acquire the practice, you realize that some of the estate planning clients have large estates that involve complicated tax issues that you have never handled before.

Q. What should you do?

The purchasing lawyer also has an obligation to assess whether he or she can competently handle all of the client matters that are pending in the seller lawyer's firm. Paragraph 11 of the Comment to Rule 1.17 states:

> **Other Applicable Ethical Standards**
>
> [11] Lawyers participating in the sale of a law practice or a practice area are subject to the ethical standards applicable to involving another lawyer in the representation of a client. These include, for example, the seller's obligation to exercise competence in identifying a purchaser qualified to assume the practice **and the purchaser's obligation to undertake the representation competently (see Rule 1.1)**; the obligation to avoid disqualifying conflicts, and to secure the client's informed consent for those conflicts that can be agreed to (see Rule 1.7 regarding conflicts and Rule 1.0(e) for the definition of informed consent); and the obligation to protect information relating to the representation (see Rules 1.6 and 1.9) [emphasis added].

Rule 1.1 *Competence* of the ABA Model Rules states:

> A lawyer shall provide competent representation to a client. Competent representation requires the legal knowledge, skill, thoroughness and preparation reasonably necessary for the representation.

A. The Comments to Rule 1.1 explain that, depending on the type of legal matter, lawyers may provide adequate representation in a field they are unfamiliar with so long as they undertake necessary study or if they associate themselves with other lawyers who have expertise in the matter.

D. Avoidance of Conflicts of Interest

The purchasing lawyer should be careful to avoid conflicts of interest that may emerge once the sale is consumated. See, e.g., North Dakota opinion 00-02 (2000) that cautioned a purchasing lawyer about potential conflicts in a situation where he represented a client who had interests that were potentially adverse to a former client of the seller's firm. See the following digest of the opinion as it appears at page 1101:6707 of the *ABA/BNA Lawyers' Manual on Professional Conduct*:

> A law firm purchasing a law practice may represent a surviving spouse seeking to review her rights under documents drafted for the decedent by the selling firm if the selling firm's files in the matter, which it closed, do not contain any confidential information about the matter. The purchasing firm is considered to have knowledge of the contents of the selling firm's closed files and is obligated

to maintain their confidentiality. If the closed files do contain confidential information, the purchasing firm must decide if its responsibility to keep the information confidential may adversely affect the new representation. Even though Rule 1.9 does not by its terms apply to this situation, its framework may be helpful in resolving the issue.

1101 *Law. Man. Prof. Conduct* 6707.

III. Law Firm Mergers

Law firm mergers pose many complicated conflicts of interest and confidentiality issues concerning present and former clients of both merging firms. To the extent that the two firms have clients who have interests that are adverse, Rules 1.7 *Conflict of Interest: Current Clients,* 1.9 *Duties to Former Clients,* and 1.10 *Imputation of Conflicts of Interest: General Rule* may be implicated.

A. The "Hot Potato" Doctrine

A recurring theme in the area of law firm mergers is the "hot potato" doctrine, which applies when a law firm attempts to withdraw from the representation of one client due to a conflict of interest so that it may continue to represent another more lucrative client. The use of the term "hot potato" to describe this scenario appears to have originated in *Picker International, Inc. v. Varian Associates, Inc.* 670 F. Supp. 1363 (1987). In *Picker,* the court stated:

> A firm may not drop a client like a hot potato, especially if it is in order to keep happy a far more lucrative client. *See* Bar Assoc. of Nassau City. Comm. on Professional Ethics, Op. No. 86-1, Law. Man. on Prof. Conduct (ABA/BNA), Curr. Rpts. Vol. 2 at 96 (Feb. 19, 1986) (attorney may not drop one client in order to sue that client on behalf of a more lucrative second client, *even if the first client consents*); *H.G. Gallimore, Inc. v. Abdula,* No. 85 C 7190, Law. Man. on Prof. Conduct (ABA/BNA), Curr. Rpts. Vol. 3 at 41–42 (N.D.Ill., Jan. 28, 1987) (firm may not cure disqualification by disassociating from adverse party in other matters).
>
> The rationale behind this rule is that a firm owes a client a duty of undivided loyalty. *See generally* Law. Man. on Prof. Conduct (ABA/BNA) 51:102–103 and cases cited therein. This is true even though a firm may cease representing a client before the disqualification motion is made. Otherwise, a firm could avoid D.R. 5-105 by simply converting a present client into a former one.

Picker at 1366.

Subsequent caselaw has examined the "hot potato" doctrine and related issues in the context of law firm mergers. See, e.g., *Cavender v. US Xpress Enterprises, Inc.* 191 F. Supp 2d 962 (2002). *Cavender* involved a situation where the plaintiff in an employment discrimination suit moved to disqualify opposing counsel because of ongoing merger negotiations between the plaintiff's former firm and the defendant's law firm. The plaintiff's former firm had withdrawn from the representation due to the merger negotiations. Countering the disqualification motion, the defendant's lawyers stated that they would erect a "Chinese Wall" around the members of the plaintiff's former firm who were going to be parties to the merger. The court declined to grant the motion, since the merger had not yet been consummated. However, the court made it clear that it would grant such a motion once the merger was completed. The court, citing precedent from an earlier Tennessee Supreme Court case, *Clinard v. Blackwood*, 46 S.W.3d 177 (2001) in which the lawyer representing a party in a matter withdrew and joined the opposing lawyer's law firm, held that disqualification would be required if the situation in the current case became similar to that described in the *Clinard* case.

> Under this analysis, then, the establishment of a Chinese Wall is not a complete defense to disqualification but merely a relevant consideration to be taken into account . . . After considering these factors including the Chinese Wall, the Tennessee Supreme Court stated joining the opposition's law firm in the middle of a case would appear to the common man as if the attorney "has not only switched teams, [but] has switched teams in the middle of the game after learning the signals." *Id*. at 188. The appearance of impropriety was too strong in this instance to allow the law firm to continue to represent a party in the litigation. *Id*. at 188–89. In *Penn Mut. Life Ins*. 841 F. Supp. at 817, Chief Judge R. Allan Edgar held the same ("For all practical purposes, the lawyers *968 have switched sides. Clients must feel free to share confidences with their lawyers. This will not occur if we permit lawyers to be today's confidants and tomorrow's adversaries."). Based upon the reasoning expressed in *Clinard* and *Penn Mut. Life Ins.*, the Court holds that in situations similar to those in these two cases disqualification is required.

Cavender at 967.

In *James v. Teleflex, Inc*., 1999 WL 98559 (E.D.Pa.), the District Court for the Eastern District of Pennsylvania disqualified the plaintiff's lawyer after he merged with a law firm that had represented the defendant in matters that the court found to be substantially related to the current case. After the merger, the firm withdrew from the representation of the defendant. Pennsylvania Rule 1.10(b) permits screening, but the court held that the firm had not complied with the Rule:

> I conclude that the Court's interest in protecting the integrity of the proceedings and maintaining public confidence, as well as Teleflex's interest in attorney loyalty, would best be served by disqualification in this case. The fact that Duane Morris and Dunham purportedly have withdrawn their representation of Teleflex does not cure the conflicts presented by Duane Morris' representation of James in this lawsuit. The fact that Dunham withdrew, or at least told Teleflex that he was withdrawing, as counsel for Teleflex in the Aeroutfitters and other matters when the conflict of interest was brought to his attention indicates behavior that violates an attorney's duty of loyalty to his client. *See International Longshoremen's Association*, 909 F. Supp. at 293 ("However, an attorney may not drop one client like a 'hot potato' in order to avoid a conflict with another, more remunerative client."); *Harte Biltmore Ltd. v. First Pennsylvania Bank, N.A.*, 655 F. Supp. 419, 422 (S.D.Fla.1987) ("Public

confidence in lawyers and the legal system must necessarily be undermined when a lawyer suddenly abandons one client in favor of another").

James v. Teleflex, Inc., 1999 WL 98559 (E.D.Pa.).[1]

B. Screening

The ABA Model Rules do not permit screening as a means to avoid imputed disqualification under Model Rule 1.10. They do, however recognize screening in circumstances involving former judicial officers, arbitrators, and third party neutrals or former or current government lawyers under Rules 1.11 *Special Conflicts of Interest for Former and Current Government Officers and Employees* and 1.12 *Former Judge, Arbitrator of Third Party Neutral*. Model Rule 1.0(k) defines screening as follows:

> (k) "Screened" denotes the isolation of a lawyer from any participation in a matter through the timely imposition of procedures within a firm that are reasonably adequate under the circumstances to protect information that the isolated lawyer is obligated to protect under these Rules or other law.

In 2003, the Ethics 2000 Commission proposed an amendment to Rule 1.10 that would have permitted screening, but it was not approved.[2]

Some jurisdictions permit screening either by court decision or by provisions in their rules of professional conduct but in various contexts that may not be directly applicable to the law firm merger scenario. States that have adopted screening rules include Arizona, Illinois, Ohio, Oregon, Massachusetts, Michigan, Pennsylvania, Washington, and Wisconsin.[3]

---

[1] For scholarly analysis of the ethics issues implicated in law firm mergers, *see* RONALD D. ROTUNDA AND JOHN S. DZIENKOWSKI, *The Hot Potato Doctrine*, *in* LEGAL ETHICS: THE LAWYER'S DESKBOOK OF PROFESSIONAL RESPONSIBILITY § 1.7-5 (7ed 2006); RONALD D. ROTUNDA AND JOHN S. DZIENKOWSKI, *Merger of Law Firms*, 91 *in* LAWYER'S MANUAL OF PROFESSIONAL CONDUCT; Sylvia Stevens, *Hot Potatoes—When Can a Lawyer Drop a Client?* 58 OR. ST. BAR BULL. 27 (1998); and Lauren C. Ravkind, *Note, Imputed Disqualification? Law Firm Mergers and the Need for Change*, 8 TEX. REV. OF LITIGATION 93 (1998).

[2] For a discussion of the debate concerning this proposed amendment, *see* Susan Shapiro, *If It Ain't Broke . . . An Empirical Perspective on Ethics 2000, Screening, and the Conflict-of-Interest Rules* U. ILL. L. REV. 1299 (2003).

[3] For an analysis of the caselaw and other authorities on screening, *see* RONALD D. ROTUNDA AND JOHN S. DZIENKOWSKI, *Waiver and Screening Under the Model Rules*, *in* LEGAL ETHICS: THE LAWYER'S DESKBOOK ON PROFESSIONAL RESPONSIBILITY (2006–2007) § 1.10-2. *See also* the chapter entitled *Merger of Law Firms* that appears at page 91:901 of the ABA/BNA LAWYERS' MANUAL ON PROFESSIONAL CONDUCT and the annotations that follow Rule 1.10 in the 2003 edition of the ABA ANNOTATED MODEL RULES OF PROFESSIONAL CONDUCT, and Jason T. Hungerford, *Working with What We've Got: Toward a Modern Approach to Ethical Screens*, 18 GEO. J. LEGAL ETHICS 823 (2005).

For information on how to put together an effective screen, *see* Christopher J. Dunnigan, *Conflict of Interest: The Art Formerly Known as the Chinese Wall: Screening in Law Firms: Why, When, Where and How*, 11 GEO J. LEGAL ETHICS 291 (1998), and for suggested forms including internal firm procedures and sample consent letters to clients concerning screens, *see* Task Force on Conflicts of Interests, Section on Business Law, A.B.A., *Conflicts of Interest Issues*, 50 BUS. LAW. 1381, 1402 (1995).

In view of the varied approach taken towards screening state by state and in the federal courts, it is crucial to check your local rules of professional conduct and caselaw before attempting to use screening as a method to cure a conflict of interest.

C. ABA Ethics Opinions

ABA ethics opinions, while not directly addressing law firm mergers, have touched on some of the issues implicated. See, e.g., ABA Formal Opinion 90-357 (1990), which discusses the consequences of a lawyer being of counsel to more than one firm and the consequent linking together of all of the firms for the purposes of imputed disqualification:

> A lawyer can surely have a close, regular, personal relationship with more than two clients; and the Committee sees no reason why the same cannot be true with more than two law firms. There is, to be sure, some point at which the number of relationships would be too great for any of them to have the necessary qualities of closeness and regularity, and that number may not be much beyond two, but the controlling criterion is "close and regular" relationships, not a particular number. *As a practical matter, nonetheless, there is a consideration that is likely to put a relatively low limit on the number of "of counsel" relationships that can be undertaken by a particular lawyer: this is the fact that, as more fully discussed below, the relationship clearly means that the lawyer is "associated" with each firm with which the lawyer is of counsel.* In consequence there is attribution to the lawyer who is of counsel of all the disqualifications of each firm, and, correspondingly, attribution from the of counsel lawyer to each firm, of each of those disqualifications. See Model Rule 1.10(a). In consequence, the effect of two or more firms sharing an of counsel lawyer is to make them all effectively a single firm, for purposes of attribution of disqualifications [emphasis added].

Formal Opinion 90-357 at page 5.

Formal Opinion 94-388 (1994) discussed the conflicts that can arise when law firms belong to a "network" of firms and the necessity of disclosing to clients the existence of conflicts that may arise when different members of the network represent clients with adverse interests:

> At some point the client of law firm A is entitled to know whether law firm B, with whom law firm A has a relationship, represents interests adverse to the client of law firm A. This is certainly so if a client, in going to law firm A, will have law firm B working on its matter. In this situation the client is the client of both firms, and is entitled to the full protections of Model Rule 1.7 as to both firms. A client is also entitled to know of conflicting commitments where, as described in Formal Opinion 84-351, the relationship between the two firms is "close and regular, continuing and semi-permanent, and not merely that of forwarder-receiver of legal business." In that relationship one firm was "available to the other firm and its clients for consultation and advice."

Formal Opinion 94-388 at page 7.

In the context of negotiating for employment with a law firm that represents an adverse party, ABA Formal Opinion 96-400 (1996) states that a lawyer may avoid such conflicts by withdrawing from the particular matter that gives rise to it:

> A means that may be available, in some circumstances, to avoid the conflict that would be presented by a lawyer's employment negotiations with a firm he opposes in a matter is for the lawyer to withdraw from the adverse representation before having a substantive discussion of employment with the firm. Such withdrawal is clearly permitted if the client consents. Alternatively, such withdrawal could be made without consent pursuant to Model Rule 1.16(b), if applicable. Under Rule 1.16(b), a lawyer may withdraw from a representation "if withdrawal can be accomplished without adverse effect on the interests of the client". . . . Rule 1.16(b) may be invoked, for example, in some situations in which the lawyer is one of several on the engagement, and not the one in charge.

Law firms involved in mergers sometimes try to avoid conflicts or problems by withdrawing from the representation of the client who has the conflict pre-merger so that the client would be considered to be a former client under Rule 1.9. Such an approach is generally disfavored. See the chapter "Merger of Law Firms" of the *ABA/BNA Lawyers' Manual on Professional Conduct* 901 at 907. The discussion in opinion 96-400 should not be read to endorse such tactics in the law firm merger context because (1) the opinion explicitly states that it does not apply to law firm mergers and (2) the opinion states that Rule 1.10 may not be directly applicable for the job negotiating lawyer, since he or she would not necessarily have the same interests as the lawyers who remain with the firm.

D. State Bar Opinions

State bar ethics opinions have addressed some of the ethical issues implicated in law firm mergers in a variety of contexts. For example, see Connecticut Bar Association Opinion 05-09 (2005). This opinion addressed a situation where a law firm that represented developers before a town's zoning board was going to merge with a firm that served as town attorney. The Committee stated that the firm could continue to represent both clients but only if it stopped representing the town in any land-use matters and obtained the informed consent of both clients for each new representation of a developer. The opinion also suggested that the firm screen any lawyers who had information that could be used to the detriment of either client. In Connecticut Bar Opinion 94-9 (1994), the Committee stated that a law firm that was representing a husband in a divorce could merge with a firm that had represented the wife in a personal injury matter so long as they took steps to ensure that no information gleaned from the former representation was used to the wife's detriment.

Rhode Island Opinion 94-77 (1994) discussed circumstances surrounding the merger of two legal services agencies. The opinion stated that the merged agency could not represent clients with adverse interests and further that it could not represent a client that had interests adverse to any of its former clients. The opinion also urged the merging agencies to develop a system whereby they could identify conflicts of interest.

Pennsylvania Opinion 98-55 (1998) stated that a lawyer may not represent the executor of a deceased client's estate if a law firm, with which the lawyer's firm has since merged, drafted the client's surviving spouse's will, even though that was 12-years ago and the lawyer who drafted the will has had no contact with the surviving spouse since then.

Missouri Opinion 990050 (1999) discussed the conflicts issue where two firms were undergoing merger negotiations while they had clients in litigation with one another. The opinion, using a rationale similar to ABA Formal Opinion 96-400, stated that the firms could continue with the negotiations only if both clients consented. The opinion stated further that clients would need to be informed that a merger was being contemplated.

South Carolina Opinion 00-13 (2000) stated that a law firm can continue to represent the executor of an estate when it merges with the law firm that represents the beneficiaries so long as they seek identical relief and the representation will not be adversely affected. South Carolina Opinion 92-23 (1992) stated that a law firm may continue to represent a client in a litigation matter where the lawyer for the opposing party joins the firm so long as the formerly adverse lawyer does not reveal any information about the adverse party.

IV. Duties of a Lawyer Who Acquires the Practice of a Deceased Sole Practitioner

ABA Formal Opinion 92-369 (a copy of which can be found at the end of Chapter 10) discusses the obligations of a lawyer who assumes responsibility for a deceased sole practitioner's client files:

> A lawyer who assumes... responsibility (for the deceased sole practitioner's client files) must review the client files carefully to determine which files need immediate attention; failure to do so would leave the clients in the same position as if their attorney died without any plan to protect their interests. The lawyer should also contact all clients of the deceased lawyer to notify them of the death of their lawyer and to request instructions, in accordance with Rule 1.15.
>
> Because the reviewing lawyer does not represent the clients, he or she should review only as much of the file as is needed to identify the client and to make a determination as to which files need immediate attention.

ABA Formal Opinion 92-369 (1992) at page 6.

Several state and local bar association ethics opinions discuss the obligations of a lawyer who assumes responsibility for a deceased sole practitioner's client files. Most of them address the duties of lawyers who are either the executors of the deceased lawyers' estates or who are partners of or shared office space with the deceased lawyers. These opinions stress the importance of the executor/partner/officemate's careful review of the files in order to determine if any action need be taken to protect client's interests. For example, Ohio State Bar Association Opinion 00-02 (2000) states:

> What then, is required of the person who assumes responsibility for these files? First, the attorney should make, in light of the age of the files, a reasonable

effort to locate the client for whom he or she has files. If the client can be located, then he or she should be notified and asked to pick up the material or authorize its disposal. If this effort is unsuccessful, and given the age of some of these files, it seems likely that it will be, then the question arises as to the proper disposition of the files.

If the effort to locate the clients of the deceased lawyer is unsuccessful, the attorney should nevertheless review the files and remove and retain "items that clearly or probably belong to the client." In particular, care should be taken to preserve original documents, and other similar materials, in the client files, the return of which could reasonably be expected by the client.

See also New York County Lawyers' Association Opinion 709 (1996), (partner of deceased attorney must give notice of the death to clients for whom the deceased attorney was handling ongoing matters); Connecticut Bar Association Opinion 95-13 (1995), Nassau County Opinions 89-43, (1989), 92-27 (1992) (lawyer who received all active and closed files of deceased attorney has the same ethical obligations for the files as if they were his or her own files or if designated a "guardian" of the files by agreement with the deceased attorney or estate); and Mississippi Opinion 114 (1986).

A digest of Maryland Opinion 89-58 (1989) states:

> A lawyer who shared office space with another lawyer and handled that lawyer's cases when he died . . . has the following responsibilities . . . (1) the lawyer must review every file in his possession and notify clients or third parties if the lawyer has property belonging to them; (2) the lawyer may dispose of files in cases he handled for the deceased lawyer as he would dispose of his own client files; (3) the lawyer must turn over all other client files to the representative of the deceased's estate and explain the legal significance of retaining those files; (4) the lawyer must keep information contained in all the files confidential regardless of whether or not he handled the cases.

901 *ABA/BNA Lawyers' Manual on Professional Conduct* 4327. *See also* Kentucky Opinion E-405 (1998) and Wisconsin Opinion E-879 (1987).

Many of the state and local bar opinions cite to ABA Informal Opinion 1384 (1977) (Disposition of a Lawyer's Closed or Dormant Files Relating to Representation of or Services to Clients) for authority on the issue of retention and disposition of the deceased lawyer's client files.[4]

These opinions also stress that any lawyer reviewing client files must take steps to preserve client confidentiality and may not disclose client confidences without the client's consent. See Maine Board of Bar Overseers Opinion 143 (1994) and Philadelphia Bar Association Opinion 97-4 (1997).

Some states have statutory guidelines for the appointment of a receiver to manage a deceased lawyer's practice in the event that no partner, associate, executor, or other responsible party capable of conducting the lawyer's affairs is known to exist. See, e.g., Illinois Supreme Court Rule 776, Appointment of Receiver in Certain Cases, Ill.Ann. Stat. ch. 110A, Par. 776 (SmithHurd 1991). See also Rule 28 of the *ABA Model Rules*

---

[4] Informal Opinion 1384 listed the guidelines relating to the disposition of closed or dormant client files. See "Forms, Guidelines, and Checklists" at the end of this chapter.

for Lawyer Disciplinary Enforcement (1989). This rule also outlines procedures for the appointment of a receiver after the lawyer's death.[5]

V. Conclusion

Although a lawyer's ethical obligations applicable to the sale, merger, or management of a deceased sole practitioner's law practice are varied, the common elements predominate. Preserving client confidentiality, identifying and avoiding conflicts of interest, and timely communications with clients are implicated in all three scenarios.

When confronted with ethics issues in a particular jurisdiction, bear in mind that the ABA Model Rules of Professional Conduct and ethics opinions are advisory only. Always check the applicable local rules of professional conduct, ethics opinions, and case law in your jurisdiction.

Forms, Guidelines, and Checklists

A. Informal Opinion 1384: Guidelines to the Disposition of Closed or Dormant Client Files

A. Informal Opinion 1384: Guidelines to the Disposition of Closed or Dormant Client Files

1. Unless the client consents, a lawyer should not destroy or discard items that clearly or probably belong to the client. Such items include those furnished to the lawyer by or in behalf of the client, the return of which could reasonably be expected by the client, and original documents (especially when not filed or recorded in the public records).

2. A lawyer should use care not to destroy or discard information that the lawyer knows or should know may still be necessary or useful in the assertion or defense of the client's position in a matter for which the applicable statutory limitations period has not expired.

3. A lawyer should use care not to destroy or discard information that the client may need, has not previously been given to the client, and is not otherwise readily

---

[5] Rule 28. Appointment of Counsel to Protect Clients' Interests When Respondent Is Transferred to Disability Inactive Status, Suspended, Disbarred, Disappears, or Dies.

    A. Inventory of Lawyer Files. If a respondent has been transferred to disability inactive status, or has disappeared or died, or has been suspended or disbarred and there is evidence that he or she has not complied with Rule 27, and no partner, executor or other responsible party capable of conducting the respondent's affairs is known to exist, the presiding judge in the judicial district in which the respondent maintained a practice, upon proper proof of fact, shall appoint a lawyer or lawyers to inventory the files of the respondent, and to take such action as seems indicated to protect the interests of the respondent and his or her clients.

    B. Protection for Records Subject to Inventory. Any lawyer so appointed shall not be permitted to disclose and information contained in any files inventories without the consent of the client to whom the file relates, except as necessary to carry out the order of the court which appointed the lawyer to make the inventory.

available to the client, and which the client may reasonably except will be preserved by the lawyer.
4. In determining the length of time for retention of disposition of a file, a lawyer should exercise discretion. The nature and contents of some files may indicate a need for longer retention than do the nature and contents of other files, based upon their obvious relevance and materiality to matters that can be expected to arise.
5. A lawyer should take special care to preserve, indefinitely, accurate and complete records of the lawyer's receipt and disbursement of trust funds.
6. In disposing of a file, a lawyer should protect the confidentiality of the contents.
7. A lawyer should not destroy or dispose of a file without screening it in order to determine that consideration has been given to the matters discussed above.
8. A lawyer should preserve, perhaps for an extended time, an index or identification of the files that the lawyer has destroyed or disposed of.

Further Reading

Dimitriou, Demetrios. "Purchase or Sale of a Solo Practice: The Ethical Issues" in K. William Gibson's *Flying Solo: A Survival Guide for the Solo and Small Firm Lawyer,* 4e. Chicago, IL: American Bar Association Law Practice Management Section, 2005.

Hildebrandt International. *Anatomy of a Law Firm Merger: How to Make—or Break—the Deal,* 3e. Chicago, IL: American Bar Association, 2005.

Poll, Edward. "Purchase or Sale of a Solo Practice: The Financial Issues," in K. William Gibson's *Flying Solo: A Survival Guide for the Solo and Small Firm Lawyer,* 4e. Chicago, IL: American Bar Association Law Practice Management Section, 2005.

Rotunda, Ronald D. *Legal Ethics in a Nutshell,* 3e. Eagan, MN: Thomson/West, 2007.

Chapter 3

Valuation of a Law Practice
by James Cotterman

I. Introduction

Valuing a business concern is difficult. When that concern is a closely held business, the task is complicated by several factors. When the closely held business is a professional practice, the task is complicated further. And when the professional practice is in the field of law, the task becomes most difficult of all. What is the fair value of a lifetime of work building a law practice? This chapter discusses the issues and methods to answer that question.

> ### *Key Points*
> - There are different methods for valuing the business and valuing the practice.
> - Valuing and selling goodwill is complex and remains a state-defined issue.
> - A firm can be perceived as either an income generator or an investment and as such must be valued differently.
> - There are specific earnings, multiples, and process steps appropriate in valuing law firms.
> - Several methods of creating a range of values are feasible, including internal reviews, the multiple of income approach, the capitalized cash flow approach, and the capitalized excess earnings method.

II. What Is Being Valued—What Is Being Transferred?

This question of what is being valued and what is being transferred is often the one most overlooked. One cannot value a law practice without answering what's being transferred, although many people try.

In the sale of a law practice, the seller is providing the accumulated efforts of establishing trust-based relationships with clients, building relationships with contacts and referral sources, creating a market presence professionally and among desired clients, and developing the infrastructure to deliver legal services.

The buyer is looking for an ongoing stream of income that is represented primarily by the client base and referral sources of the seller. The buyer is hopeful that he or she can assume the trust position with clients and market presence of the seller. In addition, there are hard (often called tangible) assets and intangibles, such as an established business operation, that make up the practice's infrastructure.

The clients are looking for consistent advice and counsel; more directly, they are looking for solutions to problems or issues from someone who understands them and their needs and someone they trust.

A. Valuing the Business

In essence, what's being transferred can be separated into two components that will be valued separately: the business and the practice.

The business consists of the operating intangibles and the hard assets less any outstanding debt or lease obligations that are a part of the business. Such assets and obligations may include:

- Cash, deposits, and prepaid expenses;
- Land, building, and improvements thereto (or possibly a long-term lease);
- Computer systems and other equipment;
- Library and reference materials (although the Internet age has altered this aspect of the business);
- Furnishings and fixtures;
- Accounts receivable;
- Unbilled fees and clients costs;
- Accounts payable and accrued expenses not yet paid;
- Loans and capital lease obligations; and
- Client funds held in trust.

The practice of law is not a capital-intensive business. Large land holdings are not required. There is minimal investment in raw materials (unless you consider the cost of attending law school!). The inventory is modest, amounting to a few months of the lawyer's time value expended on client matters (except possibly in certain contingent fee practices). There is no need for expensive equipment, as in many medical practices. Yet what investments there are have grown more expensive and require more rapid replenishment than in the past—for example, that typewriter for your secretary that used to last twenty years is now a laptop for the lawyer and a desktop computer for the assistant, and both pieces of equipment need replacement every few years.

B. Valuing the Practice

The practice is the source of the immediate stream of revenues, as well as the network of contacts and referrals that assist in generating the future stream of revenues. Access is the first step and client trust is the ultimate requirement. This is where there is significant value, or not. And this is the area where it is most difficult to determine what value there is and how much of it can be transferred from seller to buyer. This last question requires seller, buyer, and client input. This is a further reason why law practices have less value than comparably sized businesses in different settings.

A further complication arises if one looks to other professions where there is data on purchases and sales. Such transactions, often expressed as a multiple of earnings or revenues, may include some but not all of the assets and liabilities just described. One needs to be careful when looking at multiples to understand just what is included or what is not from the balance sheet. Unfortunately there are no databases of comparable transactions for law firms. The only available guidance are the surveys that look at internal transfers, which represent an okay but not ideal proxy for valuation. One must separate the buy-out of an ownership interest from any retirement benefit funded by the firm. In most instances these are co-mingled and not readily separable.

III. The Special Problem of a Law Practice

If, in essence, the most valuable asset conveyed in the transfer of a law practice is the ongoing and future access to contacts, referral sources, and clients, along with the trust they have in the seller, then essentially what is conveyed is the **professional goodwill** of the lawyer. The courts remain divided on this issue. And the complexity is seen in the various cases where goodwill has and has not been recognized. Clearly in some fact situations there may be an ongoing concern that is independent of the seller. It is also clear that fact situations exist where this is not the case.

Historically, the profession and the courts held that, as a matter of public interest and policy, clients are *not* property and can*not* be sold, and clients are ultimately free to select and change their legal representative at any time.

In matrimonial matters, both equitable distribution and community property jurisdictions have been inconsistent in their treatment of goodwill and value of practice, but this is the general area in which goodwill has traditionally been found, often embodied in the value of the professional license.

A. ABA Guidelines

Before 1990, the ABA position was that it was unethical to sell a law practice. And that was the position adopted by the state bar associations. Then in 1990 the ABA adopted Rule 1.17, *Sale of Law Practice*.[1] The rule provides for a sale or purchase of a law practice, or an area of a law practice, by a lawyer or firm if certain conditions are met. The rule further provides for the recognition of goodwill in such sales.

The ethical considerations present problems and risks for both the seller and the buyer and center on protecting clients' rights, property, and confidences. Ethical considerations cover a broad gamut of issues including client communication, lawyer

---

[1] For more information on this rule, see Chapter 10, which contains the text of this rule, and the annotations found in ANNOTATED MODEL RULES OF PROFESSIONAL CONDUCT, published by the ABA's Center for Professional Responsibility. Lawyers should also check their State's Rules, as they may vary from the ABA's guidelines.

of record, client confidences, client files/property, client funds, conflicts of interest, competency, misrepresentation by seller of purchaser's qualifications, and errors of selling lawyer discovered by buyer, among other issues.

Financial aspects covered in the rule that are important in the negotiation of the transfer are the right to have a not-to-compete provision and that the buyer must purchase an entire practice or an entire practice area. The buyer may *not* select individual matters and clients, but rather must accept the entire portfolio.

IV. Valuing Partner/Shareholder Interests (The Internal Transfer)

The spectrum of law firm valuation and withdrawal entitlement theory can be characterized by two polar positions. The first considers the firm as a means to generate income (compensation), with modest, if any, value beyond the cash basis capital account. This is currently the dominant view in the profession, and has resulted in the vast majority of firms valuing only the cash basis balance sheet for internal withdrawal rights. The second considers the firm as an investment, much like most other commercial endeavors.

There is readily acknowledged value in the establishment of a business enterprise. Starting a business involves creating business contacts, banking relationships, and vendor relationships; designing and outfitting space; finding and training staff; creating forms and procedures; and generating cash flow. These items comprise **institutional goodwill**. Any individual who has started a business understands the value of an ongoing entity. It is for this reason that many firms will still provide something to founders upon retirement beyond the cash basis capital account. At times, the cost of buying out the founders is spread across two or three generations in order to facilitate the transfer.

When this is done for founders and in those firms that still provide some form of unfunded buy-out, the typical methodology is to establish the adjusted net cash-basis book value of the firm plus a multiple of some average of past earnings. At a minimum, this multiple will recognize the value of unbilled time and accounts receivable that are not shown on the balance sheet. In some circumstances, and with higher multiples, some recognition of the goodwill or going concern value of the business will be factored into the buy-out.

The buyers, in this instance, have an advantage in that they know the seller, the clients, the infrastructure required to serve those clients, and the practice methodologies being acquired. The clients should know and have relationships with some of the acquiring partners (at least if succession was planned properly), resulting in a more likely successful transition. And this is essentially the exclusive means by which law firms handled the retirement of partners before the tax law changes in the early 1980s permitted qualified pension programs for partnerships.

V. The Earnings Multiple

The earnings multiples for service businesses are lower than those for manufacturing concerns. In professional service firms the multiples are lower yet, and law firms are generally even lower than other professional service firms. Manufacturing concerns typically have ongoing franchises and productive machinery to sustain them.

Value in a law practice is largely personal to the lawyer and that individual's ability to attract and retain clients.

This is not to say that some firms have not created a "brand identity" that is separate and distinct to the institution. It is just that those firms are rare and not the subject of this chapter.

Complicating this task is the fact that even when client relationships are transferred, it is ultimately the new lawyer's personal ability and relationship with the client that determines whether the client will stay or leave. Therefore, the transfer of a practice is a complex blend of seller, buyer, and client interaction. It is for these reasons that multiples are so low.

> Sustaining the profitability of a law firm, however, greatly depends upon whether the firm is able to retain and develop its base of clients and the lawyers responsible for attracting them.

> The lawyer has knowledge, experience, skill, judgment, and reputation—all elements of **professional goodwill**. As long as clients primarily hire lawyers, as opposed to firms, this will remain a guiding principle in valuing law practices.

A. Developing the Standard Multiple

Buy-outs beyond the return of cash basis capital in a law firm can be valued and paid in many different ways. Some plan designs are simple, while others are very complex. This variety makes comparisons of buy-outs among firms difficult. However, a present value analysis allows the various plans to be reduced to a common, comparable stated amount. Once that amount is calculated, a comparison can be made between that amount and partner earnings at withdrawal. The result is a standard multiple of compensation (earnings) that is common in the legal profession for a buy-out.

B. Adjusting the Multiple

Once the standard multiple is determined, it is adjusted up or down to reflect the facts and circumstances of that firm, practice, and market. Here are the common factors considered to adjust the multiple:

- Market demographics and location,
- Stability and quality of the client base,
- Source of clients and referral sources,
- Nature of relationships (institutional or transactional),
- Ability of remaining lawyers to perpetuate the business,
- Name recognition and reputations (firm and lawyers) in the community served,
- Type of practice and pricing/billing/payment norms,
- Concentration of revenues,
- Profitability of practice relative to comparatives,

- Size of firm,
- Stability of partner group,
- Profits reinvested into the firm to fund growth,
- Level of risk undertaken, and
- Quality of infrastructure.

The process of establishing an adjusted multiple is both subjective and judgmental. There is more art than science in the assignment of bonus points or risk reserves based upon various factors.

Generally, earnings multiples fall within a range of 1.0 to 4.25. That means the value of the practice is in a range from one year of normalized annual earnings to four and one-quarter times normalized annual earnings. A second multiple often referred to is a multiple of revenues. Generally ranging from .50 to 1.50 in value, such multiples are considered less appropriate because they ignore risk and return—two critical elements of value. Page 36 has a conversion chart for comparing revenue multiples to adjusted earnings multiples at various profit margins.

The following table depicts how one might assign factors and points for a small law firm to arrive at a reasonable multiple. Based on the table, a benefit of 2.15 to 3.10 times earnings would appear appropriate.

Valuation Factor	Multiplier Points Low Range	Multiplier Points High Range
Base multiplier	1.00	1.50
Positive factors		
Core client group is stable and obtained through direct contact	.15	.25
Seller is young enough to effect an orderly succession	.20	.30
Consistently a very profitable practice	.50	.75
Senior partner (and then firm) are known as the "go to" firm for these services	.75	1.00
Negative factors		
Remaining partners too reliant on senior partner for rainmaking and leadership	−.30	−.45
Firm is tied to a bad regional economy	−.15	−.25
Valuation Multiplier	2.15	3.10

C. Structure of Payments

In this instance, the seller (retiring partner) would receive two payments for a buy-out. The first payment would be for the cash basis capital account, adjusted upward for any additional sums owed to the partner and downward for any debt the partner owed to the partnership. This amount will most likely be paid over a short one-to-three year period and is most often the same amount of time granted new partners buying-in to the practice.

The second payment would be the earnings multiple. The definition of earnings can vary but the most common is an average three-to-five years of total compensation. There are variations on this theme, such as the average of the highest three of final five or of the last five drop the high and low and average the middle three. Total compensation includes all taxable income (wages, fringe benefits, employer paid pension, and employer paid payroll taxes for those practicing in a professional corporation setting). This payment would most often be amortized over a three-to-seven year period of time. For example, if the high multiple were used over seven years, then the partner would receive 44 percent of his or her average total compensation for each of the next seven years. In addition, most firms would condition such payments on the actual retirement of the partner from the practice of law.

D. Insurance

> Sellers (retiring partners) should not forget to have the firm acquire a tail errors and omissions insurance policy in addition to the payments for capital and retirement.

And if the partner has retired before age 65 or has a spouse under age 65, some provision for health insurance continuation should be provided. Often this would be done with the premiums paid by the retired partner. But it may complicate the mechanics of the transaction in order to comply with the insurance carrier's contract.

A special note for estate and contingent fee practices or firms with a material amount of estate or contingent fee work: these practices require extra care and special analysis, as there is future potential value that must be considered arising from past services.

VI. Valuing the External Transfer

When the buyer is not associated with the seller's firm, the transfer is handled a bit differently. The buyer and seller will often know of each other, but the buyer may not fully understand the seller's practice.

The first step is to learn about the seller. This is standard business due diligence. Interview other lawyers, judges, bankers, accountants, and other contacts who can tell you something about the individual. Discuss the practice, the clients, pricing, and billing policies.

The buyer should look to the seller to assist in the transfer of the client relationships and referral contacts. It is for this reason that so many of these deals have lives of one-to-three years and sometimes longer. A common procedure to facilitate a deal is the acquiring lawyer and the selling lawyer operating as a "firm" for a period of time.

VII. Value the Business

The method to value another lawyer's business is very similar to the internal transfer method of valuing the capital of a partner. Essentially, the business is valued on the net book value cash basis balance sheet. Reasonable due diligence should be conducted as for any business transaction. Extensive due diligence checklists are available from the author at info@altmanweil.com. Rarely will a firm have assets that require separate fair market adjustments. This usually occurs with antiques, artwork, and the like. However, often those assets are the personal property of the seller and will not be part of the transaction. See the checklist "Items to Consider When Valuing the Business" at the end of this chapter for a more comprehensive list.

VIII. Value the Practice

Review the factors provided above that affect the value of earnings multiples for internal transfers. These same factors are critical at arriving at an appropriate understanding of the practice value (appropriate multiple) for an external transfer.

A. Internal Transfers and Past Transactions

Valuing a practice can involve a number of methodologies. Internal transfers as well as past transactions for that firm are one good source to use to begin to develop a valuation. Organizational documents may set forth a methodology that the owners have agreed to with respect to valuation. Remember that buy-ins are as instructive as buy-outs in determining how the owners feel about value. Look to see how that compares to any prior transactions at the firm. Unfortunately these internal reviews may involve documents and transactions that are not recent. And such deals could have objectives other than fair market value driving the ultimate agreements reached.

B. Multiple of Income Approach

A second methodology used is known as the multiple of income approach. This method is founded on the principle that value is predicated on what an informed and rational investor would pay for the company's future earnings. Profits must be "normalized" or adjusted for those items that would reflect the company's operating characteristics going forward after a sale.

- Use five years of financial statements to see the sustained level of and direction of performance.
- Eliminate non-recurring revenues and expenses as well as items that are not indicative of economic performance for each year.
- Consider the appropriate mix of past years of revenue to use as going forward revenues.
- Review historical gross profit margin and profit margins to see how direct costs and selling, general, and administrative (SG&A) relate to revenues to determine what direct costs and SG&A expenses to subtract from the going forward revenues.
- Calculate for each year an adjustment to normalize earnings by adding back benefits, "perks," and compensation to reported net income and subtracting a reasonable compensation package. Determine what adjustment is appropriate for the going forward analysis.

- ♦ Calculate the multiple using a methodology similar to what has been described above.
- ♦ Multiply the normalized earnings by the multiple.

While a common methodology, this approach requires skill in determining the economic income, future growth, and appropriate multiple. This method will often include most of the balance sheet as those assets and liabilities are necessary to the production of the income. Excessive net assets require an addition to the final value.

C. Capitalized Cash Flows

A third methodology is capitalized cash flows. This method is predicated on the present value of future cash flows (as opposed to earnings). This means that earnings are adjusted for non-cash expenses such as depreciation and amortization and non-expense cash flows such as repayment of debt. The capitalization rate is the return a prudent investor would require, after adjusting for risk over a five year period. We have used a balanced market index investment portfolio, adjusted for risk, for this methodology.

- ♦ Use five years of financial statements to see sustained and direction of performance.
- ♦ Eliminate non-recurring revenues and expenses as well as items that are not indicative of economic performance for each year.
- ♦ Add back depreciation and amortization and subtract out repayment of debt to determine cash flows for each year.
- ♦ Calculate for each year an adjustment to normalize earnings by adding back benefits, "perks," and compensation to reported net income and subtracting a reasonable compensation package.
- ♦ Determine net cash flows for each year. Then calculate average and weighted average (determine what weights are appropriate to reflect the direction of performance) net cash flows for the five years.
- ♦ Determine the capitalization rate.
- ♦ Calculate the practice value using the capitalization rate computed above.

The same concerns exist for capitalized cash flows as for the multiple of earnings method above.

D. Capitalized Excess Earnings

A fourth methodology is capitalized excess earnings. This method essentially is calculated as follows:

- ♦ Determine the firm's net tangible assets on an accrual basis.
- ♦ Reconstruct net income by adding back benefits, "perks," and compensation to reported net income and subtracting a reasonable compensation package.
- ♦ Calculate reconstructed net income for three to five years and average.
- ♦ Multiply net tangible assets from above by a reasonable return rate.

- Subtract the reasonable return from average reconstructed net income. The result is excess net income.
- Capitalize the excess net income to arrive at goodwill.

This is a widely used valuation method, but it requires considerable skill and judgment to do well. And in a professional practice, the concept of excess earnings is a very difficult concept to work with. See the author's article, "Unreasonable Compensation for P.C. Shareholders," which is available free of charge from the author's website, www.altmanweil.com.

IX. Structuring the Deal

You have probably used all of the above methods and now have a series of value ranges. See if you have any that are significantly different from the rest. If you do, then go back and understand why that occurred. Generally you will see a pattern of value that you can feel comfortable using.

You have used a mixture of historical information and adjustments to project the future economic performance of the practice. But what if you are wrong? What if the clients do not stay with the practice? Consider a structure that pays prospectively. If you are buying a future stream of income, then pay based on the *future* income. It's riskier to the seller, which may mean a higher multiple for the valuation, but at least it is self-funding. Since the seller is needed to assist in the transfer, this could be structured as an earn-out. The best result is that you pay even more because the combination of the seller's efforts and yours results in even more business during the transition years.

X. The Seller's Perspective

The seller of a law practice is primarily interested in ensuring that his or her clients will be provided with quality legal services, payment is received, and personal liability is protected.

There is risk to the seller if the buying lawyer is not competent to handle certain areas of the practice being acquired. Clients may not continue their relationship with the new lawyer. Payments may not be made. Therefore, a selling lawyer must undertake due diligence that includes:

- Verification of the purchasing lawyer's expertise and credentials;.
- Verification of the purchasing lawyer's reputation;
- Assessment of the purchasing lawyer's philosophical approach to clients and practice and if there will likely be an effective relationship between seller's clients/referrals and the purchasing lawyer; and
- Determination of availability of "tail" insurance coverage.

XI. Conclusion

Valuing a law practice differs if you are selling or buying. The buyer is interested in qualifying the validity of the business and in confirming that the price paid will match the investment. The seller is interested in verifying that his or her clients will be provided with quality legal services, and so values the buyer's practice to ensure continued success and payments. Even though valuing client relationships and goodwill are subjective and judgmental, there are earnings multiples and several valuation methods that can track the financial reality of such firm elements. The organized firm will know itself well enough to be able to confirm such value.

Forms, Guidelines, and Checklists

A. Checklist: Items to Consider When Valuing the Business
B. Revenue Multipliers for Law Firms
C. Earnings Multipliers for Law Firms
D. Revenue Multiplier—Adjusted Profit Margin/Adjusted Earnings Equivalents

A. Checklist: Items to Consider When Valuing the Business

- Review copies of *filed* federal income tax returns for the past three-to-five years.
- Protect yourself against the quality of the work-in-progress and accounts receivable and the level of debt and accounts payable. Although you may not be buying these assets and liabilities, you could inherit the problems that are hidden within.
- Review title to all assets and a detail of assets included in the transaction.
- Review all debt agreements, equipment and office leases, maintenance contracts, and subscription agreements. Look for capital leases improperly classified as operating leases.
- Review all business and payroll tax returns that are required to be filed for the last three-to-five years.
- Review the malpractice insurance policy *and* applications. Determine the availability of "tail" and "prior acts" coverage.
- Review all other liability, fire, and theft policies and applications.
- Interview the staff and review salaries, bonuses, and benefits. Review performance evaluations, if any.
- Interview the office manager and conduct a procedures and practices, audit to look for general compliance with applicable rules and regulations.
- Test for prepaid expenses, accounts payable, accrued expenses, and deferred income taxes.
- Examine the trust account asset and liability, including the detail ledgers supporting the balances. Is the trust account properly established?
- Review annual client fee lists for several years and compare the fee detail lists to fees reported on the tax returns. Do a conflicts check.
- Review practice management procedures (file opening procedures, tickler systems, conflict check systems, and the like).
- Review open matters, deadlines.

B. Revenue Multipliers for Law Firms

Low	Likely Range	High
.50	.75–1.25	1.50

C. Earnings Multipliers for Law Firms

Low	Likely Range	High
1.00	1.50–3.50	4.25

D. Revenue Multiplier—Adjusted Profit Margin/Adjusted Earnings Equivalents

Adjusted Profit Margin

Revenue Multiplier	30%	35%	40%	45%	50%	55%	60%	65%
.25	0.833	0.714	0.625	0.556	0.500	0.455	0.417	0.385
.50	1.667	1.429	1.250	1.111	1.000	0.909	0.833	0.769
.75	2.500	2.143	1.875	1.667	1.500	1.364	1.259	1.154
1.00	3.333	2.875	2.500	2.222	2.000	1.818	1.667	1.538
1.25	4.167	3.571	3.125	2.778	2.500	2.273	2.083	1.923
1.50	5.000	4.286	3.750	3.333	3.000	2.727	2.500	2.308
1.75	5.833	5.000	4.375	3.889	3.500	3.182	2.917	2.692
2.00	6.667	5.714	5.000	4.444	4.000	3.636	3.333	3.077
2.25	7.500	6.429	5.625	5.000	4.500	4.091	3.750	3.462
2.50	8.333	7.143	6.250	5.556	5.000	4.545	4.167	3.846

Further Reading

Bower, Ward. "Is This Merger Worth Pursuing?" *Law Practice Management*. v. 28, part 7 (2002): p. 35.

Bower, Ward. "The Sale of a Law Practice in South Carolina: The Impact of Model Rule 1.17 on Sole Practitioners and Their Clients." *South Carolina Law Review* v. 50, no. 4, (Summer 1999): p. 1029.

Cotterman, James D. "How to Value a Law Practice." *The Practical Lawyer*, v. 41 (March 1995): pp. 29–36.

Fishman, J. E., and W. J. Morrison. "Business Valuation Case and Commentary: Excess Earnings and Discounted Future Earnings to Value a Law Practice Interest." *American Journal of Family Law*, v. 15, part 4 (2001): pp. 311–314.

Orenstein, Theodore P. and Gary N. Skoloff. "When a Professional Divorces: Strategies for Valuing Practices, Licenses, and Degrees" chapter in Theodore Orenstein's *When a Lawyer Divorces*, 2d (Chicago: American Bar Association 1999).

Schultz, Carl E. "Valuing a Law Practice." *Wisconsin Lawyer* v. 64 (December 1991): pp. 11–12.

Chapter 4

Setting a Price on a Law Practice: Checklist for Valuation

by Shannon Pratt, CFA, FASA, MCBA, CMCAA

I. Introduction

Law practices come in all flavors, shapes and sizes, so that it is not possible to set a price on a law practice as a rule of thumb, as it might be possible to do with some other kind of business. Nonetheless, most law practices—whether a solo practice or a multiple-office law firm with hundreds of lawyers—can be accurately valued provided the right questions are asked and the right documents are provided. The following checklist is a starting point for such a valuation.

The following is a generalized checklist for valuation of a law firm for any purpose, including sale of all or part of a practice, divorce, partnership dispute, or tax issues.

II. Checklist for Valuing a Law Practice

A. THE ASSIGNMENT

- ❏ Name of practice
- ❏ Interest to be valued (% of partnership, etc.)
- ❏ Date(s) of valuation
- ❏ Statutes/case law of what state
- ❏ Instructions regarding inclusion or exclusion of various assets/liabilities—e.g., work in progress, personal vs. practice goodwill—as applicable
- ❏ Standard of value (e.g., fair market value, fair value, etc., perhaps with reference to statutes or cases)
- ❏ Format and content of report (e.g., oral, full report in accordance with Uniform Standards of Professional Appraisal Practice, etc.)
- ❏ Name of client

B. APPRAISER(S)

- ☐ Name of appraisal firm
- ☐ Name(s) of lead appraiser(s)
- ☐ Appraisal credentials of lead appraiser(s)
    - ☐ American Society of Appraisers
        - ☐ FASA (Fellow)
        - ☐ ASA (Senior)
        - ☐ AM (Accredited Member)
    - ☐ American Institute of Certified Public Accountants
        - ☐ ABV (Accredited in Business Valuation)
    - ☐ Institute of Business Appraisers
        - ☐ MCBA (Master Certified Business Appraiser)
        - ☐ CBA (Certified Business Appraiser)
    - ☐ National Association of Certified Valuation Analysts
        - ☐ CVA (Certified Valuation Analyst)
    - ☐ Institute of Chartered Financial Analysts
        - ☐ CFA (Chartered Financial Analyst)

C. DOCUMENTS AND INFORMATION

- ☐ Five years of balance sheets
- ☐ Five years of income statements
- ☐ Five years of tax returns
- ☐ Cash or accrual basis accounting
- ☐ Partnership/operating agreements
- ☐ History of transactions in partnership interests
- ☐ Aged accounts receivable/payable lists
- ☐ Costs advanced on behalf of clients
- ☐ Work in progress
- ☐ History of collections, especially on contingent work
- ☐ Referral sources/system for generating revenues
- ☐ Client list/history of repeat business
- ☐ Asset values (current fair market values)
- ☐ Leases
- ☐ Hours worked
- ☐ Billing records
- ☐ Professionals' compensation (salary, partnership withdrawals, benefits, personal expenses, etc.)
- ☐ Charitable contributions
- ☐ Malpractice insurance and applications, including prior acts and tail coverage
- ☐ Contracts/subscription agreements
- ☐ Insurance policies
- ☐ List of partners, with % interests
- ☐ Description of practice
- ☐ Assets in excess of those needed for practice

- ❑ Covenants not to compete (could be existing covenant or newly created covenant in connection with sale)
- ❑ Firm brochures
- ❑ Law library

D. NORMALIZING THE FINANCIAL STATEMENTS

- ❑ Adjusting compensation
- ❑ Sources of reasonable compensation

_____
_____
_____

- ❑ Adjusting lease charges
- ❑ Source of reasonable lease rate

_____

- ❑ Adjusting nonrecurring and extraordinary items
- ❑ Adjusting balance sheet items to fair market value
  - ❑ Accounts receivable
  - ❑ Work in process inventory
  - ❑ Supplies inventory
  - ❑ Equipment
  - ❑ Leasehold improvements
  - ❑ Intangible assets
  - ❑ Accrued liabilities
  - ❑ Deferred liabilities (deferred revenues, deferred expenses, deferred income taxes)
  - ❑ Lease obligations
  - ❑ Long-term debt
  - ❑ Contingent liabilities and/or assets
  - ❑ Real estate
  - ❑ Capital/drawing accounts

E. EVALUATION OF BUYER

- ❑ Credentials
- ❑ Expertise
- ❑ Probable relationships with existing clients
- ❑ Availability of tail insurance coverage

F. VALUATION METHODS

- ❑ Market value
- ❑ Source(s) of comparable sales

_____
_____

- ❏ Partnership agreement
- ❏ Excess earnings method
- ❏ Discounted cash flow (or other variable representing economic income)
- ❏ Capitalization of normalized cash flow (or other economic income variable)

G. QUESTIONS TO ASK

- ❏ What definition of value did you use?
- ❏ What was the source of that definition of value?
- ❏ What appraisal credentials do you hold?
- ❏ What adjustments did you make to the financial statements?
- ❏ For each adjustment:
    - ❏ Why did you make that adjustment?
    - ❏ Explain how you arrived at the amount of the adjustment
- ❏ What valuation methods did you use and why?
- ❏ If the market approach, where did you get the transactions that you relied on?
- ❏ If the excess earnings method was used,
    - ❏ How did you determine the reasonable return on tangible assets?
    - ❏ What measure of earning power did you use (e.g., net cash flow, net income) and why?
    - ❏ How did you determine the capitalization rate for the excess earnings?
- ❏ If the discounted future benefits method was used, what variable did you discount (e.g., net cash flow, net income)? Why?
    - ❏ What was the source of the projections?
    - ❏ How did you determine the discount rate?
- ❏ If the capitalization method was used, what variable of income did you capitalize? Why?
    - ❏ How did you verify that the amount of income capitalized was reasonable?
    - ❏ How did you determine the capitalization rate?

Chapter 5

Tax Consequences of "Retiring" a General Partner's Interest in a Law Partnership

by John Clynch

I. Introduction

Liquidation, or "retirement," of a general partner's interest is "the termination of the general partner's entire interest in a partnership by means of a distribution, or a series of distributions, to the partner by the partnership."[1] The purpose of this chapter is to address tax issues involved when "retiring" a general partner's interest in a partnership.

Key Points

- I.R.C. § 736 deals with the liquidation of a partnership by retirement.
- A retiring partner receiving payments under I.R.C. § 736 is regarded as a partner until the entire interest of the retiring partner is liquidated.
- As a general proposition, if a distribution is in liquidation of a general partner's interest in a service partnership, such as a law firm, unrealized receivables and unstated goodwill are treated under § 736(a). However, there are exceptions. Under § 736(a), payment is taxed as ordinary income to retiring partner and is deductible by remaining partners.
- Goodwill represents a significant asset of a partnership. Inclusion of goodwill under § 736(b) requires a provision within the partnership agreement providing for a payment in respect of goodwill at liquidation. Under § 736(b), payment is taxed as capital gain to retiring partner and is not deductible by remaining partners.
- Currently, the IRS does not apply § 409A restrictions for deferred compensation programs to payments made under § 736.

---

[1] Internal Revenue Code (I.R.C.) § 761(d); Treasury Regulation § 1.761-1(d).

- A retiring partner receiving § 736(a) payments may be subject to self-employment tax.
- A covenant not to compete, without mentioning goodwill, is not considered a provision within the partnership agreement for a payment with respect to goodwill.
- The typical retiring partner receives a series of installment payments over more than one year. This complicates allocation of §§ 736(a) and 736(b) payments.
- Only passive income can be sheltered by both passive and active loss.
- Scenarios at the end of this chapter tie in several concepts.
- Actions by partners and partnerships that technically comply with Subchapter K could invoke anti-abuse provisions if inconsistent with the intent of Subchapter K.
- Retain independent counsel when negotiating a partnership agreement that specifies terms of liquidation of partner.

II. Description of a Partnership

A partnership is generally treated as an entity that is separate from its partners for purposes of calculating partnership income.[2] The terms "partner" and "partnership" are intended to apply to all persons and entities that are treated as partners and partnerships for tax purposes under the Internal Revenue Code, including members of Limited Partnerships, Limited Liability Partnerships, and Limited Liability Companies (LLCs) and the LLCs themselves if they do not elect to be treated as corporations for tax purposes.

> Under I.R.C. § 702(b), the character of each item of partnership income and loss is determined at the partnership level and reflected in partnership income according to the method of accounting adopted by the partnership.[3,4] Once the partnership income is calculated, the partnership acts as a conduit through which the income passes. The partnership is not subject to tax.

Instead, under I.R.C. § 702, each partner is required to take into account separately in his or her return and his or her distributive share, whether or not distributed, of each class or item of partnership income, gain, loss, deduction, or credit.[5]

Under I.R.C. § 731, when the income is eventually distributed to the partner by the partnership, it is not taxed a second time unless it exceeds the amount previously included in income by the recipient (plus the recipient's own contribution to the partnership and his or her share of any debt).[6] Under I.R.C. § 704, a partner's distributive share of income, gain, loss, deduction, and credit are, except as otherwise provided, determined by the partnership agreement. Partners have a great deal of freedom in allocating and distributing this income, gain, loss, deduction, and credit.

---

[2] United States v. Basye, 410 U.S. 441, 448, 93 S. Ct. 1080, 35 L. Ed. 2d 412, 1973 U.S. LEXIS 187, 73-1 U.S. Tax Cas. (CCH) P9250, 31 A.F.T.R.2d (RIA) 802 (1973).

[3] Podell v. Commissioner, 55 T.C. 429, 432, 1970 U.S. Tax Ct. LEXIS 17 (1970).

[4] See Kenneth W. Gideon, *ABA Tax Section Members Comment on Application of § 409A to Partnership Transactions*, TAX NOTES TODAY, May 24, 2005 TNT 99-28.

[5] Treas. Reg. § 1.702-1(a).

[6] See *supra* note 4.

III. Retirement of a Partner: Section 736

When a partner seeks to withdraw from a partnership that will continue to operate after the withdrawal, the retiring partner has options. The available options are dependent upon the provisions of the partnership agreement and applicable state law. In most cases, the partner could sell his or her interest to the remaining partner or partners or to a third party. I.R.C. §§ 741 and 751 govern the tax consequences of this type of sale, and the selling partner generally will recognize capital gain and loss except to the extent of his or her share of § 751 assets (unrealized receivables and inventory items).

Alternatively, the partner could liquidate his or her interest in the partnership, which resembles a corporation's redemption of a shareholder's stock. I.R.C. § 736 addresses distributions in liquidation of a partner's interest in a partnership. This liquidation of a partner's interest is referred to as the retirement of a partner.[7] The retirement of a partner will not necessarily invoke immediate termination of the partnership. A retiring partner receiving payments under I.R.C. § 736 is regarded as a partner until the entire interest of the retiring partner is liquidated. Alan Kennard states in his article "Continuation of a Partnership: Avoiding Adverse Tax Consequences":

> Therefore, if one of the members of a two-person partnership retires under a plan whereby that member is to receive payments under § 736, the partnership will not be considered terminated, nor will the partnership year close for either partner, until the retiring partner's entire interest is liquidated, since the retiring partner continues to hold a partnership interest in the partnership until that time.[8]

Section 736 is divided into two sections. Section 736(b) applies to distributions by the partnership in exchange for the partner's interest in partnership property. Section 736(a) applies to all other distributions. However, § 736(b) does not apply to unrealized receivables held by the partnership or to goodwill of the partnership if (1) capital is not a material income-producing factor for the partnership, and (2) the retiring partner was a general partner in the partnership.

As a general proposition, if a distribution is in liquidation of a general partner's interest in a service partnership, such as a law firm, unrealized receivables and unstated goodwill are treated under § 736(a). However, there are exceptions.

Unrealized receivables are described in I.R.C. § 751(c) as rights to payment for (1) goods delivered or to be delivered that are not capital assets, or (2) services rendered or to be rendered. The unrealized receivables cannot have already been included in income under the method of accounting used by the partnership. The portion of receivables that is already included in the partner's basis falls under § 736(b). As of 1993, various recapture items (§ 1245 property) are no longer considered unrealized receivables for purposes of § 736, and so all liquidating payments for recapture items

---

[7] STEPHEN A. LIND, STEPHEN SCHWARZ, DANIEL J. LATHROPE, AND JOSHUA D. ROSENBERG, FUNDAMENTLS OF BUSINESS ENTERPRISE TAXATION (University Casebook Series) 311 (est, 3rd ed. 2005).

[8] 2003 TAX NOTES, Vol. 100, No. 11, September 15, 2003.

are treated under § 736(b).[9] In footnote 11 of *The Logic of Subchapter K: A Conceptual Guide to the Taxation of Partnerships*, authors Laura and Noel Cunningham state that this significantly increases the chances that liquidating payments will be brought under § 751(b) as disproportionate distributions.[10]

Goodwill represents a significant and valuable asset of a partnership. Because goodwill is usually built during the existence of a partnership, it will generally have a low or no adjusted basis. (An instance when goodwill will have other than a zero basis is when the partnership previously acquired a business and allocated a portion of the purchase price to goodwill.[11]) Therefore, there will be a substantial amount of appreciation upon liquidation.[12]

> Should the parties wish to have the goodwill included under § 736(b), they will need to include a provision within the partnership agreement providing for a payment in respect of goodwill at liquidation.[13]

This provision may be included in any written or oral modification to the original partnership agreement made in any year prior to the date of filing an income tax return for the year of the liquidation.[14] However, to the extent of its basis, goodwill is § 736(b) property even in the absence of a specific provision in the partnership agreement concerning payments with respect to goodwill.[15]

Capital is not a material income-producing factor where substantially all of the business of the entity consists of fees, commissions, and other payment for personal services.[16] A law partnership that has invested heavily in equipment is considered a partnership in which capital is not a material income-producing factor because the equipment is incidental to the rendering of services.[17]

Finally, premium payments, which are payments that exceed the value of the retiring partner's share of partnership property, are also treated under § 736(a).

Whether the property is distributed under § 736(a) or § 736(b) will create different tax results. Section 736(b) distributions are treated as acquisitions by the remaining partners of the withdrawing partner's interest in the partnership property. Any gain recognized on the distribution will be capital gain for the withdrawing partner and will not be deductible by the remaining partners. However, to the extent there are cash liquidating payments, payments for § 751 recapture items generating ordinary income to the recipient under § 751(b).[18] Distributions that are not treated as made in

---

[9] Laura E. Cunningham and Noel B. Cunningham, The Logic of Subchapter K: A Conceptual Guide to the Taxation of Partnerships 210–211 (West Group, 3rd ed. 2006).

[10] *Id.* at 211, fn. 11.

[11] See *supra* note 7, at 319.

[12] William P. Prescott and Kamran Idrees, *Try to Take it Personally: Revisiting the Role of Goodwill in the Sale of a Professional Service Corporation*, The Practical Tax Lawyer, Spring 2006, at 8.

[13] I.R.C. § 736(b)(2)(B); Treas. Reg. § 1.736-1(b)(3).

[14] See *supra* note 7, at 320.

[15] William S. McKee, William F. Nelson, and Robert L. Whitmire, Federal Taxation of Partnerships and Partners 22-9–22-10 (Warren Gorham & Lamont, 4th ed. 2007).

[16] I.R.C. §§ 401(c)(2) and 911(d).

[17] See *supra* note 7, at 319.

[18] See *supra* note 15, at 22-10.

exchange for the partner's interest in partnership property are treated under § 736(a) either as part of the retiring partner's distributive share under § 704(b), if the amount is determined with respect to the income of the partnership, or as a guaranteed payment described in § 707(c) if it is not.[19]

> A retiring partner's distributive share, of course, is excluded from the determination of the other partners' income; this is the economic equivalent of a deduction. Under this regime, the character of partnership income flows through to the recipient. A liquidating payment treated as a guaranteed payment is ordinary income to the recipient in all events. Although guaranteed payments often are subject to § 263, the common understanding is that guaranteed payments under § 736(a)(2) are deductible in all events.[20]

David L. Cameron and Philip F. Postlewaite in "The Lazarus Effect: A Commentary on In-Kind Guaranteed Payments," are not happy with the above result:

> The most disturbing aspect of section 736 lies in the fact that service partnerships may treat distributions in exchange for a general partner's interest in the goodwill of the partnership as a distribution under section 736(a) rather than section 736(b). Although such distributions will effectively be taxed as ordinary income to the withdrawing partner, they will give rise to an immediate deduction to the partnership. Consequently, partners in service partnerships are effectively able to currently deduct payments for the purchase of goodwill from a withdrawing partner while all other taxpayers confront a unified regime under section 197 that requires the amortization of acquired goodwill over a 15-year period.[21]

In footnote 177, which is appended to the above statement, it is pointed out that even if the goodwill falls under I.R.C. § 736(b) because it is specified in the partnership agreement, the remaining partners may be able to amortize the goodwill under I.R.C. § 197(f)(9)(E) if the partnership makes a § 754 election and the anti-churning rules[22] do not apply.[23]

IV. Brief History of Section 736

In order to understand the impacts of recent developments related to application of § 736, one has to understand more about its origins. I.R.C. § 736 was enacted in 1954 to settle the tax treatment of payments by a partnership to a retiring partner or to the successor of a deceased partner in liquidation of the partner's interest.[24] At that time, there were no statutory provisions dealing with income tax aspects of payments

---

[19] See *supra* note 9, at 210.
[20] *Id.* at 210.
[21] 7 FLA. TAX REV. 339, 397 (2006).
[22] The anti-churning rules of I.R.C. § 168(f)(5) deny taxpayers favorable accelerated cost recovery system treatment for property acquired in certain related party transactions.
[23] See *supra* note 21, at fn. 177.
[24] Philip F. Postlewaite and Adam H. Rosenzweig, *Anachronisms in Subchapter K of the Internal Revenue Code: Is it Time to Part with Section 736?*, 100 NW. U.L. REV. 379 (2006).

by a partnership to a retiring partner.[25] Section 736 clarified when payments from a partnership to a retiring partner should be attributable to (1) the retiring partner's interest in the partnership assets, including goodwill, (2) partnership receivables, or (3) deferred compensation benefits.[26]

Section 736 represented a tradeoff where the partnership would receive a current deduction only if the retiring partner incurred ordinary income treatment. The thought was that the inherent adversity between the partner and the partnership would foster the proper characterization of payments for items of partnership property.[27] Instead, the complexity led to mistaken application and abuse.[28] Congress came up with two alterations to the Tax Code to address this abuse. Section 736(b)(3) was added, which restricted the application of § 736(a) to goodwill of service partnerships when the general partner was retiring. Also, Congress enacted § 197, which allowed for the amortization of goodwill.[29]

When § 736 was initially enacted, the idea was that the ordinary income characterization of payments to retiring partners, combined with a current deduction to the partnership, provided a form of deferred compensation for services previously rendered.[30] Senate Report No. 83-1622 explains:

> Where a retiring partner receives a lump sum or fixed payments determined without regard to the income of the partnership, the portion of such payments attributable to the capital interest of the retiring partner is to be treated as the purchase of a capital interest by the remaining partners. The balance, however, will be treated like a salary paid by the partnership.... Thus, to the extent that payments to a retiring partner ... are not in exchange for a capital interest, they are treated as deductions to the remaining partners and as income to the withdrawing partner or his successor irrespective of over how long a period they may be paid.[31]

The Tax Equity and Fiscal Responsibility Act (TEFRA), enacted by Congress in 1982, allowed partners in a partnership to participate in retirement programs on a similar basis as shareholder-employees in a corporation. However, § 736 allows retiring general partners a deferred compensation alternative without having to comply with the significant procedural safeguard requirements of § 401 and § 416 required under TEFRA.[32]

In 2004, Congress enacted I.R.C. § 409A. Section 409A addresses when and how a deferred compensation program will be respected for federal income tax purposes. It specifies that no deferral will qualify unless the deferral election is for a fixed period of time and the fixed deferral period generally cannot be accelerated. There

---

[25] *Id.* at 381–382.
[26] *Id.* at 385.
[27] *Id.* at 385–386.
[28] Foxman v. Commissioner, 41 T.C. 535, 551 n.9, 41 T.C. 535, 1964 U.S. Tax Ct. LEXIS 163 (1964), *aff'd*, 352 F.2d 466 (3d Cir. 1965).
[29] See *supra* note 24, at 392.
[30] *Id.* at 395.
[31] Senate Report No. 83-1622, at 296 (1954), reprinted in 1954 U.S.C.C.A.N. 4621, 4731.
[32] See *supra* note 24, at 395–396.

are significant penalties (interest and an additional 20 percent income tax)[33] for any deferred compensation that does not qualify under the rules.[34]

The legislative history of § 409A does not address its effect on § 736. Because of this, the IRS adopted a temporary interim solution. In Notice 2005-1, the IRS states that, until otherwise provided in applicable REGULATIONS, it will not apply § 409A to payments made under § 736.[35] The IRS also requested comments, and Kenneth W. Gideon of the Tax Section of the American Bar Association responded, stating:

> Obviously, in the case of a terminated partner, the partner frequently is receiving a share of income that he or she did not directly help to generate. However, it does not follow that the payments are deferred compensation. In many cases, they are for unrealized receivables or goodwill and are subject to Section 736(a) (even though unrealized receivables or goodwill are really just types of property) solely by virtue of Section 736(b)(2)(A).
>
> . . . .
>
> Treating payments for goodwill as deferred compensation is inappropriate because goodwill is an asset of the partnership as a whole, reflecting its value as a going concern, which can and does exist even when all of the partners were fully compensated for their services on an annual basis. Payments for goodwill are, in substance, payments for property regardless of how they might be treated under Section 736(b).[36]

In *Federal Taxation of Partnerships and Partners*, William S. McKee, William F. Nelson, and Robert L. Whitmire state that partnership arrangements under § 736 are not subject to § 409A

> unless they fall within § 1402(a)(10) (dealing with retirement payments to individuals after all capital has been returned and which continue at least until death).[37]

I.R.C. § 1402(a) addresses net earnings from self-employment. Should § 1402(a)(10) apply (in that the retirement payments continue after all capital has been returned and continue at least until death), the payments will still be excluded from § 409A provided that:

1. The partner rendered no services pertaining to trade or business of the partnership during the taxable year;
2. No obligation exists from the other partners except for retirement payments under the plan; and

---

[33] WILLIAM S. MCKEE, WILLIAM F. NELSON, AND ROBERT L. WHITMIRE, FEDERAL TAXATION OF PARTNERSHIPS AND PARTNERS, CUMULATIVE SUPPLEMENT NO. 4 § 13.02[4][c] (Warren Gorham & Lamont, 2006).

[34] See *supra* note 24, at 396.

[35] *Id.* at 396 & fn.54

[36] Kenneth W. Gideon, *ABA Tax Section Members Comment on Application of §409A to Partnership Transactions*, TAX NOTES TODAY, May 24, 2005.

[37] See *supra* note 33, at § 13.02[4][c].

3. The partner's share of the capital of the partnership has been paid in full before the close of the partnership's taxable year.[38]

V. Section 736 and Self-Employment Tax, Covenants Not to Compete, Installment Payments, and Passive Activity Losses

A. Self-Employment Tax

Arthur Willis, John Pennell and Philip F. Postlewaite in *Partnership Taxation* state:

> A retiring partner may be surprised and dismayed to discover that any § 736(a) payments received from the partnership in liquidation of the partnership interest may be subject to self-employment tax for purposes of the Federal Insurance Contributions Act (Social Security) even though the partner renders no services to the former partnership.[39]

The authors explain that since a retiring partner receiving payments under § 736 is a partner until his or her partnership interest is liquidated, and payments under § 736(a) are considered as distributive shares of partnership income, the liquidating payments are income from a trade or business carried on by the partnership and the retiring partner.[40] The net income from the trade or business translates to net earnings from self-employment, and falls subject to the self-employment tax.[41] A retiring partner may avoid the self-employment tax if the amounts received are:

> pursuant to a written plan of the partnership which provides for periodic payments on account of retirement to partners generally, or to classes of partners, if the payments continue at least until the partner's death.[42]

However, the payments must constitute bona fide retirement income with retirement based on age or physical condition or years of service in order to qualify under the exclusion.[43]

B. Covenants Not to Compete

A covenant not to compete is an agreement in which the covenantor agrees for a specific period of time and within a particular area to refrain from competition with the convenantee. The remaining partners in a partnership may be hesitant to provide payment for goodwill to a retiring partner without the assurance that the retiring

---

[38] I.R.C. § 1402(a).
[39] ARTHUR WILLIS, JOHN PENNELL, AND PHILIP F. POSTLEWAITE, PARTNERSHIP TAXATION, 15-68 (Warren, Gorham & Lamont 6th ed. 2006).
[40] *Id.*
[41] *Id.* at 15-68.
[42] *Id.* at 15-69.
[43] *Id.* at 15-69.

partner will not take his or her clients away from the firm. The remaining partners will want the retiring partner restricted by a covenant not to compete.

A covenant not to compete, without mentioning goodwill, is not considered a provision within the partnership agreement for a payment with respect to goodwill. In other words, the covenant not to compete does not turn unstated goodwill to stated goodwill per § 736(b)(2)(B).

It is important to determine if covenants not to compete are ethical in your jurisdiction. Rule 5.6(a) of the American Bar Association's Model Rules of Professional Conduct, *Restrictions on Right to Practice*, states:

A lawyer shall not participate in offering or making:

(a) a partnership, shareholders, operating, employment, or other similar type of agreement that restricts the right of a lawyer to practice after termination of the relationship, except an agreement concerning benefits upon retirement.[44, 45]

The comment to Rule 5.6 states:

[1] An agreement restricting the right of lawyers to practice after leaving a firm not only limits their professional autonomy but also limits the freedom of clients to choose a lawyer. Paragraph (a) prohibits such agreements except for restrictions incident to provisions concerning retirement benefits for service with the firm.

. . . .

[3] This Rule does not apply to prohibit restrictions that may be included in the terms of the sale of a law practice pursuant to Rule 1.17.[46]

Model Rule of Professional Conduct 5.6(a) and Comment 5.6[1] were adopted in whole by the State of Washington (my home) in Rule of Professional Conduct 5.6(a).[47] However, the Washington State Bar Association has interpreted RPC 5.6(a) as not precluding such provisions when a lawyer is selling a law practice to another lawyer and will not be in private practice in the same geographic area.[48]

C. Installment Payments

> The typical retiring partner receives a series of installment payments over more than one year.

In this scenario, the aggregate payments first must be allocated between §§ 736(a) and (b), and then each year's installment payments must be allocated.[49] Unless there is an agreed

---

[44] American Bar Association's Model Rules of Professional Conduct (2007).

[45] According to the American Bar Association's website, http://www.abanet.org, 47 states have adopted the ABA Model Rules of Professional Conduct. While it is not stated, the 47 states have adopted the rules in whole or in part.

[46] American Bar Association's Model Rules of Professional Conduct.

[47] State of Washington Rules of Professional Conduct, http://www.courts.wa.gov.

[48] GAIL MCMONAGLE, ED., WASHINGTON LEGAL ETHICS DESKBOOK, § 6.3(4)(c) (Washington State Bar Association, 2003).

[49] Treas. Reg. § 1.736-1(b)(5) & (6).

allocation within the partnership agreement, the rules governing installment payments under § 736 differ depending on whether the payments are fixed in amount. If the retiring partner receives a fixed amount over a set number of years, the portion of each annual payment allocated to § 736(b) is determined according to the following formula:

§ 736(b) Portion = (Total Fixed Agreed Payment for Taxable Year) × (Total Fixed § 736(b) Payments/Total Fixed § 736(a) & (b) payments)[50]

The balance is treated under § 736(a). If the payments are contingent rather than fixed, the payments are first treated as § 736(b) payments to the extent of the partner's interest in partnership property, and then as § 736(a) payments.[51] If the parties want to avoid the hassle of dealing with the above, they may allocate the annual payment between § 736(a) and § 736(b) in any manner agreed so long as the total amount allocated to property under § 736(b) does not exceed the fair market value of that property at the date of death or retirement.[52]

Along with allocation rules are timing options for § 736 payments. Section 736(a) payments are taxable to the retiring partner in his or her taxable year with or within which ends the partnership's taxable year for which the payment is a distributive share, or in which the partnership may deduct the amount as a guaranteed payment.[53] Alternatively, § 736(b) payments are not recognized by the retiring partner until he or she receives the payment.[54]

Recognition of § 736(b) payments at receipt gives the retiring partner the advantage of reporting the distribution as an open transaction, a method normally not available for deferred payment arrangements:

> This open transaction treatment is available because § 736(b) payments are treated as distributions. The result arguably would be different if there were a "disposition," in which event the installment sale rules in § 453 would apply and ordinarily foreclose open transaction reporting.[55]

If there is any loss, recognition is deferred until the year of the final distribution.[56] However, a partner who will receive a fixed amount of § 736(b) payments may elect to annually report a pro rata portion of gain or loss over the distribution period, similar to the installment method under § 453.[57, 58]

---

[50] See *supra* note 7, at 328–329.
[51] Treas. Reg. § 1.736-1(b)(5)(ii).
[52] Treas. Reg. § 1.736-1(b)(5)(iii).
[53] Treas. Reg. § 1.736-1(a)(5).
[54] *Id.*
[55] See *supra* note 7, at 329, fn. 9.
[56] Treas. Reg. § 1.731-1(a)(2).
[57] Treas. Reg. § 1.736-1(b)(6).
[58] See also *supra* note 7, at 329, fn. 9.

D. Passive Activity Losses

> One of the advantages of a partnership over a corporation is the ability of the partners to use passive losses in reducing taxes owed on other income. Only passive income can be sheltered by both passive and active loss.[59]

To reach this point, the losses passed through to the partner cannot be greater than the partner's basis in his or her partnership interest and the losses are limited to the amount that the partner has at risk. Finally, the loss must satisfy the passive loss rule of I.R.C. § 469, where losses passed through from a passive activity can only be offset by passive income from a different source.[60] Under I.R.C. § 469(c), passive activity means any activity that involves the conduct of any trade or business in which the taxpayer does not materially participate.[61]

Thus, one who receives passive income as opposed to active income benefits, as they are able to offset both active and passive loss with the passive income, while one with active income can only offset with active loss.

Material participation, which defines a partner's level of participation, determines active as opposed to passive activity. A partner who shows "regular, continuous and substantial" involvement is deemed to materially participate while a limited partner is presumed to not materially participate.[62]

So what about a general partner who has retired? Treasury Regulation § 1.469-2(e)(2)(iii) addresses payments in liquidation of a partner's interest in partnership property. Section 1.469-2(e)(2)(iii)(A) states that any gain or loss of a retiring partner as a result of a payment under § 736(b) is passive only if the gain or loss would have been passive if it had been recognized at the time the liquidation of the partner's interest commenced.[63] Therefore, the fact that the partner is no longer participating in the partnership does not determine whether the activity is passive. Section 1.469-2(e)(2)(iii)(B) addresses payments in liquidation of a partner's interest in unrealized receivables and goodwill under § 736(a). Again, one looks at whether the payment would have been included in passive income that the retiring partner

> would have recognized if the unrealized receivables and goodwill had been sold at the time that the liquidation of the partner's interest commenced.[64, 65]

Finally, temporary Treasury Regulation § 1.469-5T(a) details specifics as to when an individual materially participates in an activity. Under § 1.469-5T(a)(6), an individual materially participates in a personal service law firm only if he or she materially

---

[59] Dwight J. Drake, Business Planning; Closely Held Enterprises 46 (West Law School Publications, 1st ed. 2006).
[60] *Id.* at 45.
[61] I.R.C. § 469(c)(1)(A) and (B).
[62] See *supra* note 59, at 46.
[63] Treas. Reg. § 1.469-2(e)(2)(iii).
[64] Treas. Reg. § 1.469-2(e)(2)(iii)(B).
[65] The bottom line is that the general partner wants to have passive income after retirement, as he or she can offset passive losses against this income. If the income remains active after retirement, passive losses cannot be offset by this income.

participates for any three taxable years (whether or not consecutive) preceding the taxable year at question.[66]

VI. Retiring Partner Scenarios

The following are examples of how allocations are made to a retiring partner.[67] In each of these scenarios, JAC is a law firm/personal service partnership. J, A, and C have been one-third general partners for several years. The partnership's balance sheet is as follows:

Assets	Inside Basis	FMV*	Capital	Outside Basis	FMV*
Cash	$60K	$60K	J	$30K	$250K
Accounts Receivable	0	$300K	A	$30K	$250K
Capital Assets	$30K	$90K	C	$30K	$250K
Goodwill	0	$300K			
Total	$90K	$750K		$90K	$750K

*FMV = Fair Market Value

A. Scenario #1

J receives $300K cash in liquidation, and there is no goodwill provision. Since this is a service entity, $250K will fall under § 736(a), which accounts for $100K Accounts Receivable (one-third of $300K), $100K Unstated Goodwill (one-third of $300K) and a $50K premium (as the total amount that J is receiving is $50K greater than the one-third value of the JAC firm). All § 736(a) payment is ordinary income to J, and a $250K deduction to the partnership. The remaining $50K distribution (one-third of $60K FMV of cash asset and one-third FMV of Capital Assets) falls under § 736(b). Because the $50K exceeds J's Outside Basis of $30K, J will have a long-term Capital Gain of $20K per I.R.C. § 731(a)(1).

JAC only has $60K in cash. Therefore, the partnership will have to come up with additional funds to "retire" J. This is an example of why upfront payouts are difficult for partnerships that do not have significant amounts of capital to cover a retirement, which is common when there are only a few partners. It is not realistic for JAC to collect on their accounts receivables for the payout, as even if they were able to collect the amount due, JAC will need these funds for maintaining the partnership. JAC can take out a loan. JAC will likely get a better interest rate if it takes out a recourse loan. A partnership liability is recourse to the extent that any partner (or related person) bears the economic risk of loss.[68] A partnership liability is nonrecourse to the extent that no partner (or related person) bears the risk of loss.[69] A and C will share the

---

[66] Treas. Reg. § 1.469-5T(a) outlines the specifics as to what it means to materially participate.

[67] See *supra* note 7, at 326. The examples in this chapter were adapted from these examples.

[68] Treas. Reg. § 1.752-1(a)(1).

[69] Treas. Reg. § 1.752-1(a)(2).

liability and will hold J harmless. Under § 1.752-2(j), all parties are assumed to live up to their obligations.

B. Scenario #2

J agrees to receive $300K in liquidation, $150K cash in year one, and $15K cash per year in each of the next ten years. The income and deductions have not changed from Scenario #1. The issue is the timing. As in scenario #1, $50K out of the $300K total in payments to J falls under § 736(b) and $250K falls under § 736(a). Now use the installment formula mentioned earlier, where the portion of each annual payment allocated to § 736(b) is determined according to:

§ 736(b) Portion = (Total Fixed Agreed Payment for Taxable Year) × (Total Fixed § 736(b) Payments/Total Fixed § 736(a) & (b)payments)

Thus, $25K = $150K x $50K/$300K.

$50K (16.67%) out of $300K total is § 736(b) payment; $250K (83.33%) is § 736(a) payment. Of the $150K payment in the first year, 83.33%, or $125K is ordinary income to J with a $125K deduction to the partnership, and $25K can be used to recover $30K in basis, or the basis can be allocated pro rata to all § 736(b) payments. If the latter, there is $10K long-term Capital Gain in Year One. For all $15K annual payments, $12.5K is § 736(a) ordinary income and $2.5K is § 736(b) payment.

Again, JAC will need to take out a loan. However, as the initial payment is $150K rather than $300K, the amount of the loan will be less. Depending on the success of the firm, the $15K yearly payments may be able to be paid through profits of the firm.

C. Scenario #3

Same as #2, but J's Outside Basis is $70K. 83.33% of all payments are still § 736(a) ordinary income, with offsetting deduction for the partnership. 16.67% is § 736(b) payment and applied against Basis. In this scenario, there is a $20K loss. The loss could be recognized in last year's of payments, or pro rata over payments. If pro rata, there will be $10K of long-term Capital Loss in Year One, and $1K of long-term Capital Loss in each of the next 10 years. See scenario #2 regarding a loan.

D. Scenario #4

Same as #2, but J receives $150K in Year One, and 10% of profits for the next 10 years. Profits are estimated to be $150K per year. Since the amount of the profits is not a fixed amount, this is treated as an open transaction, with all § 736(b) payments first, then § 736(a). Therefore, in year one, $30K of the $150K is applied against J's $30K Outside Basis. $20K of the $150K is also § 736(b), representing J's gain on Capital Assets, and thus J has $20K long-term Capital Gain under § 731(a)(1). The remaining $100K for year one is § 736(a). Over the next ten years, all $15K yearly payments are

§ 736(a) payments. All § 736(a) payments are ordinary income to J and deductible by the partnership. See scenario #2 regarding a loan.

E. Scenario #5

Same as #1, but $100K is received for goodwill per agreement. The $100K in stated goodwill falls under § 736(b), increasing J's § 736(b) payments to $150K and reducing J's § 736(a) payments to $150K. Thus, J has $150K of ordinary income and $120K long-term Capital Gain (instead of $20K). J prefers this goodwill treatment because it converts $100K of ordinary income to long-term Capital Gain. As stated earlier in this article, even if the goodwill falls under I.R.C. § 736(b), because it is specified in the partnership agreement, the remaining partners may be able to amortize the goodwill under IRC § 197(f)(9)(E). So while the partnership cannot deduct the goodwill, they will benefit due to the amortization. See scenario #1 regarding a loan.

VII. Anti-Abuse Provisions and Purchase of Partnership that Falls under Section 736

Anti-abuse provisions, starting with Treasury Regulation § 1.701-2, were introduced so that actions taken by partnerships and partners that technically complied with Subchapter K would be disallowed if they were inconsistent with the intent of Subchapter K. However, Treasury Regulation § 1.701-2(a)(3) excepted specific rules in Subchapter K, which in essence trumped the anti-abuse regulation. Given this, Philip F. Postlewaite and Adam H. Rosenzweig pose this question:

> [D]oes the use of a partnership to make section 736(a) payments to a withdrawing partner for his share of partnership goodwill or as payment of deferred compensation violate the intent of Subchapter K in light of sections 197, 401, 416, and 409A or, does section 736 meet the "specific rule" exception to the anti-abuse provision?[70]

Postlewaite and Rosenzweig then present the following example involving an individual wishing to purchase another's professional practice for cash and deduct part of the cost of the acquisition. If the purchaser were to make a direct acquisition, he or she would not be allowed a current deduction for the cost attributable for goodwill. However, this may be possible through the formation of a partnership with the use of § 736(a) payments for goodwill upon the "retirement" of the "seller" from the partnership after a period of "service." The authors cite to the *Bluebook*, which states that:

> Under present law, a prospective buyer of a business may structure the transaction so as to currently deduct such an amount by first entering into a partnership with the seller and then liquidating the seller's partnership interest.[71]

---

[70] See *supra* note 24, at 397.
[71] See *supra* note 24, at 397 and fn.58.

The authors conclude that a literal reading of § 736 would allow for an immediate deduction for the payments, although this arrangement would appear to be the type of abuse for which the anti-abuse regulations were promulgated. Also, the argument could be raised that the enterprise did not constitute a partnership for purposes of § 7701 because there was no intent to share income, gain, loss, or deductions of the business or that there was a deemed sale of the withdrawing partner's partnership interest under § 707.[72]

VIII. Conclusion

As with most Internal Revenue Code statutes, § 736 is a great tool once one is aware of its uses. For the law partner who wants to retire and the remaining partnership, § 736 may be the way to go—and at least a discussion of the options can lead to a more informed decision. It is clear from the cases that I have read regarding the retirement of a partner that partners need to clearly state their intentions in the partnership agreement in regard to items such as goodwill (if they choose to mention goodwill), and make certain that the parties maintain consistent positions.

> My research backs my advice to encourage the partners to consider retaining independent counsel when negotiating the partnership agreement that specifies the terms of liquidation of a partner.

Further Reading

Cunningham, Laura E. & Noel B. *The Logic of Subchapter K: A Conceptual Guide to the Taxation of Partnerships.* West Group, 3rd ed. 2006. 210–211

Drake, Dwight J. *Business Planning; Closely Held Enterprises.* West Law School Publications, 1st ed. 2006.

Lind, Stephen A., Stephen Schwarz, Daniel J. Lathrope, and Joshua D. Rosenberg. *Fundamentals of Business Enterprise Taxation University Casebook Series.* West, 3rd ed. 2005.

Postlewaite, Philip F. and Adam H. Rosenzweig. "Anachronisms in Subchapter K of the Internal Revenue Code: Is It Time to Part with Section 736?" 100 *Nw. U. L. Rev.* (2006)

---

[72] See *supra* note 24, at 398 and fn.59.

Chapter 6

Merging Law Firms
by Ward Bower

I. Introduction

Since 2000, there have been between 40 and 70 law firm mergers annually in the United States—about one per week, on average. Some of these mergers, including some of the largest, have involved foreign firms as well. Clearly, the legal profession is consolidating by merger. Since lawyers generally are independent thinkers and competitive individuals, a decision to merge with another entity owned by other independent thinking, competitive individuals is not made easily. The business case for the merger of firms must be compelling, effectively articulated, and communicated broadly within both ownership groups.

> ### *Key Points*
> - The pace of consolidation of the legal profession has been slower than in other professional service industries due to a different, more restrictive regulatory environment. Conflict of interest rules for lawyers are a greater impediment to law firm mergers than conflict rules are to mergers of financial services firms.
> - Several external factors are driving law firm mergers, including overall economic conditions, the convergence movement of corporate law departments, and the sophistication of recent law graduates.
> - Scope mergers are those that involve adding a complementary business component to the firm; scale mergers are those that create depth in existing locations and practice areas to attract bigger clients and matters or to retain a growing client.
> - The business case for any merger includes determining scope or scale, compatibility factors, negotiation items, due diligence, the term sheet, and integration plans.

II. The Consolidation of the Industry

Consolidation frequently occurs as industries mature. It has already happened in other professional and service industries such as accounting, consulting, banking, and insurance. Consolidation by merger is the primary method by which the Big Four accounting firms emerged, and mergers continue in financial services industries, as regulation allows, both intra-industry (e.g., banking) and inter-industry (e.g., insurance and investment brokerage, and banking and insurance). Until inhibited by provisions of the Sarbanes-Oxley Act, combined accounting/consulting/law firms, in the form of Multi-Disciplinary Partnerships (MDPs), had emerged on an international scale, led by major global accountancies.

A. Prospects for Success

The question often asked is "how many of these 40 to 70 law firm mergers per year are successful?" In 2003, Altman Weil provided a partial response in a study of 17 significant mergers of law firms that had occurred in the preceding two to five years. That study looked at profits per partner pre- and post-merger, as a measure of the success of law firm mergers, assuming that no one merges firms in order to become less profitable. Obviously there can be other measures, but this one is viewed as fundamental. The 17 law firm mergers examined involved 300 or more lawyers and a total of 33 firms (one firm was involved in two of the mergers). The details of the study are reported in the September 2003 issue of the Altman Weil *Report to Legal Management*, and this article is accessible via the Altman Weil website at www.altmanweil.com. The following is a summary of the findings of the study:

- 11 of the 17 firms experienced increased profits per partner in the first year post-merger; three experienced reductions.
- Of the 16 firms whose mergers had occurred two or more years earlier, 14 reported a year-on-year increase in profit per partner from year one, while two remained the same.
- Three of the mergers appeared to be scale mergers, while nine were primarily scope mergers, and five appeared to be equally both scale and scope in their strategic intent.
- Scope or combined scope and scale mergers generally produce greater improvement in profit per partner than pure scale mergers.
- Geographic and practice area scope mergers both increased profits per partner more and faster than combination geography/practice area scope mergers.
- In the seven mergers occurring four or more years earlier, profits per partner increased 21 percent over the previous four years, while AmLaw 100 profits per partner overall increased 13 percent.

> The study suggests that although transaction and integration costs may result in lesser profitability in the first year post-merger, by year two profitability of merged firms has almost always increased, on average more so than in firms that have not merged.

Although the mergers selected for the 2003 Altman Weil study were anecdotal (based upon this author's recollection of then-recent law firm mergers), these results are revealing. Altman Weil plans to replicate that study in 2007, using a more comprehensive approach to identification of law firm mergers for analysis.

B. Why Do Law Firms Merge?

Many reasons are given for law firm mergers. Some are more persuasive, or more valid, than others. Merger is *not* a legitimate business goal in and of itself. Rather, it is a strategy to achieve a goal (such as growth) or a tactic employed to achieve a strategy (such as diversification or geographic expansion). Sound mergers of law firms are those intended to add new specialized services needed by a law firms' clients, to add clients needing a law firm's specialized services, to gain access to new and better clients, to extend geographical reach to new markets, to fill age or experience gaps, to achieve critical mass in a consolidating marketplace, or to achieve market dominance or enhanced market position by becoming a "top tier" firm in one's market.

"Short lists" of top tier firms generally are considered for engagement by corporations in the absence of an established relationship with firms in the marketplace.

Mergers can be defensive, intended to avoid disintegration or demise of a firm due to lack of leadership or declining performance. Defensive mergers often do not include all of the components of a weakened or threatened firm. However, mergers of two economically unsuccessful firms almost never succeed. Predictably, such mergers result in a larger, economically distressed firm, which is in turn vulnerable in the marketplace.

Law firm mergers have been attempted for other reasons that are not generally valid: to fuel egos of founding partners, to remedy poor economics, or because everyone else seems to be doing it. Mergers to achieve economies of scale are suspect, as economies of scale are limited in law practice. Bigger firms on average spend more, not less, on overhead, on a per lawyer basis. Statistical surveys, such as the Altman Weil *Survey of Law Firm Economics*, have demonstrated this for decades.

The result of a consolidation is bigger law firms. Bigger is not necessarily better, although statistical surveys consistently show greater profits per partner in larger law firms than smaller ones, driven by higher revenues per lawyer. Bigger is only better if the value proposition presented to clients (breadth or depth of practice, achievement of critical mass needed to handle bigger matters, extended geographic reach, etc.) results in the ability to generate more work and/or work for which clients are willing and able to pay higher rates.

> Recent studies show merger is one of the top business techniques employed by large law firms.

A 2005 survey by Altman Weil asked AmLaw 200 firms (the 200 highest-grossing law firms in the U.S.) to identify which of 24 management techniques they had employed and how successful they were. Almost two-thirds of responding firms had merged within the preceding two years, and almost 90 percent of those firms indicated their experience with the merger was either "very successful," or "successful." Figures 1 and 2 depict the complete results with respect to merger as a management technique in larger law firms.

C. Law Firm Mergers vs. Corporate Mergers

Law firm mergers are different and more difficult than corporate mergers. Corporate mergers generally create more profitable businesses when economies of scale reduce unit costs of production. For example, when banks merge, increased productivity and

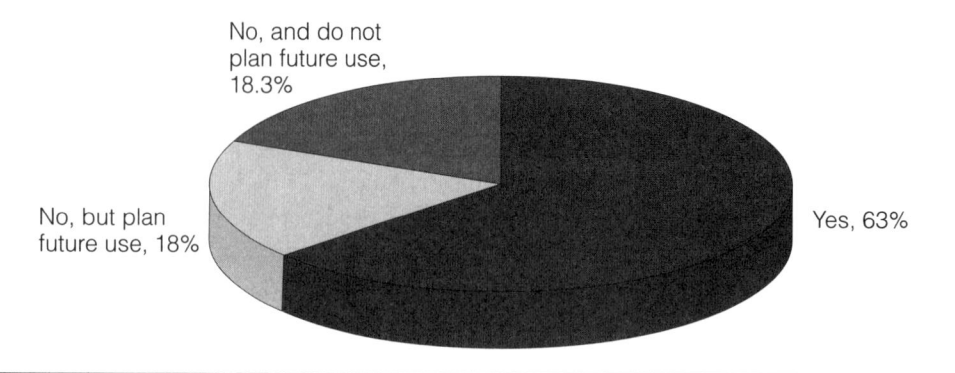

FIGURE 1. Merger/Acquisition Combining with other firm as a means of growth/expansion.

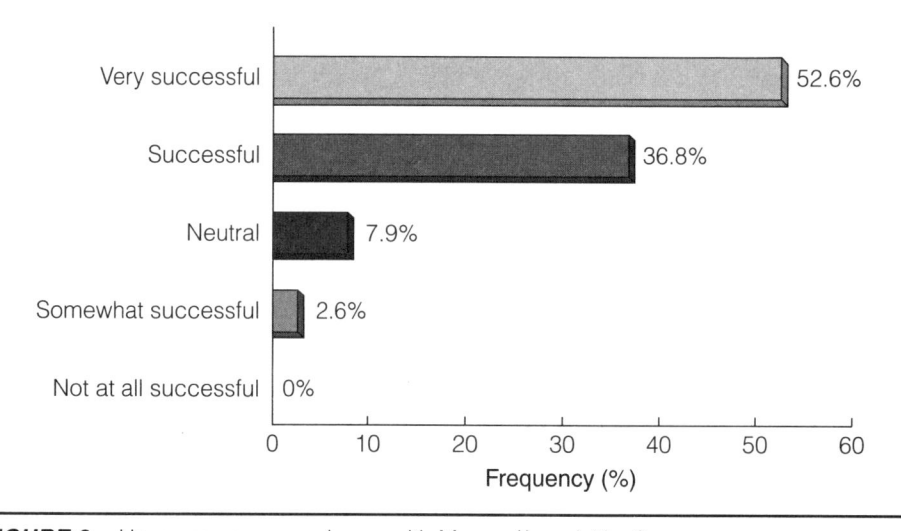

- Yes, 63%
- No, but plan future use, 18%
- No, and do not plan future use, 18.3%

FIGURE 2. How was your experience with Merger/Acquisition?

- Very successful: 52.6%
- Successful: 36.8%
- Neutral: 7.9%
- Somewhat successful: 2.6%
- Not at all successful: 0%

profitability generally result from reductions in staffing and increased application of information technology. However, since production in law firms is tied directly to professional staffing, opportunities to increase profits through downsizing are limited. Cost reductions through elimination of redundancies in law firm mergers are generally offset by transaction and integration costs, or increased costs inherent in operation of a larger law firm.

Corporate mergers can be accomplished when managements of two companies decide to merge and order the integration to occur, or when management of one or both companies persuade shareholders of the company to be acquired or to vote for a proposed merger or takeover. Once the merger is announced, management has authority to order the integration to occur. Some corporate takeovers are "hostile," and occur despite the desire of management or shareholders of one firm to remain independent.

Unlike the hierarchical corporate governance model, law firms are generally flat, horizontal organizations where owners and managers are also producers, and much greater buy in is required to approve and implement successful mergers than is the case in a corporate environment. The Chairman of an AmLaw 100 firm that pulled out of merger talks with an AmLaw 50 firm in early 2007 cited the difficulty in getting large numbers of owner-lawyers to "buy in" to a law firm merger as the major impediment to that proposed deal. See "Orrick-Dewey Law Firm Merger Scrapped," *Silicon Valley San Jose Business Journal,* January 4, 2007.

D. External Drivers of the Consolidation

Law firm consolidation by merger is driven not only by the internal business needs of law firms, but also by events in the larger economy as a whole. For one, clients are getting bigger. The most desired clients of most U.S. law firms are corporations, both publicly and privately owned. Since 2000, corporate mergers and acquisitions are occurring at unprecedented rates, increasing dramatically in 2006 according to the *Wall Street Journal* (January 2, 2007) and, barring unforeseen political, economic, manmade, or natural disasters, expected to continue into 2007. Larger clients generally look to larger law firms to provide the breadth and depth of specialized legal services that they require. They also have need for legal services delivered on the ground in more geographic locations than ever before. Law firms serving these ever-expanding clients find they need to grow dramatically in order to meet those client needs. Firms as large as 400 to 500 lawyers have embarked upon growth strategies focused on merger in order to attain the increased size they believe their expanding corporate clients require. Some mid-sized firms have lost clients to larger firms as corporations decide to "trade up" and employ larger, more geographically diverse and practice-area deep firms as they grow. Organic growth, through addition of newly qualified associates, and growth by lateral hiring are insufficiently aggressive to achieve the mass necessary to serve corporate clients that are rapidly growing themselves via mergers.

Another external factor fueling the consolidation of law firms is the "convergence" movement employed in recent years by corporate law departments, whereby outside legal work is reconsolidated in a smaller number of law firms, thereby facilitating management of outsourced legal work and, coincidentally, increasing the bargaining power of law departments as buyers. It is not unusual to encounter corporate law departments in the process of reducing their "panel" of outside law firms from hundreds to dozens. Larger law firms can make the strategic case that they are better able to handle a larger volume of a corporate law department's outsourced legal matters and likewise if they are capable of providing those services in multiple locations. That geographical expansion is another means by which one law firm might be able to replace many. This factor has driven some of the mergers between law firms in diverse geographic location in recent years. Increasingly local firms are becoming regional, regional firms national, and national firms international; some firms are even becoming global in their geographic reach.

Yet another external factor driving law firm mergers is the increasing sophistication of law students and new law graduates. They have a surfeit of information available to them through the legal press and through various directory services, as well as law firm websites. League tables published by the legal press and the editorial content of legal periodicals focus attention on larger law firms. Legal directories that rate the competence or reputations of law firms by practice areas also tend to focus on larger firms. This contributes to creation of "brand name" recognition of major law firms, which is attractive both to clients and to lawyers. Since law firms operate simultaneously in two marketplaces—that is, they are sellers of legal services but also buyers of legal talent—brand name recognition conveys a source of competitive advantage. In the labor marketplace for lawyers, there is a relatively finite supply of approximately 40,000 new lawyers per year, and there is an increasing demand for the best of those 40,000 new lawyers, driven by average new associate classes of 50 or more lawyers annually in just the AmLaw 200 firms. This translates to 10,000 new hires per year, approximately 25 percent of the graduating law school class. The remainder of the estimated 40,000 law firms in the U.S. can find it increasingly difficult to attract top graduates of top law schools, especially given the starting salary escalation driven by the larger firms whose economics are better able to accommodate those increases.

> Many small and mid-sized firms have found it virtually impossible to recruit quality law school graduates. This has been a factor that has led some to consider being acquired by a larger firm, as no law firm can succeed or even survive over the intermediate to long term without the continuity of a steady supply of quality new law graduates.

III. Steps in Preparing for a Merger

A. The Business Case

A first, necessary step in considering merger as a route to growth is to develop the fundamentals of a business case for a proposed merger. This requires definition of the characteristics of the required merger partner, in light of the strategic objectives to be achieved. Mergers can be characterized as those of either "scope" or "scale." Scope mergers are those that involve adding a complementary business component to the firm—a new practice area or a new office, for example. Scale mergers are those involved in creating depth in existing locations and practice areas to attract bigger clients and matters or to retain a growing client. The profile of a desired merger candidate would clearly be different depending upon the strategic objective to be achieved.

1. Scope Mergers For scope mergers, once the profile of a desired merger candidate has been developed (generally it would involve a combination of firm size, practice mix, geographic capability, and compatibility factors relating to economics and culture), a preliminary business case for a proposed merger can be developed. It is at this point that contact with the most promising of identified candidates can and should be made. The initial meeting would involve exploration and articulation of the potential business case for a merger, in order to determine whether there is enough potential to justify further investment of time, energy, and money in additional discussions. Generally speaking, the business case for a scope merger would involve a description such as appears in Checklist A at the end of this chapter. From this list, once would deduct:

1. Clients that would be lost through conflicts,

2. Lawyers (and their practices) that might be lost via merger, and
3. Referral sources that might be lost via merger.

The business case for successful scope mergers is usually obvious.

2. Scale Mergers Although absolute quantification of the components of the scale business case is impossible, some idea can be gained as to whether the positives outweigh the negatives in such a way as to present greater opportunities for increased profitability in the future than the two firms would be likely to experience separately and independently.

Generally, the scale merger business case would be based upon additional work or matters from existing clients of the two firms that might be gained by the greater critical mass of the resulting firm or greater depth of its specialized practices, plus new clients that might legitimately be attracted as a result of the combination of firms. In scale mergers, redundancy potential generally is greater, especially where integration of offices into consolidated locations occurs. In addition to accounting and administration, redundancies might include receptionists, librarians and research resources, and space devoted to common areas like reception/waiting areas, lunchrooms, and possibly even conference rooms. Of course, this needs to be offset by the same negative considerations in potential scope mergers: potential loss of clients, lawyers/practices, and/or referral sources due to the merger. However, it is worth noting again that economies of scale are minimal in the overall assessment of the proposed transaction.

B. Compatibility Factors

Once the fundamentals of the business case are established, consideration should be given to "compatibility factors" that will influence the ability to merge two law firms. Compatibility factors generally fall into one of two categories: economic factors, and cultural factors.

Economic factors involved in compatibility analysis include partner capital accounts, revenues per lawyer, average partner compensation, and profits per equity partner. Generally, these factors need to be within a range of 10 percent to 20 percent of each other, or it is unlikely that a successful merger will occur.

Cultural factors include such issues as expected time commitment to firm and clients, the balance between centralized firm authority and individual partner autonomy, methods for selecting/changing leadership, methods for determining partner compensation/ profit distribution, methods and levels of capitalization (including debt and attitudes toward the use of debt financing), existence and amounts of unfunded obligations to retired or departed partners, and leverage ratios of associates to partners and paralegals to lawyers.

Once there is general agreement with respect to these issues, three specific economic issues need to be resolved:

1. *Equity equalization.* Equity equalization is needed in order to bring capital accounts (or stock ownership/valuation) into rational balance between the owners of the two firms. In some cases, this will involve an up-front payment by one firm to another, which can be financed either out of current partner earnings

in the other firm, or by use of a source of financing, such as bank debt. In other instances, members of one firm might make capital contributions over time, until parity is achieved in the capitalization scheme agreed to as part of the merger.

2. *Compensation slotting. Compensation slotting* should also occur, so that it is clear where compensation of all partners will fall within the scheme adopted as a term in the merger agreement. It may be based on the compensation scheme of one of the two firms or an entirely new scheme developed as part of the merger negotiation.

3. *Equity/non-equity partners.* Most firms today (80 percent of AmLaw 100) have tiers of partners, with different criteria for admission and advancement to "equity" status according to 2007 AmLaw 100 List (ALM Properties, Inc. 2007). Ten years ago, less than half of AmLaw firms made such distinctions. Prospective mergers need to consider status of partners, equity vs. non-equity, in the merged firm. It is not unusual that this issue scuttles an otherwise appealing (e.g., positive business case) merger scenario, due in many cases to the supermajority vote of equity partners required to approve a merger. That is, it is hard to get the turkeys to vote for Thanksgiving.

C. Negotiation Items

Negotiations need to address the fundamental issues that will effectuate the business case driving the rationale for the merger. They also need to address the economic and cultural issues identified in the preceding section. In addition, they need to address critical elements of the resulting firm: equity/capitalization schemes and levels, compensation methodology and slotting, handling of any unfunded obligations and survival/reduction/elimination of those obligations, firm name, management structure and individuals to fill various roles and positions, transition arrangements (teams, events, etc., and other factors unique to every deal), office locations, openings, closings, new positions to be created, and in some cases anticipated future mergers to attain an agreed upon strategic vision.

The negotiation position taken will depend upon the relative size/influence of the two parties involved. Where the size/economic leverage differential between parties is 50 percent or more, generally the stronger of the two firms will dictate most of the provisions. The primary decision to be made by the less powerful of the two firms is essentially "can we (do we want to) become part of that firm?"

Where parties are closer in size, the only realistic approach is to view the merged entity as a third firm, separate and different from either of the two legacy firms. In such case, each element of the resulting firm needs to be discussed in some detail and consideration needs to be given to best practices in either of the two legacy firms or possibly creating a new approach different from that in either of the two firms. This often happens with respect to capitalization, compensation schemes, management structures, and retirement policies/arrangements.

D. Due Diligence

At the point at which it appears that negotiations are proceeding on track toward development of a term sheet or prospectus documenting the understanding of the two parties to the merger, due diligence should be conducted. Generally, this involves "opening the kimonos" of each firm for reassurance that negotiations have been open, honest, and conducted with honesty and integrity. Fundamentally, due diligence is viewed as a financial issue—that is, examining the books of the other party to verify income, expenses, client base, sources and uses of capital, benefit plans, retirement plans, and the like. In some cases this will involve use of outside agents such as the firms' accountants to conduct the process. In addition, *legal* due diligence needs to occur includes evaluation of risk factors such as potential client conflicts, outstanding or possible future professional or general liability claims against the firm, insurance coverages, vendor or landlord disputes, lease arrangements, and other legal and risk management issues.

E. Term Sheet

After both firms are satisfied that their due diligence has been completed, the next step is to draft a term sheet outlining the arrangements under which the merger will occur. This term sheet will include capital structure and any equity equalization payments, how debt will be handled, structure of the new entity, ownership of the new entity, handling of intangible assets such as accounts receivable and work-in-process, leasehold arrangements, unfunded obligations, compensation structures, benefit programs and retirement plans, firm name, and management structure and position appointments.

Since partnership agreements in law firms generally require a vote of partners (in most cases a supermajority) to approve a merger, the term sheet is often used as the basis upon which votes will be sought. In other instances firms will go so far as to prepare a corporate merger-style prospectus outlining the fundamental attributes of each of the legacy firms, the business case for the merger, and the vision of the merged entity in terms of consolidated financial statements and client bases, market position, and benefits to be derived from the merger.

Preparation for a merger vote begins well in advance with an educational effort to advise owners of each of the firms of the strategic rationale, reasons for selection of the merger partner, basics of the business case, likely components/attributes of the merged entity, advantages (and possible disadvantages) to individual partners or groups, and the like. As momentum builds toward the vote, opportunities need to be found for introduction of leadership of each of the two firms to each other and, if possible, personal interaction between all of the owners of each of the two firms, probably in a combination of formal (meeting) and informal (social) settings.

F. Integration Plans

Finally, merger integration plans should be developed, at least in outline form, prior to the merger vote. Some firms will append them to the prospectus, submitted to partners, pre-vote, where that methodology is used. Integration plans should address the points listed in Checklist B at the end of this chapter.

IV. Conclusion

Law firm mergers are always consensual, in the sense they can be executed only if owners of both firms agree. Technically, there is no such thing as a hostile takeover of a law firm. And, because law firm owners are also managers and producers of the business, there must be broad consensus to make a merger occur.

There have been some notable law firm merger disasters (Reuben & Proctor's merger with Isham, Lincoln & Beale comes to mind). However, preliminary studies have shown the vast majority of law firm mergers of significance have proven to be successful, at least as measured by incremental profitability. There is no reason to conclude that the current merger trend will abate, and many reasons to predict that it will continue as the factors driving it persist.

Forms, Guidelines, and Checklists

A. Scope Merger Checklist
B. Integration Plan Guide

A. Scope Merger Checklist

- ❑ Firm A services needed by Firm B clients.
- ❑ Firm B services needed by Firm A clients.
- ❑ New clients that might be attracted by the combination.
- ❑ Firm A clients that might be served in Firm B locations.
- ❑ Firm B clients that might be served in Firm A locations.
- ❑ New locations that might be served by the combined firms.
- ❑ Expense items that might be eliminated by redundancy (accounting, administration, etc.).

B. Integration Plan Guide

- ❑ Financial integration and financial management.
- ❑ HR integration and management.
- ❑ IT integration and management.
- ❑ Marketing integration and management, including the initial marketing and public relations plan for the merger.
- ❑ Practice management integration.
- ❑ Administrative integration.
- ❑ Office space integration.

Further Reading

Coulter, Charles R. "Evaluating the Potential Merger Partner." *Law Practice Management* 18, no. 6 (Sept. 1992): pp. 22–35.

Haserot, Phyllis Weiss. "Telling the World: Checklist for Marketing a Merger." *Law Practice Management* 26, no. 5 (July/Aug. 2000): p. 48.

O'Toole, Kevin, and J. Mark Santiago. "The Makings of a Merger." *Law Practice Management* 26, no. 5 (July/Aug. 2000): pp. 42–49.

Oppenheim, Donald H. "Will You Survive Big? Twelve Merger Pitfalls." *Law Practice Management* 26, no. 5 (July/Aug. 200): p. 44.

Shannon, Marcia Pennington. "The Recipes for Merger Success." *Law Practice Management* 26, no. 5 (July/Aug. 2000): pp. 60–62.

Wesemann, H. E. "The Alliance Option: Merger? Strategic Alliance? Joint Venture? What's Right for Your Future?" *Law Practice Management* 28, Part 7 (2002): pp. 24–29.

Chapter 7

Selling a Niche Practice

by John Ventura

I. Introduction

This chapter is about selling a niche practice. So if your firm is considered a "full service firm" offering multiple services to clients, a general practice, or a firm that does not have one primary focus, you can skip this chapter. You will find what you need in the other chapters in this book, but not this one, because selling a niche practice is different than selling other types of law practices.

> ### *Key Points*
> - A niche practice is much easier to value and sell than a general practice, and it is easier to make the transition to a new buyer. In addition, the buyer is usually experienced in the field and will not need you to help transition the practice.
> - Start early when you start to think about selling; do not expect to have it happen quickly.
> - If you represent consumers and market your law practice, you will build goodwill that will be valuable when you sell your practice.
> - Several professionals can help the niche practitioner sell: certified public attorneys, law firm management consultations, business evaluators, and business attorneys.
> - The buyer's familiarity with your niche may both complicate and ease the sale.

II. What Is a Niche Practice?

You probably already know if you have a niche practice. However, let's clarify what a niche practice is before we talk about selling one. There are several ways to describe a law practice. You can describe it by its size, by the size of the city it is in, or by what services it provides. There are solo firms, which have one lawyer practicing law alone. There are also firms where lawyers practice together in anywhere from two to hundreds. There are firms that practice in small towns and communities, and firms that practice in large cities. There are law firms that provide multiple services and are called "full service firms," and there are those that are known to do only one kind of law and have built a reputation in a specialty. A niche practice is one that concentrates in a specialty. It can be big or small and is most commonly found in big cities; however, there are exceptions. When a law firm is described as a tax firm, or real estate firm, or an insurance defense firm, what that usually means is that the firm only does that kind of law and is considered a niche practice.

I sold my niche practice and will use that sale as an example. I had a consumer bankruptcy practice. Part of my practice consisted of handling personal injury cases and the litigation of consumer claims, but 90 percent of the business was representing consumers in bankruptcy proceedings.

I had offices in four cities in the Rio Grande Valley of South Texas: Brownsville, Harlingen, McAllen, and Corpus Christi. I had 45 employees, including six lawyers, and was grossing close to $3 million each year.

A. What Is Unique to Selling a Niche Practice?

The most unique aspect of selling a niche practice is how much easier it is to sell than a general practice. It is easier to value and easier to make the transition to a new buyer. Something else that is unique to selling a niche practice is that the buyer is usually experienced in the law field already and will not want you, the seller, to stick around after the sale to help transition the practice. The reason for this is because the loyalty that old clients and employees have for you may interfere with the new owner's desire to establish his or her own authority and relationship with each of those groups of people. When a law practice is sold, it is common to have the seller stay and help with the transition. Of course, if the niche practice includes contracts with large companies rather than individual consumer cases, the buyer will want the seller's help to make sure the contracts are transferred to the buyer in instances such as when the niche practice is an insurance defense firm.

Something else that is unique about selling a niche practice is that the buyer of a niche practice usually has some sense of the need for the service in the community. The same cannot be said of a general practice.

In my experience, the buyers and sellers of niche practices are driven and passionate people who love what they do. So when they find each other, a potential buyer will be comfortable talking about the business with someone familiar with this type of practice. This can be dangerous in that the seller may reveal more than intended about the practice, and that could affect the price being offered.

If you have a small general practice, you most likely will not find the number of possible buyers as the seller of a niche practice will, and you most likely will not receive the kind of money that selling a niche practice will bring. One of the reasons for this is that a successful niche practice either has valuable clients that will go with it or will have built such a good reputation that it has a history of regular business in the community.

In my situation, there were many possible purchasers of my law practice, including a few of my competitors who would have loved to see me quit the arena so they could expand their practices and get rid of a competitor at the same time; consumer bankruptcy lawyers from other cities who wanted to buy an established law firm so they could move into new territory and expand their practice into a regional or statewide practice; bankruptcy lawyers who were tired of working for someone else and wanted to buy an established firm; and, of course, lawyers who worked for me. Ultimately I sold to one of the lawyers who had worked for me for a long time.

III. Why Do You Want to Sell Your Practice?

The most common reason lawyers want to sell their law practices is that they are ready to retire. They have worked for years building up a successful practice and now want to get the final rewards. They may have promised themselves they would stop and travel or spend more time on the links or just be home more with their spouses. Perhaps they are just tired. Other reasons lawyers would want to sell a practice include:

- They have won election to a judgeship;
- They are relocating to another city;
- They want to quit practicing law and do something else;
- Practicing law is more work then they planned;
- They are in bad health and cannot keep up the pace anymore; and
- They are going through a messy divorce and will have to give half the value of the law firm to their ex-spouse.

If these last reasons apply to you, you may want to get out of the business quickly, but be careful, as this is when you are most vulnerable and may be quick to make decisions that will cost you money. This is also the time when you need people around you who will give you the best advice and help you through difficult times. You do not want to sell your practice without proper preparation and help from experts. If you rush into the sale without proper preparation, without the assistance of the right professionals to advise you, and without taking the time to do it right, several things may happen. You may get less for your business than you should. You may also end up making an agreement that will not protect you from later consequences that could have been avoided if you had good advice from professionals around you and followed their advice during the sale. Your urgency, or lack of urgency, will affect the price you get for your practice.

A. Do You Really Want to Sell Your Practice?

Before you proceed with initiating the sale of your practice, make sure you really want to sell. I started to sell my practice seven years before I actually did. Right from the beginning, I got experts in and did it right. I even had a lawyer who worked for me for years ready to buy it. But as the years passed, I kept putting off the sale because I really wasn't ready to give up my law practice. Finally, the lawyer in my firm quit and opened his own practice in competition with me. It was another five years after he quit before I finally sold my practice.

B. What Are You Going to Do after You Sell Your Practice?

Think about what you are going to do with yourself and where you are going to live after selling your practice. If you stay where you are and get nostalgic about practicing law in a few years, you might have difficulty in starting up again in the same place. Think about this carefully. You might think you want to move some place else and work for someone else, or you could be thinking you want to stay where you are and work for someone else. There may be terms in your agreement to sell your practice that would prevent you from opening a practice in the same town or even working for someone else in the same town, and you will have to agree to those terms in order to sell the practice. This is especially important if you have spent a lot of time and money building your name and reputation in the community where you are now. This problem most often comes up in the sale of a niche practice because the seller's name is associated with one area of the law and the buyer will want to make sure that the seller will not continue to practice in the same niche of the law in competition.

IV. How Long Will It Take You to Sell Your Practice?

Expect it to take at least a year to sell a niche practice. It will take at least that long to do everything you need to do to prepare your law business for sale. You will want to look at your leases to see when they expire and plan to have the business sold near the end of those leases. You will want to make decisions about when you are going to let your staff know you are selling and have time enough to respond to their reactions to the sale. Some may decide to quit. In niche practices, support staff are highly trained individuals in the narrow specialty of the firm. If they quit before you sell your practice, it might not be easy to replace them, and you may be losing staff that a buyer would find valuable as an experienced workforce in place.

In my case I had many marketing contracts that I had to pay attention to when selling. I wanted to make sure the contracts concluded so that the new owner would be the person responsible for the future contracts. Marketing was key to the successful sale of my niche practice, and it may be essential in the sale of many other kinds of niche practices, such as a family law practice.

V. Who Do You Need to Help You Sell Your Practice?

Before you sell your practice, you will want to find the professionals you need to help you sell your niche law practice successfully. These are the same professionals needed when any law firm is sold, but it is helpful to have professionals experienced in selling a niche practice with its special needs. Experienced professionals will be knowledgeable about pricing the practice correctly in order to sell it and finding a buyer for a niche practice.

A. Certified Public Accountant

One of the professionals you will need to help guide you through the sale of a niche law practice is a certified public accountant (CPA). Hopefully you have had an accountant all along who is already familiar with your financial situation. You will need that accountant to make sure your books are in order and to prepare the financial documents you will need to present to the potential buyer. You will also need these documents

Who Do You Need to Help You Sell Your Practice? 73

to share with other professionals you will hire. The CPA will at a minimum need to prepare the following: a current profit and loss statement; a valuation schedule of all your assets; an asset and liability statement; an accounts receivable aging statement; a list of active cases; a list of equipment, furniture and fixtures; a list of real estate (if any) and a current appraisal; a list of accounts payable; a list of notes payable; a copy of all leases and bank statements including trust account statements; and a list of all annual costs not shown in the list of payables.

In addition, the CPA will explain the tax consequences of your sale. This is important in setting a price for your practice because what you sell it for may not be the amount you will actually get to keep.

The heart of a successful niche practice is its bookkeeping system. If you do not get paid for the work you do, you will not have a good practice to sell. Most buyers of a niche practice will pay special attention to this department in your operation.

B. Law Firm Management Consultant

Another professional you will need is a law firm management consultant. A consultant who has experience in selling a niche law practice will be invaluable to you. He or she will help manage the work of the other professionals you hire to help sell your law practice and will also do most of the following: prepare your law firm for a sale; prepare a prospectus to show potential buyers; help you determine the price for your practice (which will be different from the valuation); find potential buyers and qualify them; and help you conclude the sale to your satisfaction.

C. Business Evaluator

A third important professional to help you sell your practice is a business evaluator. This person will value your law practice. There are different opinions about whether valuing a practice is an art or a science. After all, how do you value goodwill and the worth of your client base? The business evaluator will give as objective a value as possible for your practice and then, with your law firm management consultant, he or she will come up with a price range for the sale, the price you will ask to be paid, and your bottomline price. Because the potential buyer will have an idea about the value of your firm if he or she already practices in that area, the evaluation will have to take into consideration the potential buyer's special knowledge.

D. Business Transaction Attorney

Finally, you will also need to hire a business transaction attorney who will prepare the sale documents. This is especially important if you are going to finance the sale yourself. The documents must take into consideration possible future litigation, explain what happens when there is a default, and make sure that you have a perfected lien on all the collateral you obtained in the negotiation. It is important that this attorney has past experience in the sale of niche law practices and knows the future problems that could come up after the sale takes place.

VI. How Do You Value Your Practice and Price It for Sale?

After you hire the right team to work with you, one of the first things you will want to do is have your law practice valued and then come up with the price you want for it.

The buyer of a niche practice is usually someone who already practices in the same area of law and who may have had experience in running such a practice. He or she will likely know what kind of overhead to expect to have as well as how much profit to expect. The potential buyer will be thinking about the rate of return on the money spent on your practice. He or she will be looking at future earnings and if it will be possible to cut overhead.

In my situation, I had employees who had been with me for years, and I had raised salaries over those years. The first thing my buyer wanted to do was fire the oldest employees because they represented most of the salary overhead. The idea was that one way for the buyer to get to the profitability desired was cutting overhead.

In putting a price on the business, you must assume some people are going to be let go. You have to ask yourself, "Do I owe these people anything for their long years of service?" If so, when you set a price, set it high enough to allow you to give those being fired severance pay.

When you come up with a value, also come up with a second number, which is the price you would take. This is not the same thing as your first number. One question you have to ask yourself is, "Is there a number below which I would not sell, but would just collect my receivables and close the practice down?"

What exactly are you going to value? Accounts receivables? Books and equipment? Client files? Goodwill? Are you going to sell your name and not compete? There are many factors that will determine the price someone will actually pay you. They could include location of the practice, competition in that area of practice, the kind of practice you are buying, current state of the law in that area of practice, size of practice, if you are going to finance the sale or if you want to be cashed out, how much time you have to sell, if you are going to get any repeat business from your clients, and how much the firm has spent on advertising and promotion of the firm name and for how long.

Hire an expert who will help put a value on goodwill, law firm hard assets, and contingency fee cases. A number of methods of valuation can be used: fair market value rule of thumb, price-earnings ratio, or discounted future cash flow.

Consider your tax liability when figuring your bottomline number. There will be some. For me this was softened by the fact that I had loaned money to the company over the years. So I negotiated that a portion of the sale price would be repayment of that loan, which would not be taxable. The law firm management consultant could be the person who will value the firm or help find a person to do that.

A. How Do You Develop a Prospectus for Potential Buyers?

You will have to create a professional prospectus to interest a potential buyer. Your law firm management consultant will prepare this for you and explain to you the information that should go into it. There will be some financial information, some historical data, and information about the potential for new business in the future.

This is a sales tool, and it has to look professionally prepared to catch the attention of potential buyers.

The prospectus is an important selling tool for the sale of a niche practice. It will be different than the prospectus for the sale of other kinds of law practices in that you will give information that will mean something to someone who already practices the same kind of law and has inside knowledge of how your kind of niche practice works.

B. How Do You Think about the Best Interests of Your Clients?

There are a number of ethical issues that you will face when you sell your niche practice. One issue concerns the reason your clients hired you. Your firm was probably hired because you where known for being a specialist in your field and had most likely earned a reputation for representing your clients well. When someone buys your firm, your clients will need to be notified that you are no longer their lawyer. You are going to have to strategize with the new buyer how you want this notification to be handled because the buyer will want to retain as many of your clients as possible.

Another issue that could come up in the sale of a niche practice is conflicts of interests. If I had sold my practice to anyone other than a lawyer who already worked for me, this could have been a problem. In my case, the bankruptcy community was very small, so it was not uncommon to have other lawyers in the community representing creditors as well as debtors. Sometimes they represented creditors in cases against my clients. Look closely at a potential buyer of your niche practice. If it is possible the buyer acted adversely to any of your clients in the past by representing an individual or company against them, then there could be conflict of interest issues. This is more common in the selling of niche practices, especially in small communities, than in the selling of other types of law firms.

C. Finding a Buyer

You are looking for a buyer who has means and motivation. This is the reason you need a law firm management consultant firm to represent you. They will find the potential buyers and can qualify them so your time is not wasted. You will come out with more money, have fewer headaches, and do less work.

Where are the potential buyers going to come from? If you have hired a law office management consultant firm, they will most likely advertise. They will be your agent for the sale.

If you did not hire a law firm management consultant firm and you want to find a buyer yourself, where would you look? Possible buyers could be new lawyers, lawyers leaving big firms for one reason or another, lawyers who compete with you and may want to grow their practices and get rid of the competition at the same time, and lawyers who work for you. If you are not thinking of selling immediately but instead some time in the future, you might want to develop your own buyer from the lawyers who work for you. Or else you might want to cultivate a buyer by bringing someone in and letting that person earn the right to buy your practice by working for a number of years.

When you find a potential buyer, do some due diligence to make sure he or she has the means to buy your practice. Selling the practice to someone I knew eliminated the need to do due diligence on a proposed buyer, but this is something you will want to do if you are selling to a stranger.

D. Negotiating the Sale

Before you negotiate the sale, figure out what your bottom price is. Be realistic: you are probably not going to get what you want, so just aim for getting the best you can, given the circumstances. Remember that the potential buyer will have most likely run or worked in an office just like yours and will have a realistic idea about the value of the practice.

Now you need to decide whether you are going to negotiate the sale yourself or get one of your professionals who is a good negotiator to do it. Since lawyers spend a lot of their lives negotiating for their clients, you might be inclined to negotiate yourself, but I would recommend that you have one of the professionals you have hired do this. There is less of a chance you will leave something on the table. You also might not know what conditions should be in the agreement. You might be a great negotiator, but it is presumed you have not had any experience in negotiating the sale of a law practice. Let professionals who have had the experience do it for you.

Among the terms you need to consider before the sale is negotiated are whether or not to agree to a covenant not to compete and whether or not to sell your name. These issues come up in the sale of a niche practice where someone has spent money marketing the name of the law firm. I did this, but it was limited to the cities and surrounding areas where I had offices. It did not include cities outside the area where I would possibly move after the sale. I was comfortable selling the name as I knew I was not going to start a practice again and I had put a lot of money into building up the name of my firm, so it had value. If you are going to live in the same areas of your former practice and there is the slightest chance you might want to practice again, give a lot of consideration to terms that limit your ability to do that.

When negotiating the sale, be sure to try to negotiate that the buyer will add you to his or her professional liability insurance for a period of time. Also discuss substitution of attorney on all active cases in litigation.

Other issues to consider include deciding what collateral you are going to ask for to secure your payments if you are going to sell and finance. Should you sell the business when there is not going to be collateral? Think about the ways to get paid. In my opinion, being cashed out is the best way, as you walk away with a lump sum and leave it all behind. Another way is to finance the sale yourself so you end up with a down payment and periodic payments over time, or you could be paid a percentage of the money that is received. However, you could run into trouble this way because of fee splitting rules in your state.

Also consider if you want to stay on as an employee of your firm. Some buyers might not want you to do that. They may feel they want to build their own relationship with staff and clients and would be afraid of continued loyalty to you.

VII. Make Sure You Follow the Rules of Professional Conduct

There are many ethical considerations in selling your law practice. It is important to investigate your state laws in this area, as your state might have specific rules that cover important areas of concern and protections for clients. This includes notifying clients about the change in ownership, assurance that cases will not be neglected during the period of sale, making sure that all litigation cases have the proper substitution of attorneys, and making sure that litigation cases are not going to suffer because you are changing lawyers in the middle of the case. You have to give notice to clients that they have the right to go to another lawyer. You cannot change rates you are charging without giving clients notices in advance and a chance to change lawyers. In certain kinds of practice a conflict check is needed and is a necessity.

It might be a good idea to check out the *ABA Model Rules of Professional Conduct, Model Rule 1.17: Sale of a Law Practice* after you have looked at your own state laws concerning the sale of a law practice. There is a lot of good information you will want to know before you begin the work of selling your practice.

Although normally you would notify your clients that you sold your business and give them a chance to hire someone else or stay, in my case, since I was selling my name and remaining of counsel to the firm, and since the lawyer buying my practice knew most of the clients already, we did not send a letter to the clients saying I sold the practice. They were told I was retired, which was the truth. This would not be the case in a normal sale. You would have to notify the clients and give them a chance to change lawyers.

If the person buying your firm is going to finish out cases you started, you are going to want to make sure your professional liability insurance will cover this situation and then maintain the insurance for as long as there are active cases. Of course you could get the new lawyer to put you on his or her policy as a condition of the sale.

VIII. Conclusion

Let me share with you some things I did to make it easier to sell my niche law practice.

One thing I did that helped with the sale was refining the operation system of my practice and then creating a manual on how to do everything that we did to run a successful firm. Our manual included everything we could think of, from how we set fees to how we marketed to get clients. It included how to set up a file as well as checklists for everything that a legal assistant or lawyer does to work up and prosecute a case. It also included things like when files should be destroyed and how to close out a case.

I also made my firm famous by building up the name. I spent hundreds of thousands of dollars marketing my firm so that everyone in my area heard of us. My firm name was familiar to the entire local population. I did this in a number of ways. I used traditional marketing but, in addition to that, I also got my own weekly radio show and wrote a weekly column for one of the newspapers. I wrote books including *Law for Dummies*. I did everything I could do to make sure people in the community heard about my firm. I even paid to advertise on the phone "time and temperature" so people who called were told "John Ventura Time." I sponsored floats in parades and little league teams. I had spent so much time and money building my name in the community that when I sold the practice, one of the valuable things I sold was the continued use of my name.

One of the things I did to prepare for the sale was thinking about it in advance. It was unfortunate that I did not sell to the first potential buyer, the lawyer who worked for me, but having to go through the steps necessary to sell was good preparation for when I finally decided to sell. So start early when you begin to think about selling and do not expect to have it happen quickly. Be prepared to wait a year or more.

If you represent consumers and market your law practice, you will build goodwill that will be valuable when you sell the practice. It worked for me. So do what you can to make your name the very first one people think about when they think of your law niche.

Forms, Guidelines, and Checklists

A. Checklist for the Sale of a Niche Practice: Matters to Be Considered When Drafting the Agreement

A. Checklist for the Sale of a Niche Practice: Matters to Be Considered When Drafting the Agreement

These are some of the terms that should be considered for the sale agreement. In addition, you would have all the clauses that make a contract binding.

- ❑ Assets that will be sold:
    - ❑ Building and real property
    - ❑ Goodwill
    - ❑ Use of firm name
    - ❑ Will it be a stock transfer or purchase of assets?
    - ❑ Equipment, furniture, and fixtures
    - ❑ Cash on hand and on deposit (which includes funds in trust account)
    - ❑ Account receivables and ongoing cases
- ❑ Nature of consideration:
    - ❑ Paying cash or note to seller
    - ❑ Assumption of debts
    - ❑ Other considerations
- ❑ Time and manner of payment
    - ❑ All cash on closing
    - ❑ Part payment on signing and balance on closing
    - ❑ Deposit held in escrow until closing
    - ❑ Installment payments
    - ❑ Collateral security
    - ❑ Other methods of payment
    - ❑ Personal guarantee of payment by buyer

- ❑ Indemnification of buyer
- ❑ Assumption by buyer of leases
- ❑ Covenant not to compete
    - ❑ Geographical areas
    - ❑ Duration
- ❑ Remedies on Default

Further Reading

DeWoskin, Alan E. "The Sale of a Law Practice." *The Compleat Lawyer* v. 14, no. 4 (Fall 1997): p. 48.

Dimitriou, Demetrios. "What Should Be Your Concerns? Purchase or Sale of a Solo Practice." *Law Practice Management* v. 19 no 8 (Nov/Dec 1993): p.44–48.

Keller, Michael E. "Law Practice for Sale." *Washington State Bar News* v. 50, no. 2 (Feb 1, 1996): 24

Shayne, Neil T. "Selling Your Law Practice. Who Says You Can't Sell Your Law Practice?" *New York State Bar Journal* v. 64, no. 6 (Sept 1992): 12.

Simon, Robert A. "Selling the Goodwill of a Law Practice: The Sole Practitioner's Perspective" *Illinois Bar Journal* v. 79 (Aug. 1991): 402–405.

Chapter 8

Checklist for Closing or Preparing for the Closing of a Law Practice

by Jay G Foonberg*

I. Introduction

This checklist has been written because there is a need for it. Many anecdotal stories have been written by widows and others describing how no one was prepared to close a law office and there was nowhere to get help.

Why is closing down a law practice any different than closing down any other business? The tasks which have to be done when closing a law practice are about the same as those which have to be done in closing any business including a medical practice. The major differences are the ethical conditions superimposed on the task, which makes the task difficult and sometimes impossible to accomplish. Most of the ethical conditions superimposed are designed either to protect the confidentiality of client information, including identity, or to prevent other lawyers from offering to help the clients because of solicitation concerns.

This checklist is only a starting point and must be used in conjunction with local ethical rules which vary greatly from jurisdiction to jurisdiction. Hopefully it will help the lawyer who is considering retiring or who has the time to do many of the things on the list before retiring. The checklist may also be of help to those who are called upon to close down the law practice of another where there was no prior preparation for closing.

Please note that in some of the steps there may be a repetition of information found in other steps. This is intentional to prevent inadvertent omissions.

Key Points

- Whether planned for or not, closing a practice requires preparation and organization.
- The reasons for closing an office can affect the steps necessary to close.
- Make certain to address all issues affecting the physical space; clients' files, accounts, and confidences; documents, computers, bills and accounts, vendors and contracts, insurance, and communications and notices.

---

*© 2007 Jay G Foonberg. All rights reserved. Reprinted with permission of the author. Visit www.Foonberglaw.com for other products and information from this author.

- There is necessary redundancy and overlap in the steps to close an office properly—proper tracking is critical to cover all areas: staff has to be kept or protected as much as possible. Occupancy must be dealt with. Records and Files disposition must be accomplished. Final tax returns must be prepared and filed and taxes paid.
- There may be hundreds or thousands of necessary communications to clients and from clients.
- Compared to medicine, dentistry and accounting, the ethical requirements are burdensome.

II. When Is It Necessary to Close a Law Practice?

A law practice may have to be closed permanently or temporarily, completely or partially, for any of the following reasons:

1. The lawyer dies.
2. The lawyer is physically or mentally unable to practice law.
3. The lawyer wants to retire.
4. The lawyer is disbarred.
5. The lawyer is disciplined.
6. The lawyer is elected or appointed to public office.
7. The lawyer accepts an employment opportunity that requires leaving practice.
8. The lawyer is drafted or activated into military service.
9. The lawyer is leaving the state.
10. The lawyer is merging practice with another firm and must get out of certain types of cases (a plaintiff lawyer is joining a defense firm, for example).
11. The lawyer is selling part or all of the practice.
12. The lawyer walks out the door due to "burn out."
13. The lawyer suffers temporary or permanent problems with drugs, alcohol, or other addictions.
14. The lawyer is under extreme personal stress due to drugs, alcohol, money problems, law school debt, etc.

III. Who Is Going to Do the Work of Winding Down or Closing the Practice?

1. The lawyer, if alive, competent, and available.
2. The executor of the lawyer's estate.
3. The conservator or guardian of the lawyer.
4. Another lawyer or firm with whom prior arrangements have been made. (Be careful about client confidentiality.)
5. The lawyer's widow, widower, or other family member.

6. Various entities that exist on an ongoing or ad hoc basis as needed. These entities may exist within the framework of the Bar, the Bar's disciplinary or ethics system, the state's judicial system, or at a local county level. These entities often get the work done by pro bono lawyers or nominally paid volunteers.

7. The purchaser or seller of the practice.

IV. Specifically, What Has to Be Done?

As it is very difficult to find a logical point to begin or end accordingly, the tasks listed may not be listed in a logical sequence. Some of the steps are included again in other steps.

A. Occupancy

1. Get a set of keys to the premises and to interior locked file cabinets and offices. If there is a safe, try to locate the combination. Ask the landlord for help. Ask the most recent employee for help. If necessary, get a locksmith. Change the locks and combinations to protect the office files and assets.

2. Contact the current or most recent staff to arrange their employment, if available on a full, part-time, or temporary basis, to help in the closing down process.

3. Open all mail as it arrives to look for information on pending client matters, bills that have to be paid, tax returns that have to be filed, income that may come in, services that have to be cancelled, etc.

4. Ask about "branch offices." The lawyer may have done some work from a home office or from a vacation house office. Check for existence of files and computer data. Old files and back up information are commonly stored off the premises.

5. Arrange with the landlord or other entity for both a cancellation of the old lease or tenancy arrangement and the creation of a new arrangement.

B. Tracking Down Information

1. Insurance

6. If there is a known CPA, bookkeeper, or file system, try to locate all existing insurance policies, including malpractice, workers' compensation, medical, life, general liability, etc.

7. Arrange with the insurance agents or companies involved for a termination of the policies or the issuance of new policies to protect the person(s) or entities closing down the practice. Determine status of employees' health, life and disability insurance.

8. Determine if the malpractice carrier will provide assistance in closing the practice.

9. Determine if a "tail" malpractice policy can be obtained to protect the lawyer's estate. ("Tail" policies generally protect a lawyer from malpractice claims, so long as the lawyer discontinues active law practice.)

2. Checking Accounts

10. Look for checkbooks, canceled checks, bank statements and incoming mail for information on existence of checking accounts, savings accounts, and safe deposit boxes. Notify banks. Determine if old accounts must be closed and new accounts opened.

11. Examine at least one year's check register or cancelled checks to determine insurance contracts in force and service contracts to be cancelled (water, cleaning, parking, messengers, etc.).

3. Taxes

12. Be extra careful in the months of January and February when IRS and state information return documents may arrive.

13. Determine which "final" and new tax returns must be filed. Consider federal, state and local payroll, occupancy, and sales taxes. Identify federal and state Employer Identification Numbers.

14. Ask local court clerks to run a computer search to determine if attorney is attorney of record on any open matters.

15. Examine all incoming mail to determine open client matters and open service contracts.

4. Assumption Attorneys

16. Be especially alert for documents indicating the possible existence of an assumption attorney. This information may be obtainable from the Bar Licensing Authorities, where required, as a condition of license renewal.

17. Determine if the attorney had an arrangement with another attorney (sometimes called an assuming attorney or assumption attorney) who has previously <u>formally or informally agree</u>d to assume the practice of the deceased or disabled attorney.

18. Ask the surviving spouse or office staff if the attorney had <u>a close friend attorney </u>who might have informally agreed to be an assuming attorney.

19. Ask local bar association(s) to send email alerts to members and public notice in bar publications announcing death or disability of the attorney and asking for information as to any assuming attorney or attorneys with client matters with the deceased or disabled attorney.

C. Computers & Electronic Information

20. Take possession and protect all computers. Get technical assistance if necessary to make back-up disks or tapes in the event something happens to the computers. Do not sell the computers.

21. Find the <u>computer passwords</u>. Change them if necessary. Find <u>the email password</u>. Hopefully a family member or employee will have them. Get a

court order if necessary to get email. Your IT people might be able to bypass the passwords.

22. Ask if there are back-up tapes, discs, or memory sticks and where they would be located. Take possession of them.

23. Older law practices might have confidential information on older forms of storage such as mag cards, magnetic tapes, paper tapes, 8-inch floppies, 5-inch floppies, 3-inch floppies, microfiche, etc. If you find such items, do not simply trash them. Read them, if possible, and destroy them by shredding before disposing. If there are old used carbon papers, they must also be shredded.

24. It is likely that any computer used in a law office contains confidential client information. Neither the lawyer nor another person can dispose of a computer by sale, gift, or just putting it into the trash until it has been purged of client-related information. "Delete" does not remove information from a computer. "Delete" simply moves the information to a different place within the computer. It is still there. "Formatting" may not always remove information. "Recovery" technicians using sophisticated equipment and sophisticated programs can recover almost any information that was ever in a computer if someone is willing to pay for the skill and time involved.

The only almost 100 percent guaranteed way to prevent disclosure of client information is to remove the hard disk, hit it beyond recognition with a sledge hammer, roll over it with a steam roller, and then burn it in flames. Even that method might not be 100 percent successful against skilled recovery technicians.

There are some commercially available products that probably are adequate for a lawyer or successor purging files. Technically, they don't remove the information; they obliterate the information by typing new information several times on top of the old information.

The U.S. Department of Defense publishes a standard for "removal of information from computers." It is called DoD 5220.22-M. Several programs claim to meet the standard. Among them are DBAN, available for free as an open source program; White Canyon, which is not free (www.whitecanyon.com); Window Washer (www.webroot.com); and Disk Wipes.

It is also possible that the existing computer contains programs to do what has to be done. Confidential information might also be stored on zip drives, USB flash drives, diskettes, etc.

Before purging anything, it may be necessary to back up and preserve the information being purged to protect the lawyer or the lawyer's estate. There are many devices available to do what needs to be done. You might be purging too much or too little.

If you properly erase or cleanse a hard drive, you will be removing everything including all programs.

I have been told, but have not verified that there are companies that will erase your hard drive for free if you give the computer to a charity.

As with all technology, changes are rapid, and this information might not be current or meet your needs. Get help if you are determined to try to sell or give away the computers.

25. Try to determine the attorney's password(s) to open his or her computer and or various applications. The attorney's spouse or secretary may have the passwords.

26. If a password cannot be obtained, look for "recovery specialists" who have the skills to find or avoid the password. "Recovery Specialists" are a recognized occupation and differ from mere "hackers."

1. Calendars

27. Look for desk calendars, computer calendars, PDA calendars, email calendars, and secretarial calendars to seek information on cases in process and due dates.

D. Client Lists: Active and Closed Files

28. There may be lists of clients divided into active files and closed files. These people will have to be notified. If there is nothing else available, a Christmas card list or Seasons Greetings card list may provide names and addresses of both clients and non-clients for notification. This list might be at a mailing service or printer. The form of notification may depend on the existence or nonexistence of a successor attorney.

29. Closed files may be kept in more than one location. Closed files may be stored in public warehouses, the attorney's garage or basement, or in the attorney's home or even with a client or neighbor or relative. All staff and family members should be quizzed to determine if they know of out-of-office locations.

30. Closed files must be examined before destruction or return to clients or their chosen attorneys. The examination of closed files (and open files) raises questions of attorney-client confidence and possible violation of confidence. The rules concerning confidentiality vary from state to state. In some states only an attorney or someone working under the direct supervision and control of an attorney can look into the file. In other states a non-attorney spouse, relative, or personal representative of the attorney's estate may be able to examine the files. In some states the attorney for the executor or personal representative can cause the files to be examined and get a court order if needed. In some states a receivership is allowed which authorizes non-attorneys designated by the court to examine the files.

31. Look for a number of things in the closed files. Anything that is the property of the client should immediately be returned to the client. Any original document should be removed from the files for return to the client. Typical items found in files include wills, stock certificates, original signed contracts, promissory notes, deeds, mortgages, and other items returned to the attorney's

office from a county recorder or governmental filing office. Items representing attorney work product generally are not given to the client, but the rules as to what must be returned to the client may vary from state to state. In California the only thing to which the client is not entitled is what is in the attorney's memory. *All* information is the property of the client, including electronic information, in some states.

1. Destruction of Closed Files

32. The rules concerning time periods for file retention and file destruction vary from state-to-state and usually turn on various statutes of limitations. Some rules are based on conversion, as though one was converting the property (the file) of the client. Some rules are based on statutes of limitations of ethics rules or breach of contract or negligence claims. Determine if the attorney had a file retention–destruction policy which had been communicated to the clients. There may be special rules for the files of minors, files in criminal matters, or files involving trust accounts. If there are no clear published rules, ask for guidance from both the malpractice carrier and the ethics authorities.

33. The safest way to destroy closed files is simply to shred them or get them shredded and then converted to pulp. Unfortunately this can be an expensive process. Often lawyers just dump closed files into the trash. This is a risky procedure as the trash is handled by many people before destruction and the file contents may be of interest to one or more of these people. The Department of Defense publishes standards of shredded particle size (e.g. 1mm x 4mm).

34. Depending on the price of paper, some paper recyclers will buy old files by weight. Paper used in law firms has high scrap value. The buyer will both buy the files and haul them away. The files get torn apart as they move down a conveyer belt. The paper is then sorted by type of paper and processed. I have personally observed the processing and I believe it is extremely unlikely that client confidences would be violated.

35. You may need to get client permission to destroy files. A letter to the client on closing a matter with wording to the effect, "the file in this matter may be destroyed without further notification to you," will be helpful as possible implied consent to destruction.

36. It may or may not be possible to find cheap storage in a farm area or in a slum area. Files could be put in this cheap storage with the hope that no one will ever need them.

37. File storage and accessing in a public storage facility can be very expensive and can delay the closing.

2. Unlocatable Clients

38. Property of unlocated clients may have to be stored until it can be abandoned and destroyed or properly disposed of.

39. Files of unlocated clients pose a special problem. If the applicable statutes of limitations have run and no one has responded to notices, the files probably

can be destroyed. Determine if the deceased lawyer's jurisdiction has a place to send unclaimed files.

40. Some states have a little-advertised procedure whereby a court file can be opened and the entire file deposited with the court for non-locatable clients. The filing fee can be expensive, as it is for only one client. Courts typically don't want to accept multi-year storage expense and responsibility for a single filing fee. It may be necessary to research the statutory provisions and demand the court accept the file(s).

41. Determine if there is a court or other depository for nonreturnable client wills and trust documents. Turn over of the wills and trust documents may be required by law.

E. Disposal of Office Furnishings and Books

42. Law books may have little or no value and are simply a disposal problem. The law school from which the deceased graduated is the most likely organization to accept them. Law schools might accept the books for fear that rejecting them might affect subsequent cash donations.

43. With rare exception, used law office equipment has relatively little value. Offer the equipment to the staff and give the balance to a charity that will get it and haul it away. Treat computers differently. Read again the section discouraging selling or giving away computers.

44. Computers contain client information that often cannot be divulged. In general a computer cannot be sold because of the client information. There are various programs that make it difficult to get client information out of the computer, but the only 100 percent answer is to remove the hard drive and smash it with a sledge hammer. Giving the computers to a charity or to employees creates client confidentiality problems. Other sections of this checklist discuss information on computers.

F. Trust Accounts

45. Determine who can sign checks on the trust account(s). Inform the bank that the account should be frozen. Determine if a nonlawyer can audit the account. Give a sense or urgency to determine which clients are entitled to the money and make distribution to the clients as rapidly as possible. Nonidentifiable balances may be subject to the state's escheat laws. Records may have to be stored in perpetuity.

G. Notices & Forwarding

46. Notify the post office or mail delivery service, building management and some nearby offices. Post office forwarding hopefully will prevent mail from being delivered and left at an empty office. Request building management and

nearby offices to collect and forward or notify you of mail, express deliveries, or anything that might be important. A post office forwarding notice might not be effective if a private mail forwarding service ordinarily picks up the mail from the post office and delivers it.

47. In smaller communities and where appropriate, post a notice on the door for clients who may drop by to seek their file or status of their matter. In the notice, inform the client of when, where, and with whom contact should be made. Do not do this if you feel the notice would serve as an invitation for a burglar or disappointed client to return and steal from or vandalize the office.

48. Notify clients and others as appropriate on the attorney website.

49. If you can obtain passwords, clear all voicemails which may contain client or other important communications. If passwords are not available, disconnect all voicemails for which there is no password and consider using a simple answering machine instead. Contact a "Recovery Specialist" if information may be important and passwords cannot be found.

50. Arrange for automatic forwarding of all emails to a mailbox of the responsible person. It is also possible to reject or answer all emails with a notice instructing the sender whom to contact. You may need the email password to do this.

51. If a database of client emails is maintained, consider notifying clients and others by email notifications. Bad email addresses can be quickly spotted. It may be possible to program emails to notify the sender when the email has or has not been opened or read.

52. Immediately upon making arrangements for a successor lawyer or firm, notify all courts, agencies, opposing counsel, etc., of the change in representation by appropriate substitution or other documents. Some courts or agencies might require a motion to make the change.

53. <u>Check to see if there is a statutory requirement of specific notices to clients.</u>

54. If arrangements for a successor lawyer or firm have not been made, it may be necessary to file an appropriate document or letter to the court to prevent a default proceeding or to otherwise protect the client.

H. Files & Accounts

55. Non-client office files and records such as books of account, bank statements, paid bills, etc. can usually be trashed after the necessary time for income tax or malpractice or other laws. Trust account records may have a longer retention period. The length of time necessary before destruction of internal non-client office records varies greatly from jurisdiction-to-jurisdiction.

56. Retiring lawyers or successors in interest may not want to devote the time or money to reviewing old client and office files with the attendant expenses of contacting clients. Many lawyers just dump the files into boxes with the file names on the outside. The boxes containing the files are then stored in

a garage, basement or "add on" backyard playhouse along with the hope that the files will never be requested. This system seems to work, although it would still seem necessary to remove original client documents from files before doing so.

57. Check local rules for a definition of "client files." In some jurisdictions it is only the personal property of the client (wills, documents, etc.). In some jurisdictions it is everything except the attorneys' "work product." In some jurisdictions attorney "work product" is included in the definition of client files. In some jurisdictions electronic data is included and must be downloaded and delivered.

58. Delivering an active file to a client, or an attorney chosen by the client, may be necessary to protect the client's interests. Some consideration must be given to photocopying or scanning what is given for malpractice protection. Active files delivered directly to clients must be carefully examined before delivery. A receipt for the file must be obtained.

59. Present and former clients should be advised (if not previously advised) that their closed files may be destroyed without any further notification to them.

60. Examine incoming mail to determine what subscriptions must be canceled. Newsletters, magazines, lawyer listings, legal supplements, yellow pages, web and Internet services, etc. must be canceled.

61. Many publications and memberships continue unless canceled. Monthly or other periodic charges might automatically be made to a credit card or by charges to a bank account. These must be canceled. Some subscription services will only allow the deceased or disappeared lawyer to close the account. A court order might be needed.

62. Notify all clients that the lawyer is dead, disabled, or leaving the practice of law.

63. Notify all clients whether or not arrangements have been made (if applicable) on who will handle the clients' matters if they agree or by default if they do not object.

64. Notify clients they can pick up their files or that the files may be destroyed without further notification.

65. Notify clients they may have their files delivered to another lawyer.

66. Notify bar associations, professional associations, and other organizations as appropriate. In addition to ending dues billing, the organizations may wish to notify others of the death of the member. (For example when I die, the ABA House of Delegates will read my name in its opening memorial service.)

I. Protection of Staff

67. Staff should be protected as much as is possible. Bonuses should be arranged for those who remain to close the practice. Individual rights for medical, life, or disability insurance may require immediate notices. COBRA or other laws

may apply for medical insurance. Get advice from the firm's insurance agent or the bar association's insurance person or an employment lawyer.

68. Unused accrued vacation, unused sick leave, or unused personal time pay may be required to be paid. Appropriate information returns may be required. Be sure all employee addresses and third person contacts are current.

For questions concerning this checklist, the author may be contacted through www.Foonberglaw.com

Chapter 9

Business Responsibilities in Closing a Law Practice

by Constance K. Putzel

"Law is Order and Good Law is Good Order."[1]
—Aristotle

I. Introduction

Law school taught us many things, but it did not teach us how to open, manage, or close a law office. According to the American Bar Association, there were 1,116,967 lawyers licensed in the United States in June 2006. The most recent available statistics indicate that 48 percent of all lawyers were solo and an additional 15 percent practiced in firms of 2 to 5 lawyers.[2] This chapter is designed to assist those who may be closing the office of another solo or small firm lawyer, or finalizing their own practices.

Key Points

- ABA Model Rule 1.17 affects the sale of goodwill for solo and small firm practitioners and governs the sale of your own or another's practice.
- Client communications, and the ethical handling of closed or inactive files, is one of the largest issues in closing a practice.
- Trust accounts (ABA Model Rule 1.15) are required for all funds belonging to clients regardless of the source.
- Steps to close one's own office should be undertaken at least six months in advance of the closing and include settling accounts, closing bank accounts and vendor and service contracts, safekeeping property, notifying licensing authority, and determining insurance needs.

---

[1] JOHN BARTLETT AND JUSTIN KAPLAN, BARTLETT'S FAMILIAR QUOTATIONS (USA: Little Brown and Company, 1992), at 78.

[2] AMERICAN BAR ASSOCIATION MARKET RESEARCH DEPARTMENT, LAWYER DEMOGRAPHICS (2006), available at http://www.abanet.org/marketresearch/lawyer_demographics_2006.pdf.

♦ Lawyers have a fiduciary obligation to keep any client (including another lawyer's client) property safe, whether it is money, documents, or tangible personal property. Some property must be promptly returned.

II. Closing Another Lawyer's Law Office

My recent experience closing the office of a law school classmate in Maryland provides one illustration of closing the office of a sole practitioner.

One December afternoon I sloshed across the muddy backyard of the house that had been my classmate's law office for the past 60 years. At the age of eighty-one she had died suddenly of pancreatic cancer while still in active practice as a solo practitioner. Her secretary had retired several years earlier and my friend, with great reluctance, had replaced both the secretary and typewriter with a computer. Until then, she prided herself on being the only lawyer in the county still filing documents on an old-fashioned Underwood with carbon paper copies. Her children explained that she bartered legal services in exchange for driveways, plumbing, and electrical work.

Although her methods may have been archaic and certainly unorthodox, she must have done something, or possibly everything, right because in nearly 60 years of practice there is no record of any disciplinary proceeding.

After my friend died, I was contacted by a retired Circuit Judge for Baltimore County, who had been appointed by the Court to serve as Conservator of her affairs. The Court Order read, in part:

> "ORDERED, that _____ be, and he is hereby appointed conservator of the client affairs of _____ with the immediate authority to take possession of all client files and related documents, to take possession of all trust accounts and business records of _____, to review all matters relevant to the clients of _____, and to take whatever action he considers necessary and proper to protect the interests of those clients."[3]

The judge requested that I act as personal representative of the estate, to handle the business aspects of the practice, as the law practice was the only asset in her estate. All other assets were jointly owned with the spouse.

The office was located in a working-class neighborhood on a busy thoroughfare in Baltimore County. The property was owned jointly with her husband. The practice consisted primarily of estate and real estate matters. For many families, she had been the family lawyer for three generations.

When I met with the judge and the family, the first question I asked was whether the practice could be sold. Since 1999, Maryland, following the lead of the ABA Model Rules, has permitted the sale of a law practice *in its entirety* only under certain limited circumstances, including death and complete and total retirement. This provision is

---

[3] Circuit Court for Baltimore County. "Petition for Appointment of a Conservator of the Client Affairs of _____: Order" (Baltimore, Maryland 2005).

more restrictive than the ABA Model Rule, which permits the sale of a *law practice or an area of law practice*. A more exhaustive discussion of the sale of a law practice can be found in Chapter 1 of this book and applicable ABA Model Rule 1.17 can be found at Appendix 9-1.

We were cautiously optimistic that sale was a possibility. In the process of searching the office, we located a letter dated approximately two years earlier from a local law firm indicating an interest in "engaging in a dialogue with sole practitioners who are interested in retiring in the next several years." The letter stated that, "Since most law practices are very distinct, financial arrangements will need to be negotiated on a 'case by case' basis." We contacted the writer and began compiling a client list and a list of the past seven years Schedule "Cs." When the gross receipts for the past several years failed to meet the criteria required by the potential purchaser, that option was foreclosed. Goodwill alone was insufficient to persuade an established downtown law firm to purchase a neighborhood practice.

We next attempted to sell the practice by posting a notice at each area law school and on listservs of the Family Law and Elder Law Sections of the Maryland State Bar Association. Although we had several inquiries, no offer was forthcoming.

Not to be discouraged, our final effort at selling the practice was with a new admittee who had expressed an interest in opening his own office with an emphasis on real estate. Following several months of negotiations, including consideration of a "package deal" for the real estate and the practice, we finally reached a verbal agreement. After consultation with family and financial advisers, the young lawyer agreed to purchase the inactive files for a reasonably small but acceptable sum. The potential purchaser contacted the judge who advised him by letter that he, the Conservator, was required to approve the sale, although I was responsible for the financial arrangements.[4] Although the order did not require court approval for sale of the practice, and Maryland Rule 1.17 only requires a court order if written notice to a client has been returned and the client cannot be located, the judge stated in his letter that he was required "to petition the Court for Baltimore County regarding the approval of any sale of the practice."[5] Because of the logistical difficulty of locating hundreds of clients whose files may go back 50 years, this was obviously the only safe way to resolve the dilemma.

The active files had already been carefully reviewed by the judge. Several pending estates that had been "works in progress" were referred for completion, funds distributed, and proportionate fees disbursed to the lawyers who had completed the work. The deceased lawyer's shares of the fees were deposited to the estate and ultimately distributed to the husband, the named legatee in the holographic will executed in the hospital during the testator's final illness. She practiced law, loved it, invested wisely, lived modestly, paid her bills, educated her four children, and led a comfortable, rewarding life doing what she loved.

---

[4] *Id.*

[5] American Bar Association, Center for Professional Responsibility: *Model Rules of Professional Conduct, Client Lawyer Relationship: Rule 1.17 Sale of Law Practice,* American Bar Association.

III. Closing Your Own Law Office

From a fiscal standpoint, closing a colleague's law office is not very different from closing your own. The sentiment departs with the files while the economics remain to frustrate. When contemplating retirement, give yourself enough time to get your office in order. Stop taking new cases for at least six months or one year. Resign from organizations, discontinue subscriptions, and consider tail insurance.

After reviewing every file in the office, active and inactive, and having disposed of the inactive ones, review all active files from a business standpoint. Does anything remain to be done? Has the complete fee been paid? Is the client due any refund? Decisions have to be made regarding each file. Close the ones that require no further work and no further financial arrangements. Take the necessary action to collect, if possible, on those where additional fees are due and refund any monies due the client. It is no different than before; it is just more concentrated and without the excitement and challenge of an active practice.

We are all repeatedly cautioned to get our affairs in order. We remind our clients to do the same, and our paralegals remind us. Some, like my own paralegal, even prepare our Advance Directives and Powers of Attorney and nag us until we sign. Otherwise, knowing that we are immortal, it stops there.

IV. Closing Any Law Office

A. Settle Accounts

A first step in closing any law office is settling accounts. When you are closing another lawyer's office, if there is a secretary or paralegal, start there and use this list as a starting point.

- Determine whether the records are computerized.
- Are there any outstanding fees to be collected?
- Have they been billed?
- Did the lawyer pay the bills or did the staff?
- Were any of them paid directly through the bank?
- Were business and personal bills paid from the same or different accounts?
- Did the lawyer pay bills from the office or from home?
- Did the lawyer have more than one office?
- Check unopened mail.

Look for an "unpaid bills" file. Failing to locate this, review the past year's checkbook to ascertain any recurring accounts, and review tax returns for the past several years. The checklist at Appendix 9-2 lists usual law office expenses.

If the lawyer is deceased, the Personal Representative of the Estate should note which creditors should be notified and whether any outstanding bills should be paid or negotiated, or if you should wait for a claim against the estate (note: check for obligation of P.A. or LLC).

B. Close Bank Accounts

If you are closing the office of another lawyer and there is a surviving partner or partners, that is discussed elsewhere in this book. If the practice was a solo, first determine whether it was a sole proprietorship, P.A., LLP, or other entity.

If you are lucky, bank records will be computerized and not too difficult to locate. If the records are not computerized, there should be checkbooks and bank statements available. The lawyer may have used a pegboard system to record time, cash receipts, disbursements, and escrow accounting. Or it may have been done totally manually, as in the office of my late friend.

ABA Model Rule 1.15 mandates a trust account for all funds received from any source for the intended benefit of clients or third persons.[6] A copy of Rule 1.15 may be found at Appendix 9-3. This account should be used for all funds belonging to clients regardless of the source. All escrow accounts for active files should follow the file. If the lawyer is a fiduciary for one or more estates, there should be a separate escrow account for each.

If any estate accounts remain open, the accounts should be transferred with the files. If an estate is closed, any funds remaining in the account should be disbursed as indicated, either to the client or, if fees, to the lawyer's personal account. There may be more than one personal account for a variety of reasons. If there is a balance in any personal account, it should eventually be returned to the lawyer whose office is being closed or to his or her estate, once you have finally determined that there are no further actual or contingent liabilities.

Any and all safe deposit boxes or in-office safes should be checked. If safe deposit keys are available, the lawyer for the estate should be able to enter the box with the key and a copy of Letters of Administration. If the key is unavailable, it may be necessary to have a locksmith enter the box for a fee.

C. Safekeeping Property

When a lawyer is given property of any kind by any person, the lawyer has a fiduciary obligation to keep that property safe, whether it is money, documents, or tangible personal property. Increasingly, storage is becoming burdensome and costly. A good suggestion is to avoid accepting original documents or personal property if possible. If this is not possible, acceptance of original documents or personal property should be documented by a receipt detailing the items, and they should be kept for as brief a time as possible.

Years ago, lawyers and law firms were inclined to retain original wills for clients. It is possible, if the client does not want to store the original, to file it with the Register of Wills. The fee is nominal.

Original documents used as exhibits at trial should be returned to the client as soon as possible after they are no longer necessary. When these documents are returned, a receipt should be provided and inserted in the file.

---

[6] American Bar Association, *Model Rules of Professional Conduct, Client Lawyer Relationship: Rule 1.15 Safekeeping Property,* available at http://www.abanet.org./cpr/mrpc/rule_1_15 .html.

ABA Model Rule 1.15(c) provides "[a] lawyer shall deposit into a client trust account legal fees and expenses that have been paid in advance to be withdrawn by the lawyer only as fees are earned or expenses incurred."[7] It is interesting to note that Maryland Rule 1.15 qualifies this language, adding "unless the client gives informed consent, confirmed in writing, to a different arrangement --------."[8] Other states may differ in other ways from the Model Rule. A copy of the Model Rule and the Maryland Rule may be found in the Appendices to this chapter.

D. Review All Leases, Equipment Leases, and Service Contracts

Another step in closing a law office is reviewing all leases and contracts. Does/did the lawyer own the building? If the lawyer owned the building, were there leases? Leases should be reviewed for terms, particularly expiration dates. Tenants must be advised about the obligations. Delinquent rents must be collected. If the building is to be sold, it may be necessary to negotiate for early termination of the lease or the property may have to be sold subject to the lease.

If the lawyer did not own the building, was he or she the primary lessee? What are the remaining obligations on the lease? Were there any subleases? Will one or more tenants take over the lease?

Are there any equipment leases or service contracts? These leases or contracts need to be reviewed for terms and conditions for termination or change. See Appendix 9-5 at the end of this chapter for a checklist of equipment.

E. Contact All Vendors

All vendors must be contacted to ascertain any outstanding obligations for ongoing goods or services. Vendors could include LexisNexis, Westlaw, and suppliers. These vendors should be advised as to whether the relationship will continue with another lawyer who is taking over at the same address or at a different address, or if it will be discontinued altogether.

F. Notify Licensing Authority

The state licensing authority must be notified of the death or disability of a lawyer or any other situation causing the law office to be closed.

In addition, all bar associations and other professional associations should be notified so that the appropriate action can be taken or recognition made. Most bar associations have memorial committees to recognize deceased members. In addition, all non-professional organizations should be contacted, especially if the lawyer was an officer or committee chairperson.

---

[7] Id.
[8] LexisNexis, *Michie's Annotated Code of Maryland: Maryland Rules 1* (MD Rule).

If any other license is in effect—i.e., real estate, CPA—these entities should also be on the list.

G. Identify Insurance Policies

Finally, whether for your own or another lawyer's office, certain insurance issues must be addressed. Consider the various insurance policies that the departing lawyer either chose or was required to maintain. These include, but are not limited to:

- Workers' compensation;
- Personal property and liability insurance (including "tail" insurance);
- Automobile insurance;
- Health and accident insurance;
- Life insurance;
- Disability insurance;
- Professional liability insurance; and
- State and federal unemployment insurance.

Most states, if not all, require workers' compensation and unemployment insurance for all employees. These are not optional. Upon closing a law office, these entities should be notified and final arrangements made to terminate coverage.

If the business owns any vehicles, the auto insurance company should be notified and advised as to the arrangements for the vehicle.

Health and accident insurance for all employees requires contact with the company or companies and then with the employee or employees to ensure ongoing coverage when possible. It is also advisable to ascertain whether there are any pending claims.

H. Determine Tail Insurance

If you are closing the office of a colleague, determine whether there is professional liability insurance, and whether there is a tail. In our litigious climate, a lawyer planning to retire or close a law practice for any reason must analyze professional liability insurance with great care. In its early days, this insurance was written based on what was termed an "occurrence policy" and provided coverage only for acts, errors, or omissions that occurred during the period that the policy was in effect. As claims against lawyers proliferated, and limitations statutes provided more exceptions, occurrence policies have been replaced with "claims made" policies. These provide coverage for claims made and reported during the policy period, regardless of when the alleged infraction may have occurred. (An excellent discussion of tail insurance previously appearing in the *Maryland Bar Journal* may be found at Appendix 9-6 at the end of this chapter.)

With the newer "claims made" policy, a lawyer is protected by insurance for acts that surfaced after the policy was in effect but that occurred prior thereto. Thus, when a lawyer fully retires, it is wise and prudent to continue insurance coverage for at least a period of time. This extended period of coverage is called a "tail" and can be purchased with several options.

V. Conclusion

Closing a law office involves more than just business responsibilities. The ethical and emotional issues involved in closing a law practice are addressed in other sections of this book and include contacting clients and destroying files. In Aristotle's perfect world, all lawyers would have completed a form similar to the one that is provided as Appendix 9-7. This form[9] provides the individual responsible for closing the law office with all the information needed to close a law office with maximum efficiency and minimum expense, loss of time, and patience.

"All's Well That Ends Well."[10]
—*William Shakespeare*

Further Reading

The American Bar Association's Law Practice Management Section publishes a number of helpful texts. These can be found on their website at http://www.abanet.org/lpm/home.shtml, and some are listed below.

Gibson, K. William. *Flying Solo: A Survival Guide for the Solo and Small Firm Lawyer,* 4e. Chicago, IL: American Bar Association Law Practice Management Section, 2005.

Munneke, Gary A. and Anthony E. Davis. *The Essential Formbook Series: Comprehensive Management Tools for Lawyers*, Volumes I, II, III, and IV. Chicago, IL: American Bar Association Law Practice Management Section, 2004.

Poll, Edward. *The Tool Kit for Buying and Selling a Law Practice*. Venice, CA: LawBiz Management Co., 1999.

Solo & Small Firm Practice Retreat, Pennsylvania Bar Institute, and Pennsylvania Bar Association, Solo and Small Firm Practice Section. *Eighth Annual Solo & Small Firm Practice Retreat*, 8e. Mechanicsburg, Pennsylvania: Pennsylvania Bar Institute, 2001.

Steele, Thomas M. *Materials and Cases on Law Practice Management: A Learning Tool for Law Students*. Newark, NJ: LexisNexis, 2004.

---

[9] Reprinted with permission of the State Bar of Arizona Sole Practitioner Section.
[10] JOHN BARTLETT AND JUSTIN KAPLAN, BARTLETT'S FAMILIAR QUOTATIONS (USA: Little Brown and Company, 1992), at 141.

Appendices

Appendix 9-1. Client-Lawyer Relationship: Rule 1.17 *Sale of Law Practice*

Appendix 9-2. Law Office Expense Checklist

Appendix 9-3. Client-Lawyer Relationship: Rule 1.15 *Safekeeping Property*

Appendix 9-4. The Maryland Lawyers' Rules of Professional Conduct: Rule 1.15 *Safekeeping Property*

Appendix 9-5. Equipment Lease or Service Contract List

Appendix 9-6. "Why Attorneys Need Tail Insurance"

Appendix 9-7. Law Office List of Contacts Inventory

Appendix 9-1

Client-Lawyer Relationship: Rule 1.17 *Sale of Law Practice*

A lawyer or a law firm may sell or purchase a law practice, or an area of law practice, including good will, if the following conditions are satisfied:

(a) The seller ceases to engage in the private practice of law, or in the area of practice that has been sold, [in the geographic area] [in the jurisdiction] (a jurisdiction may elect either version) in which the practice has been conducted;

(b) The entire practice, or the entire area of practice, is sold to one or more lawyers or law firms;

(c) The seller gives written notice to each of the seller's clients regarding:

    (1) the proposed sale;

    (2) the client's right to retain other counsel or to take possession of the file; and

    (3) the fact that the client's consent to the transfer of the client's files will be presumed if the client does not take any action or does not otherwise object within ninety (90) days of receipt of the notice.

If a client cannot be given notice, the representation of that client may be transferred to the purchaser only upon entry of an order so authorizing by a court having jurisdiction. The seller may disclose to the court in camera information relating to the representation only to the extent necessary to obtain an order authorizing the transfer of a file.

(d) The fees charged clients shall not be increased by reason of the sale.

Comment

[1] The practice of law is a profession, not merely a business. Clients are not commodities that can be purchased and sold at will. Pursuant to this Rule, when a lawyer or an entire firm ceases to practice, or ceases to practice in an area of law, and other lawyers or firms take over the representation, the selling lawyer or firm may obtain compensation for the reasonable value of the practice as may withdrawing partners of law firms. See Rules 5.4 and 5.6.

Termination of Practice by the Seller

[2] The requirement that all of the private practice, or all of an area of practice, be sold is satisfied if the seller in good faith makes the entire practice, or the area of practice, available for sale to the purchasers. The fact that a number of the seller's clients decide not to be represented by the purchasers but take their matters elsewhere, therefore, does not result in a violation. Return to private practice as a result of an unanticipated change in circumstances does not necessarily result in a violation. For example, a lawyer who has sold the practice to accept an appointment to judicial office does not violate the requirement that the sale be attendant to cessation of practice if the lawyer later resumes private practice upon being defeated in a contested or a retention election for the office or resigns from a judiciary position.

[3] The requirement that the seller cease to engage in the private practice of law does not prohibit employment as a lawyer on the staff of a public agency or a legal services entity that provides legal services to the poor, or as in-house counsel to a business.

[4] The Rule permits a sale of an entire practice attendant upon retirement from the private practice of law within the jurisdiction. Its provisions, therefore, accommodate the lawyer who sells the practice on the occasion of moving to another state. Some states are so large that a move from one locale therein to another is tantamount to leaving the jurisdiction in which the lawyer has engaged in the practice of law. To also accommodate lawyers so situated, states may permit the sale of the practice when the lawyer leaves the geographical area rather than the jurisdiction. The alternative desired should be indicated by selecting one of the two provided for in Rule 1.17(a).

[5] This Rule also permits a lawyer or law firm to sell an area of practice. If an area of practice is sold and the lawyer remains in the active practice of law, the lawyer must cease accepting any matters in the area of practice that has been sold, either as counsel or co-counsel or by assuming joint responsibility for a matter in connection with the division of a fee with another lawyer as would otherwise be permitted by Rule 1.5(e). For example, a lawyer with a substantial number of estate planning matters and a substantial number of probate administration cases may sell the estate planning portion of the practice but remain in the practice of law by concentrating on probate administration; however, that practitioner may not thereafter accept any estate planning matters. Although a lawyer who leaves a jurisdiction or geographical area typically would sell the entire practice, this Rule permits the lawyer to limit the sale to one or more areas of the practice, thereby preserving the lawyer's right to continue practice in the areas of the practice that were not sold.

Sale of Entire Practice or Entire Area of Practice

[6] The Rule requires that the seller's entire practice, or an entire area of practice, be sold. The prohibition against sale of less than an entire practice area protects those clients whose matters are less lucrative and who might find it difficult to secure other counsel if a sale could be limited to substantial fee-generating matters. The purchasers are required to undertake all client matters in the practice or practice area, subject to

client consent. This requirement is satisfied, however, even if a purchaser is unable to undertake a particular client matter because of a conflict of interest.

Client Confidences, Consent, and Notice

[7] Negotiations between seller and prospective purchaser prior to disclosure of information relating to a specific representation of an identifiable client no more violate the confidentiality provisions of Model Rule 1.6 than do preliminary discussions concerning the possible association of another lawyer or mergers between firms, with respect to which client consent is not required. Providing the purchaser access to client-specific information relating to the representation and to the file, however, requires client consent. The Rule provides that before such information can be disclosed by the seller to the purchaser the client must be given actual written notice of the contemplated sale, including the identity of the purchaser, and must be told that the decision to consent or make other arrangements must be made within 90 days. If nothing is heard from the client within that time, consent to the sale is presumed.

[8] A lawyer or law firm ceasing to practice cannot be required to remain in practice because some clients cannot be given actual notice of the proposed purchase. Since these clients cannot themselves consent to the purchase or direct any other disposition of their files, the Rule requires an order from a court having jurisdiction authorizing their transfer or other disposition. The Court can be expected to determine whether reasonable efforts to locate the client have been exhausted, and whether the absent client's legitimate interests will be served by authorizing the transfer of the file so that the purchaser may continue the representation. Preservation of client confidences requires that the petition for a court order be considered in camera. (A procedure by which such an order can be obtained needs to be established in jurisdictions in which it presently does not exist).

[9] All elements of client autonomy, including the client's absolute right to discharge a lawyer and transfer the representation to another, survive the sale of the practice or area of practice.

Fee Arrangements Between Client and Purchaser

[10] The sale may not be financed by increases in fees charged the clients of the practice. Existing arrangements between the seller and the client as to fees and the scope of the work must be honored by the purchaser.

Other Applicable Ethical Standards

[11] Lawyers participating in the sale of a law practice or a practice area are subject to the ethical standards applicable to involving another lawyer in the representation of a client. These include, for example, the seller's obligation to exercise competence in identifying a purchaser qualified to assume the practice and the purchaser's obligation to undertake the representation competently (see Rule 1.1); the obligation to avoid disqualifying conflicts, and to secure the client's informed consent for those

conflicts that can be agreed to (see Rule 1.7 regarding conflicts and Rule 1.0(e) for the definition of informed consent); and the obligation to protect information relating to the representation (see Rules 1.6 and 1.9).

[12] If approval of the substitution of the purchasing lawyer for the selling lawyer is required by the rules of any tribunal in which a matter is pending, such approval must be obtained before the matter can be included in the sale (see Rule 1.16).

Applicability of the Rule

[13] This Rule applies to the sale of a law practice of a deceased, disabled or disappeared lawyer. Thus, the seller may be represented by a non-lawyer representative not subject to these Rules. Since, however, no lawyer may participate in a sale of a law practice which does not conform to the requirements of this Rule, the representatives of the seller as well as the purchasing lawyer can be expected to see to it that they are met.

[14] Admission to or retirement from a law partnership or professional association, retirement plans and similar arrangements, and a sale of tangible assets of a law practice, do not constitute a sale or purchase governed by this Rule.

[15] This Rule does not apply to the transfers of legal representation between lawyers when such transfers are unrelated to the sale of a practice or an area of practice.

Appendix 9-2

Law Office Expense Checklist

- ❏ Federal taxes—Tax Return for previous or current year
- ❏ Other taxes
    - ❏ Federal withholding
    - ❏ State withholding
    - ❏ FUTA
    - ❏ State unemployment
    - ❏ Municipal or county
    - ❏ Personal property
- ❏ Insurance
    - ❏ Workers' compensation
    - ❏ Errors and omissions (professional liability)
    - ❏ Personal property and liability
    - ❏ Automobile
    - ❏ Health and accident
- ❏ Utilities
    - ❏ Stationary phone
    - ❏ Cell phone
    - ❏ Computer access
    - ❏ Gas & electricity
- ❏ Advertising
    - ❏ Yellow pages
    - ❏ Other directories
    - ❏ Media: radio & TV
- ❏ Car & truck expenses
- ❏ Retirement contributions
- ❏ Repairs and maintenance
- ❏ Dues and subscriptions
- ❏ Equipment leases
- ❏ Credit cards
- ❏ Storage

Appendix 9-3

Client-Lawyer Relationship: Rule 1.15 *Safekeeping Property*

(a) A lawyer shall hold property of clients or third persons that is in a lawyer's possession in connection with a representation separate from the lawyer's own property. Funds shall be kept in a separate account maintained in the state where the lawyer's office is situated, or elsewhere with the consent of the client or third person. Other property shall be identified as such and appropriately safeguarded. Complete records of such account funds and other property shall be kept by the lawyer and shall be preserved for a period of [five years] after termination of the representation.

(b) A lawyer may deposit the lawyer's own funds in a client trust account for the sole purpose of paying bank service charges on that account, but only in an amount necessary for that purpose.

(c) A lawyer shall deposit into a client trust account legal fees and expenses that have been paid in advance, to be withdrawn by the lawyer only as fees are earned or expenses incurred.

(d) Upon receiving funds or other property in which a client or third person has an interest, a lawyer shall promptly notify the client or third person. Except as stated in this rule or otherwise permitted by law or by agreement with the client, a lawyer shall promptly deliver to the client or third person any funds or other property that the client or third person is entitled to receive and, upon request by the client or third person, shall promptly render a full accounting regarding such property.

(e) When in the course of representation a lawyer is in possession of property in which two or more persons (one of whom may be the lawyer) claim interests, the property shall be kept separate by the lawyer until the dispute is resolved. The lawyer shall promptly distribute all portions of the property as to which the interests are not in dispute.

Appendix 9-4

The Maryland Lawyers' Rules of Professional Conduct: Rule 1.15 *Safekeeping Property*

<Effective January 1, 2008.>

(a) A lawyer shall hold property of clients or third persons that is in a lawyer's possession in connection with a representation separate from the lawyer's own property. Funds shall be kept in a separate account maintained pursuant to Title 16, Chapter 600 of the Maryland Rules, and records shall be created and maintained in accordance with the Rules in that Chapter. Other property shall be identified specifically as such and appropriately safeguarded. Complete records of the account funds and other property shall be kept by the lawyer and shall be preserved for a period of at least five years after the date the record was created.

(b) A lawyer may deposit the lawyer's own funds in a client trust account only as permitted by Rule 16-607 b.

(c) Unless the client gives informed consent, confirmed in writing, to a different arrangement, a lawyer shall deposit legal fees and expenses that have been paid in advance into a client trust account and may withdrawn those funds for the lawyer's own benefit only as fees are earned or expenses incurred.

(d) Upon receiving funds or other property in which a client or third person has an interest, a lawyer shall promptly notify the client or third person. Except as stated in this rule or otherwise permitted by law or by agreement with the client, a lawyer shall deliver promptly to the client or third person any funds or other property that the client or third person is entitled to receive and, upon request by the client or third person, shall render promptly a full accounting regarding such property.

(e) When a lawyer in the course of representing a client is in possession of property in which two or more persons (one of whom may be the lawyer) claim interests, the property shall be kept separate by the lawyer until the dispute is resolved. The lawyer shall distribute promptly all portions of the property as to which the interests are not in dispute.

Appendix 9-5

Equipment Lease or Service Contract List

The following is a partial list of equipment for which there may be leases or service contracts:

- ❑ Computerized research
- ❑ Computer maintenance
- ❑ Computer support services
- ❑ Copier leases
- ❑ Copier service contracts
- ❑ Fax charges
- ❑ Telephones
- ❑ Telephone service contracts
- ❑ Internet services

Appendix 9-6

"Why Attorneys Need Tail Insurance"*

One of the least understood and appreciated provisions in the typical lawyer professional liability insurance policy is the option for an extended claims reporting period, commonly referred to as the "tail" option or "tail" coverage. It is amazing how many lawyers have never read their errors and omissions policy and are completely unaware of the coverage afforded or the risks entailed in failing to understand the intricacies of their policy. The dangers of such ignorance are especially prevalent when attorneys switch insurance companies, move from one law firm to another, or retire from the active practice of law. Attorneys who would never dream of ignoring such a critical document when representing their clients, blithely assume that having purchased a policy they are "covered." Indeed, after being sued for malpractice, a significant number of attorneys claim they never received a copy of the policy, or in the alternative, ruefully admit that while they may have received the policy they have no idea what they did with this vital document. Many retiring attorneys assume that since they are no longer practicing, there is no need for continuing insurance coverage. The penalty for this cavalier attitude is often devastating. Having practiced law for decades during which they paid considerable premiums, it is the foolhardy attorney who neglects "tail" coverage during his retirement.

Many retiring attorneys' misconceptions regarding the need for continuing coverage following retirement are based upon their confusion over how insurance policies have changed in the past two decades. In its infancy, lawyers' errors and omissions policies were written on an "occurrence" as opposed to "claims made" basis. Under this system, an attorney received coverage for acts, errors or omissions which occurred during the period the policy was in effect. Thus, it was irrelevant when the claim or suit was advanced against the lawyer, so long as the alleged act, error or omission occurred during the period in which the policy was in force and effect. With the advent of the discovery rule for statute of limitations purposes, it became not only possible, but inevitable, that an error might lie fallow for many years or even decades before being "discovered" and advanced against the attorney. This created a nearly impossible situation for insurance companies because they were unable to calculate to any reasonable degree the proper premiums for the risk. Especially in the fields of estates and trusts, real estate, business transactions, and the representation

---

*This article by Edward J. Hutchins, Jr., a partner in Eccelston and Wolf, originally appeared in the *Maryland Bar Journal,* July/August 1998. This article is reproduced with the permission of the *Maryland Bar Journal,* published by the Maryland State Bar Association.

of minors, claims might lie dormant and then be asserted ten, fifteen, or even twenty years after the occurrence. As a result, every carrier writing professional errors and omissions policies abandoned the "occurrence" form and adopted some variation of the "claims made" form. This basic change necessarily altered how attorneys retiring from practice should evaluate their coverage needs.

A claims made policy provides coverage for claims made during the policy period regardless of whether the act, error or omission giving rise to the claim occurred during or prior to the policy period. Thus, the date of the occurrence became largely irrelevant, and insurance companies were able to fairly accurately predict the risk being accepted and thus charge an appropriate premium. Moreover, once the policy year expired, the insurance company, knowing that no future claims changeable to that policy would be forthcoming, could quickly analyze claims history and adjust premiums. The pure claims made policy, however, posed several problems. Since a claim is deemed "made" when a demand for damages is advanced against the Insured, it often results that the claim is not reported to the insurance company until after the policy period expires. In states such as Maryland, insurance companies cannot deny coverage in the absence of actual prejudice when an Insured fails to promptly report a claim. Thus, insurance companies were generally unable to rely upon late notice conditions to deny coverage. The Annotated Code of Maryland, Insurance Article §19-110 provides in pertinent part that:

> An insurer may disclaim coverage on a liability insurance policy on the ground that the insured or a person claiming the benefits of the policy through the insured has breached the policy by failing to cooperate with the insurer or by not giving the insurer required notice only if the insurer establishes by a preponderance of the evidence that the lack of cooperation or notice has resulted in actual prejudice to the insurer.

Most insurance companies, therefore, altered the pure claims made form to require that the claim not only be made, but also, that the claim be *reported* to the insurance company within the policy period in order to trigger coverage. Thus, most policies in current use should more properly be called claims made and reported policies. It should be noted that the Maryland courts have been reluctant to deny coverage where the claim was made against the insured during the policy period, but not reported until after the policy expired. In *St. Paul Fire & Marine Ins. v. House*, 315 Md. 328 (1989), the Court of Appeals held that even though the policy provided that the insured was required to give notice within the policy period, coverage would be afforded for a late notice claim since the policy language was ambiguous. Judge Rodowsky, in writing for a split court in which three judges dissented, relied extensively on Maryland's prejudice statute and the specific language of the St. Paul policy. It should be understood, however that where a carrier in unambiguous language, writes the policy so that coverage is not afforded if the claim is not reported within the policy period, the provision will almost certainly be upheld by the courts.

The switch from an occurrence to a claims made and reported form created a huge problem for lawyers retiring from the practice of law. With occurrence policies, there was, of course, no need to continue purchasing insurance following retirement because the retired attorney would not be committing "new" acts, errors or omissions. The retiree's old occurrence policies would therefore protect him from any claims made in the future, since they would, by definition, be based upon acts, errors or omissions which occurred during one of the earlier policy periods. However, under a claims made and reported policy, once the last policy period expired any claims made, even though based upon acts, errors or omissions which occurred while the policy was in effect, would not be covered. Hence, the need for an extended reporting period to protect the attorneys for claims made after his last policy expired, for acts, errors or omissions which occurred during earlier policy periods.

These "tails" do not provide coverage for new acts, errors or omissions, but rather, simply allow the Insured to *report* claims based on prior acts, errors or omissions following the normal expiration of the policy term. The precise terms of the extended claims reporting options differ from policy to policy. Three provisions from lawyer's errors and omissions policies are set forth below by way of example and to illustrate the widely divergent options currently available in the market. As a quick review will indicate, the coverage available varies from carrier to carrier, and the difference is often in the details.

Example 1:

If [Insurance Company] shall cancel this policy or terminate it by refusing to issue a new policy, for reasons other than the insured's non-payment of premium and/or deductible amount or other non-compliance with the terms and conditions of this policy, or if the insured shall cancel this policy, or terminates it by choosing not to renew this insurance and has paid all earned premiums in full and any deductible owed and is in compliance with the terms and conditions of the policy, then the insured upon payment of additional premiums at those rates described in Item 8 of the Declarations, shall have the option to extend the claims reporting period to an unlimited period of time, but only by reason of any act, error or omission in professional services rendered before such applicable policy termination or cancellation date and otherwise covered under this policy.

The insured's right to purchase the OPTIONAL EXTENSION PERIOD must be exercised by NOTICE in writing and payment of premium for the OPTIONAL EXTENSION PERIOD not later than thirty (30) days after the cancellation or termination date of this policy. If such notice and premium payment is not given to [Insurance Company], the insured shall not at a later date be able to exercise such right.

At the commencement of any OPTIONAL EXTENSION PERIOD, the entire premium therefore shall be deemed earned, and in the event the insured terminates the OPTIONAL EXTENSION PERIOD before its term for any reason, [Insurance Company] shall not be liable to return to the insured any portion of the premium paid for the OPTIONAL EXTENSION PERIOD.

Example 2:

In the event of cancellation or non-renewal of this policy by either the Named Insured or the Company, any insured as defined in (a), (b) or (c) of the

Persons Insured Section of this policy shall have the right, upon payment of an appropriate additional premium within 30 days of such termination, to have issued an endorsement providing an extended reporting period for all claims first made against the insured and reported to the Company after the termination of the policy period arising out of any act, error or omission occurring prior to the termination of the policy period and otherwise covered by this policy.

The appropriate additional premium and corresponding extended reporting shall be:

a. for 225 percent of the Named Insured's last annual premium an unlimited extended reporting period;
b. for 150 percent of the Named Insured's last annual premium a 6 year extended reporting period;
c. for 100 percent of the Named Insured's last annual premium a 3 year extended reporting period.

The right to the extended reporting period under this Section shall not be available to any insured where cancellation or non-renewal by the Company is due to non-payment of premium or failure of an insured to reimburse the Company such amounts paid in excess of the applicable limit of liability or within the amount of the applicable deductible.

Example 3:

As used herein, "extended reporting period" means the period of time after the end of the policy period for reporting claims by reason of an act or omission that occurred prior to the end of the policy period and is otherwise covered by this Policy.

A. *Automatic Extended Reporting Period*

If this Policy is canceled or non-renewed by either the Company or by the Named Insured, the Company will provide to the Named Insured an automatic, non-cancelable extended reporting period starting at the termination of the policy period if the Named Insured has not obtained another policy of lawyers professional liability insurance within sixty (60) days of the termination of this Policy. This automatic extended reporting period will terminate after sixty (60) days.

B. *Optional Extended Reporting Period*

1. If this Policy is canceled or non-renewed by either the Company or by the Named Insured, then the Named Insured shall have the right to purchase an optional extended reporting period. Such right must be exercised by the Named Insured within sixty (60) days of the termination of the policy period by providing:
   a. written notice to the Company; and
   b. with the written notice, the amount of additional premium described below.
2. The additional premium for the optional extended reporting period shall be based upon the rates for such coverage in effect on the date

this Policy was issued or last renewed and shall be for one (1) year at 100 percent of such premium; three (3) years at 175 percent of such premium; six (6) years at 225 percent of such premium; or, for an unlimited period at 250 percent of such premium.

C. *Death or Disability Extended Reporting Period*
1. If an Insured dies or becomes totally and permanently disabled during the policy period, then upon the latter of the expiration of: the policy period; any renewal or successive renewal of this Policy; or any automatic or optional extended reporting period, such Insured shall be provided with a death or disability extended reporting period as provided below.
    a. In the event of death, such Insured's estate, heirs, executors or administrators must, within sixty (60) days of the expiration of the policy period, provide the Company with written proof of the date of death. This extended reporting period is provided to the estate, heirs, executors and administrators of such Insured until the executor or administrator of the estate of such Insured is discharged.
    b. If an Insured become totally and permanently disabled, such Insured or Insured's legal guardian must, within sixty (60) days of the expiration of the policy period, provide the Company with written proof that such Insured is totally and permanently disabled, including the date the disability commenced, certified by the Insured's physician. The Company retains the right to contest the certification made by the Insured's physician, and it is a condition precedent to this coverage that the Insured agree to submit to medical examinations by any physician designated by the Company. This extended reporting period is provided until such Insured shall no longer be totally or permanently disabled or until the death of such Insured in which case subparagraph a. hereof shall apply.
2. No additional premium will be charged for any death or disability extended reporting period.

D. *Non-Practicing Extended Reporting Period*
1. If an insured retires or otherwise voluntarily ceases, permanently and totally, the private practice of law during the policy period and has been continuously insured by the Company for at least three consecutive years, then such Insured shall be provided with an extended reporting period commencing upon the latter of the expiration of: the policy period; any renewal or successive renewal of this Policy; or any automatic or optional extended reporting period.
2. The extended reporting period is provided until the death of such Insured in which case subparagraph C.1. hereof shall apply or, until such Insured shall resume the practice of law.
3. No additional premium will be charged for any non-practicing extended reporting period.

E. *Extended Reporting Periods Limits of Liability*
1. Automatic and optional extended reporting periods limits of liability:

a. Where the Company has the right to non-renew or cancel this Policy and it exercises that right, then the Company's liability for all claims reported during the automatic and optional extended reporting periods shall be part of and not in addition to the limits of liability for the policy period as set forth in the Declarations and Section II, Limits of Liability of this Policy.
  b. If this Policy is canceled by the Named Insured or if the Company offers to renew this Policy, and the Named Insured refuses such renewal offer, then the Company's liability for all claims reported during the automatic and optional extended reporting periods shall be reinstated to the limits of liability applicable to this Policy as set forth in Section II.A. and B. hereof.
 2. Separate death or disability and non-practicing extended reporting period limits of liability:

 The limit of liability of the Company for all claims first made against the Insured and reported to the Company during any death or disability extended reporting period or non-practicing extended reporting period shall not exceed the amount stated in the Declarations as the "Aggregate Death or Disability and Non-Practicing extended reporting period limit of liability," and shall include damages and claim expenses.

F. *Elimination of Right To Any Extended Reporting Period*
   There is no right to any extended reporting period:
   1. If the company shall cancel or refuse to renew this Policy due to:
      a. non-payment of premiums; or
      b. non-compliance by an Insured with any of the terms and conditions of this Policy; or
      c. any misrepresentation or omission in the application for this Policy; or,
   2. If at the time this right could be exercised by an Insured, such Insured's right to practice law has been revoked, suspended or surrendered at the request of any regulatory authority for reasons other than that the Insured is totally and permanently disabled.
G. *Extended Reporting Period Not A New Policy*
   It is understood and agreed that the extended reporting period shall not be construed to be a new policy and any claim submitted during such period shall otherwise be governed by this Policy.

It should be emphasized that these provisions are only three examples from the many policies currently available. The point is that the tail option provisions differ widely and it is important to be cognizant of the applicable provisions that may best suit an individual's needs.

For the solo practitioner who decides to retire, the choice seems fairly simple and straightforward. Simply put, the solo practitioner contemplating retirement should seek a policy which provides free tail coverage upon retirement or at least permits the purchase of such coverage. Either unlimited or a long-term tail provision should be sought. While the cost may seem high at a time when your income may be limited, the risks entailed are too great to forego the protection afforded. For those individuals retiring from a stable law firm, which is likely to indefinitely carry on the business, the decision is slightly more complex. Most errors and omissions policies contain a provision making a retired partner or employee an "additional insured." For example, the first policy noted above provides that the following are "additional insureds":

1. Any former partner, officer, director, stockholder or employee of the Named Insured Firm or Predecessor Firm named in the Declarations while acting solely in a professional capacity on behalf of such Named Insured Firm or Firms;
2. Any partner, officer, director, stockholder, or employee of the Named Insured Firm or Predecessor Firm named in the Declarations who has retired from the practice of law, but only for those professional services rendered prior to the date of retirement from the Named Insured Firm or Firms.

Most policies contain similar, but certainly not identical, provisions. Thus, so long as the firm stays in business and continues to purchase insurance without break from the same insurance company, the retiring attorney is covered without the need to purchase additional tail coverage. Unfortunately, the firm may dissolve shortly after the attorney's retirement, or may drop its insurance or switch to a new company whose policy will not afford coverage. For example, even if the firm continues in business and maintains insurance coverage after the attorney's retirement, in order to save on premiums, the firm might switch to a new carrier and accept a very restrictive prior acts exclusion or other limiting language. This could leave the retiring attorney in a vulnerable position. Even worse, should the firm dissolve or cease to buy coverage of any type, the retiree could be left wholly uncovered. Thus, in a subsequent lawsuit, even if the former law firm is named as one of the defendants, the retiree will most likely bear the entire brunt of any adverse judgment and the defense costs associated therewith because typically the firm is judgment proof allowing a dissolution.

Thus, a careful review of the specific provisions set forth in your policy is crucial to any determination as to your best course of action. Moreover, discussions with your insurance professional regarding the other possible policy forms available are always wise. Some companies offer a free tail provision under certain circumstances, which can be of great benefit. The third policy quoted above, for instance, offers free tail coverage for an unlimited period to retiring attorneys. With other policies, the tail periods may be available in different lengths of time and at different premiums. Standard lengths are 12, 24, 36 or 60 months, or for an unlimited period of time. With different companies, the rules change depending upon the specific circumstances, and from time to time insurance companies will alter their policies as they either more or less aggressively pursue business. Moreover, sometimes carriers will provide special endorsements, upon request, which expand coverage beyond the written terms of the standard policy form. For example, under the first provision quoted above, there is no guaranteed right to purchase the extended reporting option if you are a member of a firm and you retire. Some companies using these types of provisions may, however, permit you to purchase the tail coverage despite the fact that there is no "right" to do so under the policy. Other policies, such as the third policy quoted above, set forth in detail the rights and options available and may provide such coverage at no cost and for an unlimited period of time if certain conditions are met.

The most important aspect of any determination as to what coverage you need is a clear understanding of the options available. It is imperative that when planning for retirement you obtain and carefully review your insurance policy in order to ascertain the options available. It is also highly recommended that you discuss the various policies available with your insurance professional. If the professional you typically use offers only one product, or will not provide you with information on competing policies, do not be afraid to contact other professionals or carriers directly. At the very minimum, three years prior to contemplated retirement is not too soon to begin thinking and planning how you will protect the fruits of a lifetime of labor.

Appendix 9-7

Law Office List of Contacts Inventory

ATTORNEY NAME: _____ Social Security #: _____
OR State Bar #: _____ Federal Employer ID #: _____ State Tax ID #: _____
Date of Birth: _____

Office Address: _____
_____

Office Phone: _____
Home Address: _____
_____

Home Phone: _____

SPOUSE:
Name: _____
Work Phone: _____
Employer: _____

OFFICE MANAGER:
Name: _____
Address: _____
_____

Phone: _____

COMPUTER PASSWORDS:
(Name of person or location such as safety deposit box)
Name: _____
Address: _____
_____

Phone: _____

SECRETARY:
Name: _____
Address: _____
_____

Phone: _____

BOOKKEEPER:
Name: _____
Address: _____
_____
Phone: _____

LANDLORD:
Name: _____
Address: _____
_____
Phone: _____

PERSONAL REPRESENTATIVE:
Name: _____
Address: _____
_____
Phone: _____

ATTORNEY:
Name: _____
Address: _____
_____
Phone: _____

ACCOUNTANT:
Name: _____
Address: _____
_____
Phone: _____

ATTORNEYS TO HELP WITH PRACTICE CLOSURE:
First Choice: _____
Address: _____
_____
Phone: _____

Second Choice: _____
Address: _____
_____
Phone: _____

Third Choice: _____
Address: _____
_____
Phone: _____

LOCATION OF WILL AND/OR TRUST:
Access Will and/or Trust by contracting: _____
Address: _____
_____

Phone: _____

PROFESSIONAL CORPORATIONS:
Corporate Name: _____
Date Incorporated: _____
Location of Corporate
 Minute Book: _____
Location of Corporate
 Seal: _____
Location of Corporate
 Stock Certif.: _____
Location of Corporate
 Tax Returns: _____
Fiscal Year-End Date: _____
Corporate Attorney: _____
Address: _____
_____

Phone: _____

PROCESS SERVICE COMPANY:
Name: _____
Address: _____
_____

Phone: _____
Contact: _____

OFFICE-SHARER OR "OF COUNSEL":
Name: _____
Address: _____
_____

Phone: _____

Name: _____
Address: _____
_____

Phone: _____

OFFICE PROPERTY/LIABILITY COVERAGE:
Name: _____
Address: _____
_____

Phone: _____

Policy No: _____
Contact Person: _____

OTHER IMPORTANT CONTACTS:
Name: _____
Address: _____
_____
Phone: _____

Name: _____
Address: _____
_____
Phone: _____

Name: _____
Address: _____
_____
Phone: _____

GENERAL LIABILITY COVERAGE:
Insurer: _____
Address: _____
_____
Phone: _____
Policy No: _____
Contact Person: _____

LEGAL MALPRACTICE—PRIMARY COVERAGE:
Insurer: _____
Address: _____
_____
Phone: _____
Policy No: _____
Contact Person: _____

LEGAL MALPRACTICE—EXCESS COVERAGE:
Insurer: _____
Address: _____
_____
Phone: _____
Policy No: _____
Contact Person: _____

VALUABLE PAPERS COVERAGE:
Insurer: _____

Address: _____
_____
Phone: _____
Policy No: _____
Contact Person: _____

OFFICE OVERHEAD/DISABILITY:
Insurer: _____
Address: _____
_____
Phone: _____
Policy No: _____
Contact Person: _____

HEALTH INSURANCE:
Insurer: _____
Address: _____
_____
Phone: _____
Policy No: _____
Contact Person: _____

DISABILITY INSURANCE:
Insurer: _____
Address: _____
_____
Phone: _____
Policy No: _____
Contact Person: _____

LIFE INSURANCE:
Insurer: _____
Address: _____
_____
Phone: _____
Policy No: _____
Contact Person: _____

Insurer: _____
Address: _____
_____
Phone: _____
Policy No: _____
Contact Person: _____

WORKERS' COMPENSATION:
Insurer: _____
Address: _____
_____

Phone: _____
Policy No: _____
Contact Person: _____

STORAGE LOCKER LOCATION:
Storage Company: _____
Locker No: _____
Address: _____
_____

Phone: _____
Obtain Key From: _____
Address: _____
_____

Phone: _____
Items Stored: _____

Storage Company: _____
Locker No: _____
Address: _____
_____

Phone: _____
Obtain Key From: _____
Address: _____
_____

Phone: _____
Items Stored: _____

Storage Company: _____
Locker No: _____
Address: _____
_____

Phone: _____
Obtain Key From: _____
Address: _____
_____

Phone: _____
Items Stored: _____

SAFE DEPOSIT BOXES
Institution: _____
Box No: _____
Address: _____
_____

Phone: _____
Obtain Key From: _____
Address: _____
_____
Phone: _____
Items Stored: _____

Other Signatory: _____
Address: _____
_____
Phone: _____

Institution: _____
Box No: _____
Address: _____
_____
Phone: _____
Obtain Key From: _____
Address: _____
_____
Phone: _____
Items Stored: _____

Other Signatory: _____
Address: _____
_____
Phone: _____

Institution: _____
Box No: _____
Address: _____
_____
Phone: _____
Obtain Key From: _____
Address: _____
_____
Phone: _____
Items Stored: _____

Other Signatory: _____
Address: _____
_____
Phone: _____

<u>LEASES:</u>
Items Leased: _____

Lessor: _____
Address: _____
_____

Phone: _____
Expiration Date: _____

Items Leased: _____
Lessor: _____
Address: _____
_____

Phone: _____
Expiration Date: _____

Items Leased: _____
Lessor: _____
Address: _____
_____

Phone: _____
Expiration Date: _____

Items Leased: _____
Lessor: _____
Address: _____
_____

Phone: _____
Expiration Date: _____

LAWYER'S TRUST ACCOUNT:
IOLTA: _____
Institution: _____
Address: _____
_____

Phone: _____
Account Number: _____
Other Signatory: _____
Address: _____
_____

Phone: _____

INDIVIDUAL TRUST ACCOUNT:
Name of Client: _____
Institution: _____
Address: _____
_____

Phone: _____

Account Number: _____
Other Signatory: _____
Address: _____
_____

Phone: _____

GENERAL OPERATING ACCOUNT:
Institution: _____
Address: _____
_____

Phone: _____
Account Number: _____
Other Signatory: _____
Address: _____
_____

Phone: _____

Institution: _____
Address: _____
_____

Phone: _____
Account Number: _____
Other Signatory: _____
Address: _____
_____

Phone: _____

Institution: _____
Address: _____
_____

Phone: _____
Account Number: _____
Other Signatory: _____
Address: _____
_____

Phone: _____

BUSINESS CREDIT CARDS:
Institution: _____
Address: _____
_____

Phone: _____
Account Number: _____
Other Signatory: _____
Address: _____
_____

Phone: _____

Institution: _____
Address: _____
_____

Phone: _____
Account Number: _____
Other Signatory: _____
Address: _____
_____

Phone: _____

MAINTENANCE CONTRACTS:
Item Covered: _____
Vendor Name: _____
Address: _____
_____

Phone: _____
Expiration Date: _____

Item Covered: _____
Vendor Name: _____
Address: _____
_____

Phone: _____
Expiration Date: _____

Item Covered: _____
Vendor Name: _____
Address: _____
_____

Phone: _____
Expiration Date: _____

Item Covered: _____
Vendor Name: _____
Address: _____
_____

Phone: _____
Expiration Date: _____

ALSO ADMITTED TO PRACTICE IN THE FOLLOWING STATES:

State of: _____
Address: _____
_____

Phone: _____
Bar ID #: _____

State of: _____
Address: _____
_____

Phone: _____
Bar ID #: _____

State of: _____
Address: _____
_____

Phone: _____
Bar ID #: _____

Chapter 10

The Ethical Aspects of Winding Down a Law Practice

by Peter Geraghty

I. Introduction: The Scenario

You have developed a small solo practice over the past 30 years, concentrating in real estate, probate, and family law matters. Lately, you have been thinking about scaling back your practice so that you have time to pursue your other interests. For the past 10 years, you have been volunteering your time at a local legal assistance clinic, and you have often thought about working there on a part-time basis. You figure that now is the time to make a change.

Before you move on, you will need to close down all or part of your practice, but there are a number of questions you must deal with first:

- *Can you sell your law practice? If you can, what are the general requirements of the sale of a law practice?*
- *If you decide to simply wind down the practice without selling it, what are your obligations to your clients? What are your obligations with regard to closed or dormant client files?*

This chapter will focus on the ethical issues surrounding the sale of a law practice and also on the steps lawyers should take when they decide to simply wind down their practice without selling it. It will also discuss the plan a lawyer should have in place in the event of his or her death or disability.

When a sole practitioner considers closing down a practice, the key ethical considerations the lawyer must keep in mind are communication with clients, the protection of client confidences, and the appropriate handling of client files.[1]

---

[1] Most of the state bar ethics opinions cited in this chapter are available on their respective state bar websites. To locate them, visit the links that are included in the *Links to Other Legal Ethics and Professional Responsibility Pages* webpage that is a part of the ABA Center for Professional Responsibility (CPR) website located at http://www.abanet.org/cpr/links.html#States. The ABA Model Rules are also available on the CPR website at http://www.abanet.org/cpr/mrpc/mrpc_toc.html.

Key Points

- ABA Model Rule 1.17 *Sale of a Law Practice* provides a basic framework for the ethical issues involved when a lawyer decides to sell his or her law practice. However, significant variations in the state versions of ABA Model Rule 1.17 render it crucial for the practitioner who is contemplating selling a law practice to check the rules of professional conduct that have been adopted in the individual jurisdiction.
- When a lawyer retires or when a law firm dissolves, the lawyers involved may have joint ethical obligations with regard to client files that may continue after the lawyer retires or the firm is dissolved.
- When deciding whether to store or discard closed or dormant client files, lawyers should be aware of the guidelines for the disposition of such files as provided in various ABA, state, and local bar association ethics opinions, rules of professional conduct, and the law of the individual jurisdiction.
- A sole practitioner should have a plan in place that will provide for the protection of his or her clients' interests in the event of his or her death or disability.

II. Sale of a Law Practice

Rule 1.17 *Sale of a Law Practice*[2] was first adopted by the ABA in 1990. It was modeled after a sale of a law practice rule that was adopted in California in 1989. There are currently 41 jurisdictions that have adopted a version of the Rule.[3] Ethics committees from another three jurisdictions have issued ethics opinions approving of the practice even though they have not adopted a version of the Rule. *See* Connecticut Bar Association Ethics Opinion 99-10 (1999), District of Columbia Ethics Op. 294 (1999), and Kansas Bar Ethics Op. 93-14 (1993). Historically, the sale of a law practice was not allowed, and lawyers, especially sole practitioners, were not allowed to sell the goodwill associated with their practices. In the words of an oft-cited (at least in this context) Bar of the City of New York ethics opinion,

> Clients are not merchandise. Lawyers are not tradesmen. They have nothing to sell but personal service. An attempt, therefore to barter in clients would appear to be inconsistent with the best concepts of our professional status.

Bar of the City of New York Opinion 633 (1943).

At the time Rule 1.17 was under consideration, proponents of the Rule argued that since pursuant to retirement plans and partnership agreements, retiring lawyers in law firms were in effect allowed compensation for the goodwill they had developed

---

[2] See Appendix 1 of this chapter for the text for this rule.

[3] California Rule of Professional Conduct 2-300 has permitted the sale of a law practice, including goodwill, since 1989, predating Model Rule 1.17. Since the ABA added Rule 1.17 to the Model Rules in 1990, it has been adopted by at least 41 jurisdictions: Alaska, Arizona, Arkansas, Colorado, Delaware, Florida, Georgia, Hawaii, Idaho, Indiana, Iowa, Maine, Maryland, Massachusetts, Michigan, Minnesota, Mississippi, Missouri, Montana, Nebraska, Nevada, New Jersey, New Mexico, New York, North Carolina, North Dakota, Ohio, Oklahoma, Oregon, Pennsylvania, Rhode Island, South Carolina, South Dakota, Utah, Vermont, Virginia, Washington, West Virginia, Wisconsin, Wyoming, and the Virgin Islands.

after years of practice, solo practitioners should also have the right to be similarly compensated. They also argued that such a rule would help to prevent the neglect of client matters after the retirement or death of the sole practitioner. See report 8(a) submitted to the ABA House of Delegates in 1990.[4]

Following the recommendations of the ABA Ethics 2000 Commission (E2K), Rule 1.17 was amended in February of 2002. The Rule, as adopted in 1990, required that the practice be sold in its entirety to a single purchaser. The E2K-inspired amendments permit a lawyer to sell discrete parts of his or her practice to different lawyers. The E2K Reporter gave this explanation for the change:

> The Commission believes that the present requirement is unduly restrictive and potentially disserves clients. While it remains important to ensure the disposition of the entire caseload, it is not necessary to require that all cases must be sold to a single buyer. For example, it may make better sense to allow the sale of family-law cases to a family lawyer and bankruptcy cases to a bankruptcy lawyer. Common sense would suggest the lawyer should sell the cases to the most competent practitioner and not be limited by such a "single buyer" rule, and paragraph (b) has been redrafted accordingly.[5]

In a nutshell, Rule 1.17 permits a lawyer to sell his or her entire practice or an area of the practice if:

- The seller ceases to practice law or ceases to practice law in the area of practice that has been sold;
- The seller gives written notice to each of the seller's clients notifying them of the proposed sale, the client's right to retain other counsel or to simply take possession of the file, and that the client's consent will be presumed if the client does not object within 90 days of receipt of the notice;
- If the client cannot be given notice, the file can be transferred to the buyer only by court order; and
- The fees charged clients are not increased because of the sale.

The Comments to the Rule provide additional guidance. For example, Paragraph 11 of the Comments states that the seller has an obligation to exercise competence in identifying a purchaser qualified to assume the practice.[6]

Paragraph 7 of the Comments to the Rule also recognizes that preliminary negotiations between seller and purchaser do not violate confidentiality provisions, but that

> Negotiations between seller and prospective purchaser prior to disclosure of information relating to a specific representation of an identifiable client no more violate the confidentiality provisions of Model Rule 1.6 than do preliminary discussions concerning the possible association of another lawyer or merger between firms, with respect to which client consent is not

---

[4] This report is reproduced as Appendix 2 to this chapter.
[5] For further information on the ABA E2K Report and the E2K Reporter's explanation of changes memos, visit the ABA E2K website at http://www.abanet.org/cpr/e2k/home.html
[6] See Rule 1.1 Competence, at http://www.abanet.org/cpr/e2k/e2k-rule11.html.

required . . . providing the purchaser access to client-specific information relating to the representation and to the file, however, requires client consent. The Rule provides that before such information can be disclosed by the seller to the purchaser the client must be given actual written notice of the contemplated sale, including the identity of the purchaser, and must be told that the decision to consent or make other arrangements must be made within 90 days. If nothing is heard from the client within that time, consent to the sale is presumed.

Under Rule 1.6 *Confidentiality of Information* of the ABA Model Rules, a lawyer "shall not reveal information relating to the representation of a client unless the client gives informed consent. . . . " However, in the context of the sale of a law practice, if the seller's clients are given written notice of the contemplated sale, consent is presumed if the clients do not respond within 90 days. Subpart (c) of the Rule and Paragraph 7 of the Comments recognize the possibility that not all clients will be able to be given actual notice of the sale. Under these circumstances, client files can be transferred to the purchaser only on order of the court. For a detailed analysis of a state bar's version of subpart (c)(3) of Rule 1.17 and the corresponding Comment that is substantially similar to the ABA Model Rule, see Arizona State Bar Opinion 06-01 (2006).[7] For a

---

[7] The Arizona Opinion provides the following analysis:

1. Client-specific information
ER 1.17 was specifically intended to authorize lawyers to sell their legal practices so long as they meet certain requirements. To prevent lawyers from disclosing his or her clients' identities, for conflicts purposes, a high-level, general description of the work done for each (e.g. tax advice, business litigation) would thwart the rule's very purpose. This minimal information would be key to preliminary negotiations. As a practical matter, no reasonable lawyer would agree to pursue serious negotiations to buy another lawyer's law practice without this minimal information. Conceivably, the prospective selling lawyer could ask his or her clients for consent to disclose such information. But no reasonable lawyer would make such a request at a preliminary stage of negotiating a sale because it would jeopardize his or her ability to retain the clients if the preliminary negotiations were unsuccessful.

The sentence in the comment immediately preceding the one quoted above supports this conclusion, albeit inartfully:

Negotiations between seller and prospective purchaser prior to disclosure of information relating to a specific representation of an identifiable client no more violate the confidentiality provisions of ER 1.6 than do preliminary discussions concerning the possible association of another lawyer or mergers between firms, with respect to which client consent is not required.

ER 1.17 cmt. 7. See also *ABA/BNA Lawyers' Manual on Professional Conduct* 91:902 to 91:903 (1999) ("the compelling need to protect clients from conflicts of interest arguably provides a rationale for limited disclosure of client information in the context of serious merger negotiations"). If two law firms contemplating a merger do not need client consent to exchange basic, minimal information, such as client names to check for conflicts, then a lawyer negotiating to sell his or her solo law practice may provide similar minimal information to the prospective purchasing lawyer.

Although the selling lawyer may disclose client identities and high-level, general descriptions of the work performed, the fees paid by the specific clients over the past three years do not fall into the category of minimal necessary information. The revenue stream provided by each specific client does not facilitate the sale of a law practice.

discussion of the types of client information that can be disclosed by a lawyer to a firm to which the lawyer is considering making a lateral move, *see* Tremblay, *Migrating Lawyers and the Ethics of Conflict Checking* 19 Geo. J. Legal Ethics 489 (2006).

A. State Versions of Rule 1.17

There can be significant variations in states' versions of Model Rule 1.17.

Similar to the pre-E2K version of Rule 1.17, some states require that the practice be sold in its entirety to a single purchaser. For example, this is true in the Alaska, Colorado, Georgia, and North Dakota versions of Rule 1.17. The ABA Model Rule states that the client's consent to the transfer of the client's files to the purchaser will be presumed if the client does not object within 90 days. The Florida and North Carolina versions of the Rule require 30 days' notice; Colorado, New Jersey, and Pennsylvania require 60 days' notice.

The ABA Model Rule assumes client consent if a client who has received notice of the sale does not take any action or does not otherwise object to the notice of sale. The representation of those clients who cannot be given notice can be transferred to the purchasing lawyer only by order of the court. Subpart e(2) of Florida Rule 4-1.17 provides that:

> e) **Consummation of Sale.** A sale of a law practice shall not be consummated until:

> (2) court orders have been entered authorizing substitution of counsel for all clients who could not be served with written notice of the proposed sale and whose representations involve pending litigation; provided, in the event the court fails to grant a substitution of counsel in a matter involving pending litigation, that matter shall not be included in the sale and the sale otherwise shall be unaffected. Further, the matters not involving pending litigation of any client who cannot be served with written notice of the proposed sale shall not be included in the sale and the sale otherwise shall be unaffected.

Paragraph [5] of the Comment to Model Rule 1.17 states that if "the purchaser is unable to undertake all client matters because of a conflict of interest in a specific matter respecting which the purchaser is not permitted by Rule 1.7 or another rule to represent the client, the requirement that there be a single purchaser is nevertheless satisfied." North Carolina's Rule 1.17(d) provides that if a conflict of interest arises that

---

This interpretation of ER 1.17—that the selling lawyer may disclose without client consent client identities and high-level, general descriptions of the work performed—comes with a caveat. If there is a reasonable prospect that disclosing such information will adversely affect a client's material interest or the client has given the selling lawyer instructions not to disclose such information, then the selling lawyer may not reveal the information without client consent.

Finally, the selling lawyer's ability to release minimal information without client consent to a prospective purchaser necessarily imposes a corresponding duty on the prospective purchaser to keep that information confidential. If the sale is consummated properly under ER 1.17, the buyer then becomes lawyer for the seller's clients, with all the attendant obligations under ER 1.6. The problem arises if the selling lawyer has disclosed client names and high-level, general descriptions of the legal work, but the preliminary negotiations do not result in a sale agreement. In that situation, the former prospective purchaser has an obligation to keep the information confidential.—AZ State Bar Opinion 06-01 (2006) "prohibits the purchaser from representing the client, the seller's notice to the client shall advise the client to retain substitute counsel to assume the client's representation and to arrange to have the substitute counsel contact the seller." Subpart (c) of Michigan Rule 1.17 contains a similar provision.

The California, Florida, Maine, Minnesota, and Wyoming rules require that the purchasers be admitted to practice in their respective states.

Arkansas adds a subpart (e) to its version of Rule 1.17, which requires the selling lawyer to file an affidavit with the committee on Professional Conduct that he or she has complied with the notice requirements of the rule, proof of publication, a list of the clients notified, and a copy of the notice sent.[8]

The Pennsylvania Rule adds a subpart (e) that states as follows:

(e) The agreement of sale shall include a clear statement of the respective responsibilities of the parties to maintain the records and files of the seller's practice including client files.

The Ohio version of Rule 1.17 (effective February 1, 2007) adds the following section to the notice provision:

5) Biographical information relative to the professional qualifications of the purchasing lawyer, including but not limited to applicable information consistent with Rule 7.2, information regarding any disciplinary action taken against the purchasing lawyer, and information regarding the existence, nature, and status of any pending disciplinary complaint certified by a probable cause panel pursuant to Gov. Bar R. V, Section 6(D)(1).

As the above sampling of the variations in state versions of Rule 1.17 illustrates, the practitioner who is considering the sale or purchase of a law practice in a particular jurisdiction would be well advised to check the rules of that jurisdiction.

There are a limited number of state bar ethics opinions that have discussed sale of a law practice issues. Arizona State Bar Opinion 06-01 (2006) addressed a broad range of issues relating to the sale of a law practice, analyzing Arizona's version of Rule 1.17 that is virtually identical to the ABA Model Rule. It concluded *inter alia* that a lawyer seeking to sell his or her solo law practice may disclose certain limited client-specific information to the prospective lawyer-buyer without client consent to the disclosure; that the lawyer may continue in private practice, so long as the legal and geographic areas are different from what was sold; and that the lawyer may also negotiate a reasonable covenant not to compete with the purchaser.

Two other opinions came to differing conclusions on the question of whether a suspended or disbarred lawyer can sell his or her law practice. South Carolina Opinion 03-06 (2003) stated that a suspended or disbarred lawyer may not sell his or her law practice, and the most prudent course may be for the lawyer to petition the court for an order allowing a proposed sale. The Maine Board of Bar Overseers Opinion 178 (2002) stated that a disbarred or suspended lawyer may sell his or her practice to another lawyer but must comply with applicable rules requiring disbarred or

---

[8] This text can be found at http://courts.state.ar.us/opinions/2005a/20050303/arpc2005.html.

suspended lawyers to take specific actions, such as notifying clients of the disbarment or suspension and advising clients to obtain substitute counsel. Other opinions have noted that Rule 1.17 does not apply in situations where retiring lawyers transfer their interests to younger lawyers in the firm when there is a continuing succession in the firm's identity. See for example North Carolina Opinion 98-06 (1998) and South Carolina Opinion 02-14 (undated). See also Comment 14 to Rule 1.17.

B. Law Review Articles, Treatises

There have been several law review and bar journal articles written on the topic of sale of a law practice. One commentator, Edward Poll, has written an entire treatise on the subject in *Selling Your Law Practice: The Profitable Exit Strategy* (LawBiz Management Co. 2005). Other treatises devote separate chapters to the subject, and include Ronald D. Rotunda and John S. Dzienkowski's "Sale of a Law Practice" from Rotunda and Dzienkowski, *Legal Ethics: The Lawyer's Deskbook on Professional Responsibility* §§ 17-1 (2007–2008 ed.), "Sale of a Law Practice," 91 *ABA/BNA Lawyer's Manual on Professional Conduct*, 801 (last updated 1999), and the analysis of Model Rule 1.17 in Geoffrey C. Hazard, Jr. & W. William Hodes' *The Law of Lawyering* § 21.1 (Aspen Law & Business, 3rd ed., 2003). See also Overton, George, "Are Lawyers for Sale?" 15-APR *CBA Rec.* 64 (2001), DeWoskin, Alan "When a Solo Takes Down the Shingle," from *A Lawyers' Guide to Retirement* (David A. Bridewell ed., 3d ed., published by the ABA Senior Lawyers Division 1998); Coy, Gayle "Permitting the Sale of a Law Practice: Furthering the Interests of Both Attorneys and Their Clients," 222 *Hofstra L. Rev.* 969 (1994); Schoenwald, Scott, "Model Rule 1.17 and the Ethical Sale of Law Practices: A Critical Analysis," 7 *Geo. J. Legal Ethics* 395 (1993). Other sources address the practical concerns involved in the sale of a law practice. See, for example, Shaw, Betty "Winding Down, Closing Up Or Selling Out," 61-NOV *Bench & B.* Minn. 12 (2004), Poll, Edward, "Selling A Law Practice: Prospects and Pitfalls" 16 NO. 11 *Acct. & Fin. Plan. for L. Firms* 1 (2003), Crawford, Barton, "The Sale of a Legal Practice in North Carolina: Goodwill and Discrimination Against the Sole Practitioner," 32 *Wake Forest L. Rev.* 993 (1997), and Dimitriou, Dimitrios "What Should Be Your Concerns? Purchase or Sale of a Solo Practice," 19 *Law Prac. Mgmt.* 44 (1993)

III. Winding Down the Practice

Similar to the sale of a law practice, key ethical issues that relate to the winding down of a law practice include communication with clients, the protection of client confidences, and the appropriate handling of client files.

There have been some state bar opinions that have addressed a broad range of issues as they relate to the winding down of a law practice. These include State Bar of Louisiana Opinion 05-RPCC-001 (2005), a digest of which states as follows:

> A lawyer closing her practice should surrender client files to the client or new counsel, return client property and unearned fees, and give clients adequate notice to enable them to employ other counsel. With respect to matters in litigation, the lawyer should inform clients of pending court

dates, advise them to obtain new counsel as soon as possible, and file a motion to withdraw as appropriate. The lawyer should analyze any client file she has not been asked to surrender and advise that client how to protect his or her interests. If a client's whereabouts are unknown, the lawyer should send a form letter to the last known address notifying the client of the lawyer's termination of the representation and of the opportunity for the client to obtain his or her files and property. Rule 1.15 requires that a lawyer keep records of all client property and trust account funds for five years after termination of the representation. Rules 1.15, 1.16. 1201 Law. Man Prof. Conduct 4001.

See also State Bar of Michigan Opinion RI-100 (1991), Maryland Opinions 2005-01 (2004) and 92-2 (1992), Illinois State Bar Opinion 94-14 and New Jersey Opinion 692 (supplement) (2002).

To the extent that a sole practitioner's retirement from and subsequent dissolution of his or her practice is in effect a withdrawal from the representation, Model Rule 1.16, *Declining or Terminating Representation*, may be implicated. For example, subpart (c) of Rule 1.16 requires that a lawyer must get the court's permission to withdraw for those matters currently pending before the court, and that the lawyer must continue with the representation if ordered by the court to do so.

A. Client Confidences

Lawyers who either retire from practice or assume responsibility for the client files of a dissolved law firm must protect their client confidences. See, for example, Oregon State Bar Opinion 2005-23 (2005) which addressed whether a retired lawyer could turn over his former client files to a third party:

> Absent consent from the affected client or some other applicable exception, it would be improper for lawyer either to turn over files to an educational institution or to inform a new lawyer for the same client about any prior confidences or secrets.

See also Pennsylvania Opinion 94-51 (1994) that addresses confidentiality issues from the successor lawyer's perspective, a digest of which states as follows:

> A lawyer who is the successor attorney for several former clients of a law firm that is now dissolved may grant access to the clients' files to a former partner from the firm who requests information in connection with an arbitration proceeding regarding the dissolution. The successor lawyer must distinguish between information obtained since the dissolution when a new attorney-client relationship came about; this information may not be disclosed without client consent. A distinction must also be made between access and possession of the files. The former partner may be allowed access to information provided before the law firm dissolved, but may not take possession of the files unless the client consents. Rules 1.6, 1.9, 1.15.

B. Client Files

As the sole practitioner winds down the practice, there will no doubt be file cabinets and boxes of old closed and dormant client files that the lawyer has accumulated during the years he or she has been in practice. One of the most frequently asked questions to the ABA ETHICSearch service is what the lawyer's obligations are with regard to these old files.

There are a great many state bar ethics opinions that have addressed the disposition of closed and/or dormant client files. See, for example, State Bar of California Ethics Opinion 2001-157 (undated), Maine Board of Bar Overseers Opinion 187 (2004), Missouri Opinion 2004–0052 (undated), West Virginia Opinion 2002-01 (2002). Digests of all of theses opinions are available in the ABA/BNA Lawyers' Manual on Professional Conduct. ABA Informal Opinion 1384, *Disposition of a Lawyer's Closed or Dormant Files Relating to Representation of or Services to Clients* (1977),[9] while dated, is still very widely cited in more recent state bar opinions that have addressed this issue.[10] Informal Opinion 1384 listed the following guidelines relating to the disposition of closed or dormant client files:

1. Unless the client consents, a lawyer should not destroy or discard items that clearly or probably belong to the client. Such items include those furnished to the lawyer by or on behalf of the client, the return of which could reasonably be expected by the client, and original documents (especially when not filed or recorded in the public records).

2. A lawyer should use care not to destroy or discard information that the lawyer knows or should know may still be necessary or useful in the assertion or defense of the client's position in a matter for which the applicable statutory limitations period has not expired.

3. A lawyer should use care not to destroy or discard information that the client may need, has not previously been given to the client, and is not otherwise readily available to the client, and which the client may reasonably expect will be preserved by the lawyer.

4. In determining the length of time for retention of disposition of a file, a lawyer should exercise discretion. The nature and contents of some files may indicate a need for longer retention than do the nature and contents of other files, based upon their obvious relevance and materiality to matters that can be expected to arise.

---

[9] This opinion is reproduced as Appendix 3.

[10] Many state ethics committees have also addressed this question, many prior to ABA Informal Opinion 1384. Digests of these opinions are from the ABA/BNA *Lawyers' Manual on Professional Conduct*, which carries thousands of state and local bar association ethics opinions as well as articles on current developments in professional responsibility. A copy of the manual should be available at your local law library and is also accessible through Westlaw and Lexis. An excellent article entitled "Records Retention in the Private Legal Environment: Annotated Bibliography and Program Implementation Tools" by Lee R. Nemchek, is available here. This article includes a comprehensive list of articles and ethics opinions on file destruction/retention.

5. <u>A lawyer should take special care to preserve, indefinitely, accurate and complete records of the lawyer's receipt and disbursement of trust funds.</u>
6. In disposing of a file, a lawyer should protect the confidentiality of the contents.
7. A lawyer <u>should not destroy or dispose of a file without screening it in order to determine that consideration has been given to the matters discussed above.</u>
8. A lawyer should <u>preserve, perhaps for an extended time, an index or identification of the files that the lawyer has destroyed or disposed of.</u>

Some state bar opinions have addressed the joint obligations partners have with regard to client files when they retire from a partnership or when the partnership they are associated with is dissolved. For example, the following extract of New York State Bar Opinion 623 (1991) appears at page 1001:6103 of the *ABA/BNA Lawyers' Manual on Professional Conduct*:

> A lawyer who leaves a law practice, due either to retirement or dissolution of a law firm, has joint and several responsibility with other firm members for the proper disposition of client files. In the case of closed client files, the lawyer may destroy all documents that belong to him without notice to the client unless extraordinary circumstances exist. As for documents belonging to the client, the lawyer must offer to make them available to the client and may follow the client's instruction as to their disposal. If the client fails to respond in a reasonable period of time, the lawyer should review the files to determine which files he must salvage because of legal requirements or because the documents establish client rights. The lawyer may then destroy the remainder of the files in a manner that preserves client confidentiality. He must notify the client of any documents that must be salvaged and forward any documents the client is required by law to maintain. If the client is deceased or incapacitated, the lawyer may deliver the files to the client's representative. If delivery to the client or his representative is not possible, the lawyer must retain these files until the expiration of the legal retention period or the period of reasonably foreseeable need by the client but may charge the client the cost for maintaining the files.

Nassau County Bar Association 93-23 (1993) discusses the joint ethical obligations of the lawyers who were formerly partners in a now dissolved law firm. The lawyers who withdrew made arrangements to store their inactive files with the lawyers who remained to form a successor law firm. The successor firm then contacted the former partners and gave them a list of the files the firm had in storage. The former partners instructed the firm to send them approximately 30 percent of the files and destroy the rest. The successor firm inquired as to its obligations with regard to the remaining files in its possession. The opinion states:

> Neither the fact that inquiring counsel and his present partners have no knowledge of the files which remain in their custody, changes their obligations with respect to the files. . . .
>
> Moreover, if there are any members of inquiring counsel's current firm who are not members of the predecessor law firm in the present firm, of which

they are members, has custody of the files ... an attorney voluntarily assuming custody of the files of another lawyer's client has the same ethical obligations for the files as if they were his or her own files.

Thus, while the private contractual agreement may have the effect of allocating among the former partners the economic burden of dealing with particular files ... it cannot shift the ethical burden which is joint and several as to (a) all the former partners, both "withdrawing partners" and those remaining at the successor firm and (b) any new partners of the successor firm.

See also State Bar of Wisconsin Committee on Professional Ethics Opinion E-98-01 (1998), which states:

> The fact the firm has dissolved or that the lawyers maintaining the files may not have been involved in the representation does not alter the duties of either the lawyer or firm that performed the engagement or the lawyer or firm that now maintains the files. Each retains responsibilities to the client. Lawyers in firms that are dissolving should agree among themselves on the handling of client files, and shall transfer files to a departing or new lawyer upon client request. However, those arrangements do not obviate the ethical and fiduciary duty to maintain and properly handle client files. See Nassau County Bar Association Opinion 93-23 (1993). Both the lawyers who handled the engagement and the lawyers who may have voluntarily assumed custody of the file owe the same obligation to handle the return or destruction in a reasonable fashion as described above.

Committee on Legal Ethics and Professional Conduct of the Ohio State Bar Association Informal Opinion 98-2 (1998) provides the following guidance to a lawyer who wished to retire and who inquired as to what he should do with original client wills that he assumed responsibility for upon the deaths of two senior partners:

> It is the Committee's opinion that your ethical obligations with respect to these wills is to ascertain whether the makers are still living and, if so, to return the wills to them; and, if the maker is deceased, then your obligation is to locate and deliver the will to the maker's personal representative. Your ethical obligation is to make a diligent effort to locate either the client or, if the client is deceased, his or her personal representative. If, after undertaking this effort, there remain clients whose whereabouts you cannot determine, then, the Committee is of the opinion that you must preserve and retain the wills. You should leave instructions that upon your death, if there is no responsible party willing to assume appropriate responsibility, then the wills should be delivered to the chair of the local certified grievance committee or Disciplinary Counsel.

C. What Should a Lawyer Do with Client Files for Clients the Lawyer Cannot Locate?

If you cannot locate some of your clients and you have documents that they might need at some future date, what should you do? One possible solution to the storage aspect of the client file dilemma is to convert the paper in these old files into an electronic format. For matters that originated within the past 10–15 years, chances are that a great number of the paper documents in these files may have electronic duplicates on the lawyer's computer system. If a lawyer decides to store files electronically and discard the paper copies, some state bar association ethics opinions have identified legal ethics issues that can arise.

Even if a lawyer decides to store client files electronically, there may be items in a particular client file—such as original wills, deeds, or other client property—that the client may reasonably expect the lawyer will preserve in the original. See, for example, ABA Informal Opinion 1384, as discussed in Part III.B. above. Some states' Rules of Professional Conduct require that certain items in a client's files *must* be kept as originals, including Rule 3.4(a)(4) of the Maine Code of Professional Responsibility and DR 9-102(D)(8) of the New York Code of Professional Responsibility. See also New York State Bar Association Opinion 680 (1996) (referencing DR 9-102(D)(8) in the context of electronic file retention). Check your local rules and ethics opinions.

Maine Opinion 183 (2004) addressed the question of whether a lawyer is obligated to keep paper copies of correspondence generated on the client's behalf if the lawyer maintains electronic copies on his or her computer system. While the opinion concluded that in general a lawyer did not have to keep paper copies, it stated that the lawyer should consider the client's access to and understanding of technology when returning an electronic file to a client. The opinion also cautioned that a lawyer should maintain the software used to create the files so that the lawyer and the client will be able to open the files long after the software has become obsolete. The opinion stated:

> it may be necessary for an attorney to retain old versions of software in order to ensure that computerized records may be accessed or printed when requested by the client. Similarly, as part of the obligation to deliver files, an attorney may need to retain the means by which a client may review or print computerized records. While an attorney may satisfy these ethical obligations by providing paper copies of computerized records to the client, electronic file retention is also acceptable provided that the client will have meaningful access to the electronic file in the future.

State Bar of Virginia Opinion 1818 (2005) (*ABA/BNA Lawyers' Manual on Professional Conduct*, 21 Current Reports (2005)) stated that a lawyer may maintain paperless client files, but that he or she must obtain the client's consent before destroying that current client's paper documents. The opinion also stated that before destroying a client's paper file, the lawyer should carefully review the documents in the file to ensure that paper documents that have legal significance only in their paper form—such as testamentary documents, marriage certificates, and handwriting samples—are not destroyed. The opinion also indicated that a lawyer can make maintaining client files in an electronic format a condition of representation in a retainer agreement with a prospective client subject to the lawyer's obligation to keep certain documents in their original form.

Missouri Informal Opinion 20010147 (undated) stated that a lawyer may not discard the hard copies of client files after scanning them without the client's consent. Other opinions state that a lawyer who maintains client files in an electronic format should provide a client with electronic copies should the client request them. See, for example, Wisconsin State Bar opinion E-00-03 (2003), which states:

> when the client requests documents be provided on a computer disk which the lawyer has maintained electronically, the lawyer should provide those documents in the requested format, so long as it is reasonably practicable to do so.

See also *Accord*, North Dakota Opinion 01-03 (2001), which states that a client's file that is maintained in an electronic format should be provided in that same format if requested.

IV. Preparation for the Protection of Client Interests When a Lawyer Dies or Becomes Disabled

Particularly in the case of the sole practitioner, no discussion of the ethical issues implicated in the winding down of a law practice would be complete without a discussion of the need to have in place a plan for the disposition of a lawyer's practice in the event of his or her death or disability. In 1992, the ABA Standing Committee on Ethics and Professional Responsibility issued Formal Opinion 92-369, *Disposition of Deceased Sole Practitioners' Client Files and Property*.[11] This opinion addressed the need for a lawyer to have a plan in place that would provide for the protection of a client's interests in the event of the lawyer's death, and provided guidance for the lawyer who assumes responsibility for the deceased lawyer's files. The opinion states:

> The death of a sole practitioner could have serious effects on the sole practitioner's clients. . . . Important client matters, such as court dates, statutes of limitations, or document filings, could be neglected until the clients discover that their lawyer has died. As a precaution to safeguard client interests, the sole practitioner should have a plan in place that will ensure insofar as is reasonably practicable that client matters will not be neglected in the event of the sole practitioner's death.

ABA Formal Opinion 92-369 (1992).

The Opinion drew support for its conclusions from ABA Model Rules of Professional Conduct 1.1 (Competence) and 1.3 (Diligence), and from lawyers' fiduciary duties to their clients:

> According to Rule 1.1, competence includes "preparation necessary for the representation," which when read in conjunction with Rule 1.3 would indicate that a lawyer should diligently prepare for the client's representation. Although representation should terminate when the attorney is no longer able to adequately represent the client, the lawyer's fiduciary obligations of loyalty and confidentiality continue beyond the termination of the agency relationship.

ABA Formal Opinion 92-369 (1992)

---

[11] This opinion is reproduced as Appendix 4 to this chapter.

The Opinion noted that lawyers have been disciplined for the neglect of client matters due to the lawyer's ill health or personal problems. It further suggested that a lawyer who has failed to make preparations to protect his or her clients' interests in the event of the his or her death should be sanctioned, both in the hope of encouraging other lawyers to make such preparations, and to restore confidence in the bar, although the sanctions would obviously have no deterrent effect on deceased lawyers. See also Recommendation 111 of the Senior Lawyers Division to the ABA House of Delegates, which was approved at the 1997 ABA Annual Meeting. A copy of the recommendation and its accompanying report are available at http://www.abanet.org/cpr/ethicsearch/report111.pdf.

In 2002, pursuant to the ABA Ethics 2000 Commission's (E2K) recommendations, the ABA House of Delegates approved adding a paragraph to the Comment to Rule 1.3 that states as follows:

> To prevent neglect of client matters in the event of a sole practitioner's death or disability, the duty of diligence may require that each sole practitioner prepare a plan, in conformity with applicable rules, that designates another competent lawyer to review client files, notify each client of the lawyer's death or disability, and determine whether there is a need for immediate protective action. Cf. Rule 28 of the American Bar Association Model Rules for Lawyer Disciplinary Enforcement (providing for court appointment of a lawyer to inventory files and take other protective action in absence of a plan providing for another lawyer to protect the interests of the clients of a deceased or disabled lawyer).

There are several state bar associations that have issued opinions on this general topic. Arizona State Bar Opinion 04-05 (2005) addressed what should be included in a plan for the protection of clients' financial interests in the event of a sole practitioner's death. It also stated that such a plan should be a part of a larger plan to protect clients' interests in the event of the lawyer's death or disability:

> [A] lawyer's plans for the disposition of his or her client trust account should be made in concert with a broader plan for the disposition of the lawyer's practice in the event of his or her death or disability. Prudence dictates that arrangements should be made with another lawyer to notify clients of the lawyer's disability or death, and to review the lawyer's files for the limited purpose of determining whether any immediate action needs to be taken to protect those clients' legal interests. See, e.g., ABA Formal Op. 92-369 at 4 (such arrangements do not violate ER 1.6 because they are impliedly authorized in order for the lawyer to carry out a representation).

Florida Opinion 81-8M (1981) involved a situation where a lawyer was anticipating termination of his practice because of a terminal illness. A digest of the opinion reads as follows:

> After a diligent attempt is made to contact all clients whose files he holds, a lawyer anticipating termination of his practice by death should dispose of

all files according to his client's instructions. The files of those clients who do not respond should be individually reviewed by the lawyer and destroyed only if no important papers belonging to the clients are in the files. Important documents should be indexed and placed in storage or turned over to any lawyer who assumes control of his active files.

801 *ABA/BNA Lawyers' Manual on Professional Conduct* 2502.

In 1986, the ABA General Practice Section, Sole Practitioners and Small Firms Committee sponsored a program titled, "Preparing for and Dealing with the Consequences of the Death of a Sole Practitioner." One of the papers presented at this program, "A Sole Practitioner's Letters of Instruction Regarding Things to Be Done Upon His or Her Death," listed the following as items the sole practitioner should mention in a letter to the personal representative of his or her estate:

- Engaging a lawyer to wind up the law practice;
- Notifying clients of the sole practitioner's death;
- Transferring active files to the client or to the successor lawyer designated by the client;
- Disposing of closed or inactive files;
- Making arrangements to complete work on active files; and
- Securing agreements with the successor lawyers as to the handling of open files.

All lawyers should have a plan in place that will protect their clients' interests in the event of their death. This is especially true for sole practitioners who do not have partners or associates who can manage the practice in their absence. A lawyer who assumes responsibility for a deceased lawyer's client files should review them carefully to determine which files need immediate attention. The lawyer should also make all reasonable efforts to contact the deceased lawyer's clients, notify them that their lawyer has died, and request instructions. Depending on the nature and contents of the client files, the lawyer may have an obligation to preserve them. As ABA Informal Opinion 1384 (1977) states, the obligation arises if there are items in the files that clearly belong to the client and contain information that "the lawyer knows or should know may still be useful in the assertion or defense of the client's position in a matter for which the applicable statutory limitations period has not expired."

V. Conclusion

When a lawyer decides to either wind down or sell his or her law practice, he or she must carefully manage client files, take steps to preserve client confidentiality, and provide appropriate notice to clients. Model Rule 1.17 provides additional specific guidance with regard to the sale of a law practice.

The sole practitioner should also have a plan in place to protect his or her client's interests in the event of his or her death or disability.

Appendices

Appendix 10-1. Client-Lawyer Relationship: Rule 1.17 *Sale of Law Practice*

Appendix 10-2. Report 8(a)

Appendix 10-3. ABA Committee on Ethics and Professional Responsibility Op. 1384 American Bar Association

Appendix 10-4. American Bar Association Standing Committee on Ethics and Professional Responsibility: Formal Opinion 92-369, *Disposition of Deceased Sole Practitioners' Client Files and Property*

Appendix 10-1

Client-Lawyer Relationship: Rule 1.17 *Sale of Law Practice*

A lawyer or a law firm may sell or purchase a law practice, or an area of law practice, including good will, if the following conditions are satisfied:

(a) The seller ceases to engage in the private practice of law, or in the area of practice that has been sold, [in the geographic area] [in the jurisdiction] (a jurisdiction may elect either version) in which the practice has been conducted;

(b) The entire practice, or the entire area of practice, is sold to one or more lawyers or law firms;

(c) The seller gives written notice to each of the seller's clients regarding:

(1) the proposed sale;
(2) the client's right to retain other counsel or to take possession of the file; and
(3) the fact that the client's consent to the transfer of the client's files will be presumed if the client does not take any action or does not otherwise object within ninety (90) days of receipt of the notice.

If a client cannot be given notice, the representation of that client may be transferred to the purchaser only upon entry of an order so authorizing by a court having jurisdiction. The seller may disclose to the court in camera information relating to the representation only to the extent necessary to obtain an order authorizing the transfer of a file.

(d) The fees charged clients shall not be increased by reason of the sale.

Comment

[1] The practice of law is a profession, not merely a business. Clients are not commodities that can be purchased and sold at will. Pursuant to this Rule, when a lawyer or an entire firm ceases to practice, or ceases to practice in an area of law, and other lawyers or firms take over the representation, the selling lawyer or firm may obtain compensation for the reasonable value of the practice as may withdrawing partners of law firms. See Rules 5.4 and 5.6.

Termination of Practice by the Seller

[2] The requirement that all of the private practice, or all of an area of practice, be sold is satisfied if the seller in good faith makes the entire practice, or the area of practice, available for sale to the purchasers. The fact that a number of the seller's clients decide not to be represented by the purchasers but take their matters elsewhere, therefore, does not result in a violation. Return to private practice as a result of an unanticipated change in circumstances does not necessarily result in a violation. For example, a lawyer who has sold the practice to accept an appointment to judicial office does not violate the requirement that the sale be attendant to cessation of practice if the lawyer later resumes private practice upon being defeated in a contested or a retention election for the office or resigns from a judiciary position.

[3] The requirement that the seller cease to engage in the private practice of law does not prohibit employment as a lawyer on the staff of a public agency or a legal services entity that provides legal services to the poor, or as in-house counsel to a business.

[4] The Rule permits a sale of an entire practice attendant upon retirement from the private practice of law within the jurisdiction. Its provisions, therefore, accommodate the lawyer who sells the practice on the occasion of moving to another state. Some states are so large that a move from one locale therein to another is tantamount to leaving the jurisdiction in which the lawyer has engaged in the practice of law. To also accommodate lawyers so situated, states may permit the sale of the practice when the lawyer leaves the geographical area rather than the jurisdiction. The alternative desired should be indicated by selecting one of the two provided for in Rule 1.17(a).

[5] This Rule also permits a lawyer or law firm to sell an area of practice. If an area of practice is sold and the lawyer remains in the active practice of law, the lawyer must cease accepting any matters in the area of practice that has been sold, either as counsel or co-counsel or by assuming joint responsibility for a matter in connection with the division of a fee with another lawyer as would otherwise be permitted by Rule 1.5(e). For example, a lawyer with a substantial number of estate planning matters and a substantial number of probate administration cases may sell the estate planning portion of the practice but remain in the practice of law by concentrating on probate administration; however, that practitioner may not thereafter accept any estate planning matters. Although a lawyer who leaves a jurisdiction or geographical area typically would sell the entire practice, this Rule permits the lawyer to limit the sale to one or more areas of the practice, thereby preserving the lawyer's right to continue practice in the areas of the practice that were not sold.

Sale of Entire Practice or Entire Area of Practice

[6] The Rule requires that the seller's entire practice, or an entire area of practice, be sold. The prohibition against sale of less than an entire practice area protects those clients whose matters are less lucrative and who might find it difficult to secure other counsel if a sale could be limited to substantial fee-generating matters. The purchasers are required to undertake all client matters in the practice or practice area, subject to

client consent. This requirement is satisfied, however, even if a purchaser is unable to undertake a particular client matter because of a conflict of interest.

Client Confidences, Consent, and Notice

[7] Negotiations between seller and prospective purchaser prior to disclosure of information relating to a specific representation of an identifiable client no more violate the confidentiality provisions of Model Rule 1.6 than do preliminary discussions concerning the possible association of another lawyer or mergers between firms, with respect to which client consent is not required. Providing the purchaser access to client-specific information relating to the representation and to the file, however, requires client consent. The Rule provides that before such information can be disclosed by the seller to the purchaser the client must be given actual written notice of the contemplated sale, including the identity of the purchaser, and must be told that the decision to consent or make other arrangements must be made within 90 days. If nothing is heard from the client within that time, consent to the sale is presumed.

[8] A lawyer or law firm ceasing to practice cannot be required to remain in practice because some clients cannot be given actual notice of the proposed purchase. Since these clients cannot themselves consent to the purchase or direct any other disposition of their files, the Rule requires an order from a court having jurisdiction authorizing their transfer or other disposition. The Court can be expected to determine whether reasonable efforts to locate the client have been exhausted, and whether the absent client's legitimate interests will be served by authorizing the transfer of the file so that the purchaser may continue the representation. Preservation of client confidences requires that the petition for a court order be considered in camera. (A procedure by which such an order can be obtained needs to be established in jurisdictions in which it presently does not exist).

[9] All elements of client autonomy, including the client's absolute right to discharge a lawyer and transfer the representation to another, survive the sale of the practice or area of practice.

Fee Arrangements Between Client and Purchaser

[10] The sale may not be financed by increases in fees charged the clients of the practice. Existing arrangements between the seller and the client as to fees and the scope of the work must be honored by the purchaser.

Other Applicable Ethical Standards

[11] Lawyers participating in the sale of a law practice or a practice area are subject to the ethical standards applicable to involving another lawyer in the representation of a client. These include, for example, the seller's obligation to exercise competence in identifying a purchaser qualified to assume the practice and the purchaser's obligation to undertake the representation competently (see Rule 1.1); the obligation

to avoid disqualifying conflicts, and to secure the client's informed consent for those conflicts that can be agreed to (see Rule 1.7 regarding conflicts and Rule 1.0(e) for the definition of informed consent); and the obligation to protect information relating to the representation (see Rules 1.6 and 1.9).

[12] If approval of the substitution of the purchasing lawyer for the selling lawyer is required by the rules of any tribunal in which a matter is pending, such approval must be obtained before the matter can be included in the sale (see Rule 1.16).

Applicability of the Rule

[13] This Rule applies to the sale of a law practice of a deceased, disabled or disappeared lawyer. Thus, the seller may be represented by a non-lawyer representative not subject to these Rules. Since, however, no lawyer may participate in a sale of a law practice which does not conform to the requirements of this Rule, the representatives of the seller as well as the purchasing lawyer can be expected to see to it that they are met.

[14] Admission to or retirement from a law partnership or professional association, retirement plans and similar arrangements, and a sale of tangible assets of a law practice, do not constitute a sale or purchase governed by this Rule.

[15] This Rule does not apply to the transfers of legal representation between lawyers when such transfers are unrelated to the sale of a practice or an area of practice.

Appendix 10-2

Report 8(a)

At the 1988 Annual Meeting of the House of Delegates in Toronto, the State Bar of California introduced a resolution to amend the Model Rules so as to authorize the sale of an individual law practice. This resolution was modelled along the concepts of then proposed Rule 2-300 of the Rules of Professional Conduct of the State Bar of California, which has since been adopted by the California Supreme Court and has been effective since May 27, 1989. (A copy of California Rule 2-300 is attached.)

The resolution was not then pursued, because of an expressed desire of the Standing Committee on Ethics and Professional Responsibility to work with the proponents of the resolution so as to develop a proposed rule acceptable to the Standing Committee. We are pleased to say that the State Bar of California, together with the Sections of General Practice and Law Practice Management which have become co-sponsors of this resolution, worked extensively with the Standing Committee, and a proposed rule has resulted from this process. This is the rule proposed by the present resolution.

The reasons supporting a rule which would allow the sale of a law practice remain as valid now as they were in 1988 and are repeated here.

Procedural History

The California rule was the result of a study begun in 1979 by the California State Bar's Committee on Professional Responsibility and Conduct ("COPRAC") when an attorney requested COPRAC to issue an opinion as to whether he could ethically include "good will" in the selling price of his sole practice. COPRAC studied the issue in great depth and determined to draft a Rule of Professional Conduct to address the issue. The State Bar Board of Governors circulated the rule drafted by COPRAC for a 90 day public comment period. In 1985, after the public comment period, the Board referred the rule back to COPRAC for further study in light of concerns raised regarding how the recently enacted requirement that attorneys enter into written fee agreements with their clients would impact the rule.

In January, 1985, about the time COPRAC completed its review, a special committee, subsequently renamed the Commission for the Revision of the Rules of Professional Conduct ("Commission"), was appointed to review all the California rules and to recommend appropriate amendments. COPRAC transmitted its reports and recommendation about the draft rule to the Commission for its consideration.

The Commission determined to adopt the recommendations of COPRAC and included a slightly revised version of the "good will" rule drafted by COPRAC in its Discussion Draft of Proposed Amendments to the California Rules of Professional Conduct that was circulated for public comment in July, 1986. After reviewing the comments, the Commission recommended that the Board adopt the rule as part of its overall revision of the rules. The Board of Governors concurred in the recommendation of the Commission and the rule was one of several forwarded to the California Supreme Court for approval. On November 28, 1988, the Supreme Court approved rule 2-300 to become operative on May 27, 1989.

Impetus for Formulation of the Rule

Protection of Clients

Rule of Professional Conduct 2-300 and proposed Model Rule 1.17 are consumer protection measures designed to address the disparity between the treatment of the clients of sole practitioners and the clients of law firms when the attorney handling the client matter leaves the practice, by ensuring that the client matters handled by sole practitioners are attended to when the sole practitioner leaves the practice.

If the attorney leaving the practice is or was part of a law firm, in most cases, the firm continues to handle the matter. In the majority of situations, the transition for the client is very smooth. However, if the attorney was in sole practice, the transition is not so smooth because there is no law firm standing ready to continue to handle the client matter. The clients of sole practitioners who leave the practice of law are relatively unprotected because there are no regulations in place to protect them during the transition.

Sole Practitioners in Unfair Financial Position

In addition to the issues of client protection, sole practitioners are in an unfair financial position concerning the "good will" of their law practice. The "good will" of a business is "the expectation of continued public patronage." (See e.g., Cal. Bus. & Prof. Code, § 14100.) Attorneys, like other business persons, may sell the physical assets of their law practice, such as equipment, the library or the furniture. However, case authority and ethics opinions held that the sale of "good will" of a law practice is unethical and against public policy. In *Geffen v. Moss* (1975) 53 Cal. App. 3d 215, 226 [125 Cal. Rptr. 687], a case involving a sole practitioner's sale of his law practice to another sole practitioner, the court stated:

> The attempted sale of the expectation of future patronage by former and current clients of a law office coupled with an agreement to encourage said clients to continue to patronize the purchaser of the physical assets of the office, under the facts of this case, may well be said to constitute an attempt to buy and sell the good will of

a law practice as a going business, contrary to public policy, and that the portion of the agreement purported to do so is invalid and unenforceable...

(See *O'Hara v. Ahlgren* (Ill. 1989) 537 N.E.2d 730.)

Treatment of "good will" in other contexts presents a mixed picture. For example, attorneys who are members of firms with two or more members may ethically enter into retirement agreements which may require lump sum payments that implicitly include sums for the attorney's share of the firm's "good will."

The estate of a deceased attorney may receive payments from the attorney who completes the unfinished client matters of the deceased attorney. However, in the absence of a rule like that which is being proposed, the payments are limited to the "proportion of the total compensation which fairly represents the services rendered by the deceased member" and thus do not permit an allowance for "good will."

Pursuant to agreements entered into between an attorney not in sole practice and the attorney's firm, partner or associate, the estate of the attorney may receive payments over a reasonable period of time after the attorney's death. Note that there is no requirement that the payments be related to any services the attorney performed. Thus, it appears that the payments to the estate can include the value of "good will."

In marital dissolution proceedings, the "good will" of the attorney-spouse's share in his or her law practice may be valued for the purpose of determining the community or other divisible assets.

This inconsistent treatment of "good will" resulted in a series of awkward results: the estate of a sole practitioner could not receive payment for the "good will" of the law practice, while the estate of an attorney who was a member of a law firm could; upon retirement, an attorney who was a member of a law firm could receive compensation including "good will", while the compensation received by a sole practitioner could not include "good will"; the "good will" of a sole practice may be considered an asset of the marital community for purposes of a dissolution, but could not be sold.

In order to ensure that unfinished client matters would be taken care of and to avoid losing compensation for the "good will" of the law practice, some sole practitioners entered into "quickie" partnerships prior to leaving the practice. Often, clients do no benefit from such hastily assembled arrangements.

Given this situation, the State Bar of California determined to formulate a Rule of Professional Conduct to eliminate the disparity between the treatment of the clients of sole practitioners and the clients of law firms when the attorney handling the client matter leaves the practice and to permit sole practitioners to receive compensation for the value of the "good will" of their practice.

Conclusion

Proposed Model Rule 1.17, derived from California Rule of Professional Conduct 2-300, is a consumer protection measure intended to eliminate the disparity that exists between the treatment of the clients of sole practitioners and law firms when the attorney handling the matter leaves the practice. The rule also puts sole practitioners in a financial position equal to members of firms regarding the value of the "good will" of the practice. This rule should be adopted and be made the norm throughout the country.

> Respectfully submitted,
>
> Alan I. Rothenberg
> President, State Bar of California
>
> John Krsul, Jr.
> Chair, Section of General Practice
>
> Luther Avery
> Chair, Section of Law Practice Management

February, 1990

California Rule of Professional Conduct 2-300

Rule 2-300. Sale or Purchase of a Law Practice of a Member, Living or Deceased.

All or substantially all of the law practice of a member, living or deceased, including goodwill, may be sold to another member or law firm subject to all the following conditions:

(A) Fees charged to clients shall not be increased solely by reason of such sale.
(B) If the sale contemplates the transfer of responsibility for work not yet completed or responsibility for client files or information protected by Business and Professions Code section 6068, subdivision (e), then;
   (1) if the seller is deceased, or has a conservator or other person acting in a representative capacity, prior to the transfer;
      (a) the purchaser shall cause a written notice to be given to the client stating that the interest in the law practice is being transferred to the purchaser; that the client has the right to retain other counsel; that the client may take possession of any client papers and property, as required by rule 3-700(D); and that if no response is received to the notification within 90 days of the sending of such notice, or in the event the client's rights would be prejudiced by a failure to act during that time, the purchaser may act on behalf of the client until otherwise notified by the client. Such notice shall comply with the requirements as set forth in rule 1-400(D) and any provisions relating to attorney-client fee arrangements, and
      (b) the purchaser shall obtain the written consent of the client provided that such consent shall be presumed until otherwise notified by

the client if no response is received to the notification specified in subparagraph (a) within 90 days of the date of the sending of such notification to the client's last address as shown on the records of the seller, or the client's rights would be prejudiced by a failure to act during such 90-day period.

(2) in all other circumstances, not less than 90 days prior to the transfer;

    (a) the seller shall cause a written notice to be given to the client stating that the interest in the law practice is being transferred to the purchaser; that the client has the right to retain other counsel; that the client may take possession of any client papers and property, as required by rule 3-700(D); and that if no response is received to the notification within 90 days of the sending of such notice, the purchaser may act on behalf of the client until otherwise notified by the client. Such notice shall comply with the requirements as set forth in rule 1-400(D) and any provisions relating to attorney-client fee arrangements, and

    (b) the seller shall obtain the written consent of the client prior to the transfer provided that such consent shall be presumed until otherwise notified by the client if no response is received to the notification specified in subparagraph (a) within 90 days of the date of the sending of such notification to the client's last address as shown on the records of the seller.

(C) If substitution is required by the rules of a tribunal in which a matter is pending, all steps necessary to substitute a member shall be taken.

(D) All activity of a purchaser or potential purchaser under this rule shall be subject to compliance with rules 3-300 and 3-310 where applicable.

(E) Confidential information shall not be disclosed to a non-member in connection with a sale under this rule.

(F) Admission to or retirement from a law partnership or law corporation, retirement plans and similar arrangements, or sale of tangible assets of a law practice shall not be deemed a sale or purchase under this rule.

Discussion:

Paragraph (A) is intended to prohibit the purchaser from charging the former clients of the seller a higher fee than the purchaser is charging his or her existing clients.

"All or substantially all of the law practice of a member" means, for purposes of rule 2-300, that, for example, a member may retain one or two clients who have such a longstanding personal and professional relationship with the member that transfer of those clients' files is not feasible. Conversely, rule 2-300 is not intended to authorize the sale of a law practice in a piecemeal fashion except as may be required by subparagraph (B)(1)(a) or paragraph (D).

Transfer of individual client matters, where permitted, is governed by rule 2-200. Payment of a fee to a non-lawyer broker for arranging the sale or purchase of a law practice is governed by rule 1-320.

Appendix 10-3

ABA Committee on Ethics and Professional Responsibility Op. 1384 American Bar Association

DISPOSITION OF A LAWYER'S CLOSED OR DORMANT FILES RELATING TO REPRESENTATION OF OR SERVICES TO CLIENTS

March 14, 1977

Copyright (c) 1985 by the American Bar Association

You have asked for advice concerning a lawyer's professional responsibility with respect to disposition of his files relating to representation of or services to clients after the matters have terminated and the files have been closed or retired.

Your question does not involve a lawyer's retaining lien or a lawyer's right to withhold contents of a file from a client or another lawyer representing a client.

Questions can arise as to ownership of or proprietary interests in the contents of a lawyer's file. These are usually questions of law, and this Committee has no jurisdiction to determine or give opinions on questions of law.

All lawyers are aware of the continuing economic burden of storing retired and inactive files. How to deal with the burden is primarily a question of business management, and not primarily a question of ethics or professional responsibility.

A lawyer does not have a general duty to preserve all of his files permanently. Mounting and substantial storage costs can affect the cost of legal services, and the public interest is not served by unnecessary and avoidable additions to the cost of legal services.

But clients (and former clients) reasonably expect from their lawyers that valuable and useful information in the lawyers' files, and not otherwise readily available to the clients, will not be prematurely and carelessly destroyed, to the clients' detriment.

The Code of Professional Responsibility does not set forth particular rules or guidelines on the subject. This Committee had not previously issued an opinion that deals directly with the subject.

We cannot say that there is a specific time during which a lawyer must preserve all files and beyond which he is free to destroy all files.

Good common sense should provide answers to most questions that arise.

With the foregoing limitations in mind, we suggest the considerations set forth below.

1. Unless the client consents, a lawyer should not destroy or discard items that clearly or probably belong to the client. Such items include those furnished to the lawyer by or in behalf of the client, the return of which could reasonably be expected by the client, and original documents (especially when not filed or recorded in the public records).

2. A lawyer should use care not to destroy or discard information that the lawyer knows or should know may still be necessary or useful in the assertion or defense of the client's position in a matter for which the applicable statutory limitations period has not expired.

3. A lawyer should use care not to destroy or discard information that the client may need, has not previously been given to the client, and is not otherwise readily available to the client, and which the client may reasonably except will be preserved by the lawyer.

4. In determining the length of time for retention of disposition of a file, a lawyer should exercise discretion. The nature and contents of some files may indicate a need for longer retention than do the nature and contents of other files, based upon their obvious relevance and materiality to matters that can be expected to arise.

5. A lawyer should take special care to preserve, indefinitely, accurate and complete records of the lawyer's receipt and disbursement of trust funds.

6. In disposing of a file, a lawyer should protect the confidentiality of the contents.

7. A lawyer should not destroy or dispose of a file without screening it in order to determine that consideration has been given to the matters discussed above.

8. A lawyer should preserve, perhaps for an extended time, an index or identification of the files that the lawyer has destroyed or disposed of.

ABA Informal Op. 1384

Appendix 10-4

American Bar Association Standing Committee on Ethics and Professional Responsibility: Formal Opinion 92-369, *Disposition of Deceased Sole Practitioners' Client Files and Property*

Copyright © 1992 by the American Bar Association

To fulfill the obligation to protect client files and property, a lawyer should prepare a future plan providing for the maintenance and protection of those client interests in the event of the lawyer's death. Such a plan should, at a minimum, include the designation of another lawyer who would have the authority to review client files and make determinations as to which files need immediate attention, and who would notify the clients of their lawyer's death.

A lawyer who assumes responsibility for the client files and property of a deceased lawyer must review the files carefully to determine which need immediate attention. Because the reviewing lawyer does not represent the client, only as much of the file as is needed to identify the client and to make a determination as to which files need immediate attention should be reviewed. Reasonable efforts must be made to contact all clients of the deceased lawyer to notify them of the death and to request instructions in accordance with Rule 1.15.

The Committee has been asked to render an opinion based on the following circumstances. A lawyer who has a large solo practice dies. The lawyer had hundreds of client files, some of which concern probate matters, civil litigation and real estate transactions. Most of the files are inactive, but some involve ongoing matters. The lawyer kept the active files at his office; most of the inactive files he removed from the office and kept in storage at his home. The questions posed are two:

1. What steps should lawyers take to ensure that their clients' matters will not be neglected in the event of their death?
2. What obligations do lawyers representing the estates of deceased lawyers, or appointed or otherwise responsible for review of the files of a lawyer who dies intestate, have with regard to the deceased lawyer's client files and property?

I. Sole Practitioner's obligations with regard to making plans to ensure that client matters will not be neglected in the event of the sole practitioner's death

The death of a sole practitioner could have serious effects on the sole practitioner's clients. See Program: Preparing for and Dealing with the Consequences of the Death of a Sole Practitioner, prepared by the ABA General Practice Section, Sole Practitioners and Small Law Firms Committee, August 7, 1986. Important client matters, such as court dates, statutes of limitations, or document filings, could be neglected until the clients discover that their lawyer has died. As a precaution to safeguard client interests, the sole practitioner should have a plan in place that will ensure insofar as is reasonably practicable that client matters will not be neglected in the event of the sole practitioner's death.

Model Rules of Professional Conduct 1.1 (Competence) and 1.3 (Diligence) are relevant to this issue, and read in pertinent part:

Rule 1.1 Competence

A lawyer shall provide competent representation to a client. Competent representation requires the legal knowledge, skill, thoroughness and preparation reasonably necessary for the representation.

Rule 1.3 Diligence

A lawyer shall act with reasonable diligence and promptness in representing a client.

Furthermore, the Comment to Rule 1.3 states in relevant part:

A client's interests often can be adversely affected by the passage of time or the change of conditions; in extreme instances, as when a lawyer overlooks a statute of limitations, the client's legal position may be destroyed. Even when the client's interests are not affected in substance, however, unreasonable delay can cause a client needless anxiety....

According to Rule 1.1, competence includes "preparation necessary for the representation," which when read in conjunction with Rule 1.3 would indicate that a lawyer should diligently prepare for the client's representation. Although representation should terminate when the attorney is no longer able to adequately represent the client,[1] the lawyer's fiduciary obligations of loyalty and confidentiality continue beyond the termination of the agency relationship.[2]

Lawyers have a fiduciary duty to inform their clients in the event of their partnership's dissolution.[3] A sole practitioner would seem to have a similar duty to ensure that his or her clients are so informed in the event of the sole practitioner's dissolution caused by the sole practitioner's death. Because a deceased lawyer cannot very well inform anyone of his or her death, preparation of a future plan is the reasonable means to preserve these obligations. Thus, the lawyer ought to have a plan in place which would protect the clients' interests in the event of the lawyer's death.[4]

Some jurisdictions, operating under the Model Code of Professional Responsibility, have found lawyers to have violated DR6-101(A)(3) when the attorneys have neglected client matters by reason of ill-health, attempted retirement, or personal problems.[5] The same problems are clearly presented by the attorney's death, thus suggesting that a lawyer who died without a plan for the maintenance of his or her client files would be guilty of neglect. Such a result is also consistent with two of the three justifications for lawyer discipline.[6] Sanctioning of lawyers who had inadequately prepared to protect

---

[1] See Model Rule of Professional Conduct 1.16 ("... a lawyer shall not represent a client or, where representation has commenced, shall withdraw from the representation of the client if: ... (2) the lawyer's physical or mental condition materially impairs the lawyer's ability to represent the client....")

[2] See Murphy v. Riggs, 213 N.W. 110 (Mich.1927) (fiduciary obligations of loyalty and confidentiality continue after agency relationship concluded); Eoff v. Irvine, 18 S.W. 907 (Mo.1892) (same).

[3] See Vollgraff v. Block, 458 N.Y.S.2d 437 (Sup.Ct.1982) (breach of fiduciary duty if partnership's clients not advised of dissolution of partnership). A state bar association is considering creating an "archive form"—indicating the location of client files—which lawyers would complete and file with the state bar association in the event they terminate or merge their practice, thus enabling clients to locate their files. See ABA ETHICSearch, September 1992 Report. Such a form would be consistent with the duty discussed in Vollgraff, as simply informing a client of a firm's dissolution without telling the client where the client's files are located would be tantamount to saying "your files are no longer here."

[4] The Fla.Bar, Professional Ethics Comm., Op. 81-8(M) (Undated) discussed the obligations of a lawyer who was terminally ill with regard to client files:

> After diligent attempt is made to contact all clients whose files he holds, a lawyer anticipating termination of his practice by death should dispose of all files according to his client's instructions. The files of those clients who do not respond should be individually reviewed by the lawyer and destroyed only if no important papers belonging to the clients are in the files. Important documents should be indexed and placed in storage or turned over to any lawyer who assumes control of his active files. In any event, the files may not be automatically destroyed after 90 days.

[5] See In re Jamieson, 658 P.2d 1244 (Wash.1983) (neglect due to ill-health and attempted retirement); In Re Whitlock, 441 A.2d 989 (D.C.App.1982) (neglect due to poor health, marital difficulties and heavy caseload); Committee on Legal Ethics of West Virginia State Bar v. Smith, 194 S.E.2d 665 (W.Va.1973) (neglect due to illness and personal problems).

[6] See In Re Moynihan, 643 P.2d 439 (Wash.1982) (three objectives of lawyer disciplinary action are to prevent recurrence, to discourage similar conduct on the part of other lawyers, and to restore public confidence in the bar).

their clients in the event of their death would tend to dissuade future acts by other lawyers, and it would help to restore public confidence in the bar.[7]

Although there is no specifically applicable requirement of the rules of ethics, it is fairly to be inferred from the pertinent rules that lawyers should make arrangements for their client files to be maintained in the event of their own death. Such a plan should at a minimum include the designation of another lawyer who would have the authority to look over the sole practitioner's files and make determinations as to which files needed immediate attention, and provide for notification to the sole practitioner's clients of their lawyer's death.[8]

II. Duties of lawyer who assumes responsibility for deceased lawyer's client files

This brings us to the second question, namely the ethical obligations of the lawyer who assumes responsibility for the client files and property of the deceased lawyer. Issues commonly confronting the lawyer in this situation involve the nature of the lawyer's duty to inspect client files, the need to protect client confidences and the length of time the lawyer should keep the client files in the event that the lawyer is unable to locate certain clients of the deceased lawyer.

At the outset, the Committee notes that several states' rules of civil procedure make provision for court appointment of lawyers to take responsibility for a deceased lawyer's client files and property.[9] Since the lawyer's duties under these

---

[7] Obviously, sanctions would have no deterrent effect on deceased lawyers.

[8] Although the designation of another lawyer to assume responsibility for a deceased lawyer's client files would seem to raise issues of client confidentiality, in that a lawyer outside the lawyer-client relationship would have access to confidential client information, it is reasonable to read Rule 1.6 as authorizing such disclosure. Model Rule of Professional Conduct 1.6(a) ("A lawyer shall not reveal information relating to representation of a client ... except for disclosures that are impliedly authorized in order to carry out the representation.") Reasonable clients would likely not object to, but rather approve of, efforts to ensure that their interests are safeguarded.

[9] See, e.g., Illinois Supreme Court Rule 776, Appointment of Receiver in Certain Cases:

Appointment of Receiver. When it comes to the attention of the circuit court in any judicial circuit from any source that a lawyer in the circuit is unable properly to discharge his responsibilities to his clients due to disability, disappearance or death, and that no partner, associate, executor or other responsible party capable of conducting that lawyer's affairs is known to exist, then, upon such showing of the presiding judge in the judicial circuit in which the lawyer maintained his practice, or the supreme court, may appoint an attorney from the same judicial circuit to perform certain duties hereafter enumerated ...

Duties of Receiver. As expeditiously as possible, the receiver shall take custody of and make an inventory of the lawyer's files, notify the lawyer's clients in all pending cases as to the lawyer's disability, or inability to continue legal representation, and recommend prompt substitution of attorneys, take appropriate steps to sequester client funds of the lawyer, and to take whatever other action is indicated to protect the interests of the attorney, his clients or other affected parties.

statutes constitute questions of law, the Committee cannot offer guidance as to how to interpret them.[10]

A. Duty to inspect files

Many state and local bar associations have explored the issues presented when a lawyer assumes responsibility for a deceased lawyer's client files.[11] The ABA Model Rules for Lawyer Disciplinary Enforcement also address some aspects of the question.[12] A lawyer who assumes such responsibility must review the client files carefully to determine which files need immediate attention; failure to do so would leave the clients in the same position as if their attorney died without any plan to protect their interests. The lawyer should also contact all clients of the deceased lawyer to notify them of the death of their lawyer and to request instructions, in accordance with Rule 1.15.[13] Because the reviewing lawyer does not represent the clients, he or she should review only as much of the file as is needed to identify the client and to make a determination as to which files need immediate attention.[14]

---

[10] Lawyers who act as administrators of estates have fiduciary duties to all those who have an interest in it, such as beneficiaries and creditors. Questions involving the lawyer's fiduciary responsibility to the estate of a deceased lawyer are also questions of law that this Committee cannot address. See, e.g., In Re Estate of Halas, 512 N.E.2d 1276 (Ill.1987); Aksomitas v. Aksomitas, 529 A.2d 1314 (Conn.1987).

[11] See, e.g., Md. State Bar Ass'n, Inc., Comm. on Ethics, Op. 89-58 (1989); State Bar of Wis., Comm. on Professional Ethics, Op. E-87-9 (1987); Miss.State Bar, Ethics Comm., Op. 114 (1986); N.C. State Bar Ass'n, Ethics Comm., Op. 16 (1986); Ala. State Bar, Disciplinary Comm'n., Op. 83-155 (1983); Bar Ass'n of Nassau County (N.Y.), Comm. on Professional Ethics, Ops. 89-43 and 89-23 (1989); Ore.State Bar, Ethics Comm., Op. 1991-129 (1991).

[12] ABA Model Rules for Lawyer Disciplinary Enforcement (1989), Rule 28 states in relevant part:

APPOINTMENT OF COUNSEL TO PROTECT CLIENTS' INTERESTS WHEN RESPONDENT IS TRANSFERRED TO DISABILITY INACTIVE STATUS, SUSPENDED, DISBARRED, DISAPPEARS, OR DIES. A. Inventory of Lawyer Files. If a respondent has been transferred to disability inactive status, or has disappeared or died, or has been suspended or disbarred and there is evidence that he or she has not complied with Rule 27, and no partner, executor or other responsible party capable of conducting the respondent's affairs is known to exist, the presiding judge in the judicial district in which the respondent maintained a practice, upon proper proof of fact, shall appoint a lawyer or lawyers to inventory the files of the respondent, and to take such action as seems indicated to protect the interests of the respondent and his or her clients.

B. Protection for Records Subject to Inventory. Any lawyer so appointed shall not be permitted to disclose and information contained in any files inventories without the consent of the client to whom the file relates, except as necessary to carry out the order of the court which appointed the lawyer to make the inventory.

[13] Model Rule of Professional Conduct 1.15(b) ("Upon receiving funds or other property in which a client or third person has an interest, a lawyer shall promptly notify the client or third person.")

[14] Again, while issues of client confidentiality would appear to be raised here, a reasonable reading of Rule 1.6 suggests that any disclosure of confidential information to the reviewing attorney would be impliedly authorized in the representation. See note 8, supra.

B. Duty to maintain client files and property

Questions also arise as to how long the lawyer who assumes responsibility for the deceased lawyer's client files should keep the files for those clients he or she is unable to locate. ABA Informal Opinion 1384 (1977) provides general guidance in this area. We believe that the principles set out in that opinion are applicable to the instant question. Informal Opinion 1384 states as follows:

> *A lawyer does not have a general duty to preserve all of his files permanently. Mounting and substantial storage costs can affect the cost of legal services, and the public interest is not served by unnecessary and avoidable additions to the cost of legal services.*

But clients (and former clients) reasonably expect from their lawyers that valuable and useful information in the lawyers' files, and not otherwise readily available to the clients, will not be prematurely and carelessly destroyed to the clients' detriment.

Informal Opinion 1384 then lists eight guidelines that lawyers should follow when deciding whether to discard old client files. One of these guidelines states that a lawyer should not "destroy or discard items that clearly or probably belong to the client. Such items include those furnished to the lawyer by or in behalf of the client, and original documents." Another suggests that a lawyer should not "destroy or discard information that the lawyer knows or should know may still be necessary or useful in the assertion or defense of the client's position in a matter for which the applicable statutory limitations period has not expired."

There is no simple answer to this question. Each file must be evaluated separately. Reasonable efforts must be made to contact the clients and inform them that their lawyer has died, such as mailing letters to the last known address of the clients explaining that their lawyer has died and requesting instructions.[15]

Finally, questions arise with regard to unclaimed funds in the deceased lawyer's client trust account. In this situation, reasonable efforts must be made to contact the clients. If this fails, then the lawyer should maintain the funds in the trust account. Whether the lawyer should follow the procedures as outlined in the applicable Disposition of Unclaimed Property Act that is in effect in the lawyer's state jurisdiction is a question of law that this Committee cannot address.[16]

---

[15] Responding to a recent inquiry, the Committee on Professional Ethics of the Bar Association of Nassau County suggested that an attorney assuming responsibility for a deceased attorney's client files has an ethical obligation to treat the assumed files as his or her own. Bar Ass'n of Nassau County (N.Y.), Comm. on Professional Ethics, Op. 92-27 (1992).

[16] There are at least 27 state and local bar opinions that discuss a lawyer's obligations when the lawyer cannot locate clients who have funds in lawyer trust accounts. See, e.g., State Bar of S.D., Ethics Comm., Op. 91-20 (1991); State Bar of Ariz., Comm. on Rules of Professional Conduct, Op. 90-11 (1990); R.I.Sup.Ct., Ethics Advisory Panel, Op. 90-21 (1990); Alaska Bar Ass'n, Ethics Comm., Op. 90-3 (1990); Md.State Bar Ass'n, Inc., Comm. on Ethics, Op. 90-25 (1990); Bar Ass'n of Nassau County (N.Y.), Comm. on Professional Ethics, Op. 89 (1990).

Chapter 11

Preservation of Files: To Destroy or Not to Destroy

by Jay G Foonberg*

I. Introduction

The purpose of this chapter is to encourage the reader to begin the process of file destruction at the earliest possible opportunity, from womb to tomb, from the beginning of a practice to the closing of a practice. File maintenance, closing, and destruction should be part of an in-place system in the law practice of every lawyer.

Key Points

- File management is an ongoing process that, if successfully maintained, enhances the value of and eases the transitions of a law practice.
- A file should be opened and closed with the client understanding that eventual file disposal or destruction is part of the process.
- The definition of "the file" varies greatly from jurisdiction to jurisdiction and may include all information concerning the case, including all electronic data.
- A file should be considered "closed" when all necessary work has been done, all fees and costs paid, and the contents will no longer be needed for future work by the firm.
- The rules for file destruction are state-specific and case-type specific. No general rule is applicable to all jurisdictions or type of matter, nor necessarily is there any uniformity within a single jurisdiction.

II. File Maintenance, Preservation, and Destruction

File destruction and file preservation are, of course, opposite sides of the same coin. For purposes of this chapter, the file process will be divided into three phases:

1. The opening of a file. A file should be opened, at the very latest, when facts are obtained and/or professional responsibility commences.

---

[*] © 2007, Jay G Foonberg. All rights reserved. Reprinted with permission of the author.

2. The closing of a file. A file should be "closed" when there is nothing more to be done on that matter. If there are any unpaid fees, the file should not be closed until a decision has been made to give up the claim for fees or until collection efforts are abandoned. If the file will require future work but not current work, it should be kept open.

3. The destruction of the file. The file should be destroyed as soon as possible after the closing of the file—at the very latest, on the closing of the file plus a period of time as required by law to comply with local rules or statutes of limitations, if any.

A file should be opened and closed with the client's understanding that eventual file disposal or destruction is part of the process. The proper closing of an active file will trigger and facilitate the subsequent destruction of the file.

A. Why Destroy the File?

A good file destruction system presents a win-win opportunity both for the law firm and the client as well as the successors in interest to the lawyer, the firm, and the client. Possession of, and responsibility for, a closed file presents a storage, retrieval, and space occupancy problem for an active lawyer.

> Without a file closing and destruction system in place, the lawyer or firm becomes a permanent unpaid warehouse service or bailee for the file.

Storage of old files costs money for rental space on an ongoing basis. An old file can cost many dollars in rental occupancy costs if it sits long enough.

A closed file also may present the problem of locating the client or making other disposition should the lawyer decide to sell the practice or close the practice, and it could present an even bigger problem for those who must close or transfer the practice of a deceased or disabled lawyer—the family or executors of a deceased or disabled lawyer won't have the lawyer's memory to help them.

File destruction should begin long before file storage space becomes a problem or before a lawyer dies or a decision is made to close the office for any reason, especially retirement.

B. Old Files, New Lawyers

Many states have a system of court-appointed receiverships to take possession of the client files and liquidate the practice if the lawyer is dead, disappeared, or incompetent. Some bar associations have volunteer committees to take over and liquidate the practice of a deceased, incompetent, or disappeared attorney. Some states have a successor attorney requirement wherein every lawyer is supposed to have a successor lawyer to assume the practice if the first lawyer becomes disabled. A lawyer who accepts the position of being a successor lawyer should insist on file destruction as a precondition of remaining a successor lawyer.

III. Defining "The File"

The definition of "the file" varies greatly from jurisdiction to jurisdiction. We lawyers are accustomed to thinking of "the file" as being the paper contents with local rules variations distinguishing between:

- Paper entirely in the handwriting of the lawyer;
- Paper that has been mechanically printed or typed and which has handwritten notations of the lawyer on the paper;
- Paper containing the results of legal research;
- Paper prepared by or for the lawyer containing the lawyer's "work product;" and
- Correspondence directed to the attorney or firm, or to or from a succession lawyer.

It comes as a shock to some lawyers (it did to me) that the definition of "the file" includes all information concerning the case, including all electronic data. Thus, when a client wants "his file" or the lawyer wants to destroy the "the file," the lawyer may have to do a complete search on the current and former computer hard drives and backups in order to first find out what information he or she has to either give to the client or destroy.

IV. Closing the File

A file should be considered "closed" when all necessary work has been done, all fees and costs paid, and the contents will no longer be needed for future work by the firm.

You should go through the physical file page by page, piece by piece, to look for at least three specific types of items to be removed before closing the file.

1. Items that are the property of the client. Common items would include deeds; mortgages; birth, marriage, and death certificates; citizenship certificates; photography; unused trial exhibits; any document with an original signature; or any other item of personal property belonging to the client.
2. Items that have been misfiled and belong in another client's file.
3. Multiple copies of documents that are no longer needed.

Many firms purge electronic data that is no longer needed relative to the matter, such as electronic computer documents and billings, by scanning the data and transferring it onto a disk or other storage medium to get it out of the computer and into the closed file.

A. Implied Consent to Destruction

When a file is closed, I recommend an "implied consent" to destruction paragraph in the file closing letter or even a separate letter to the client. (See the "Implied Consent to Destruction Letter" in the Forms, Guidelines, and Checklists section of this chapter on page 177.)

Note that this letter refers to a new numbering system for the file, which reflects the month, year, and date when the file was closed (e.g., 2007 12-12). The new numbering system will facilitate the file destruction process—all of the files closed in a given year should be stored together and can be destroyed in accordance with your local rules.

It is my opinion that a client who has received this letter and has taken no further action for 30 days has implicitly consented to the new closed file system, including the "destruction without further notice" provision. It is preferable, but not normally required, for the client to sign and return a copy of the letter. You might want to check this with your bar counsel.

B. Disposal of Files of Unlocatable Clients

When a file is closed, the lawyer normally has a then-current address for the client. The longer a lawyer waits to contact the client, the more difficult it is to find the client or determine the client's successors in interest. Having to locate long-disappeared clients to get rid of their files is the nightmare of every lawyer. Clients change residences and names, making it difficult or impossible to locate them. In some cases the "client" no longer exists owing to death or bankruptcy or other form of dissolution. There may or may not be a locatable successor in interest, or the successor may no longer be locatable. This leaves the lawyer with client files and nowhere to send them.

The lawyer or successor lawyer has to make "reasonable" efforts to find the missing client. What constitutes "reasonable" is of course a question of fact under the circumstances. Internet searches or Google or other search engines are a good way to start. Sending mail to the last known address and saving the returned letters as proof that the client is unlocatable is also a good way to start. You should consider photocopying the client's driver's license at the beginning of the case or as soon as is convenient (assuming photocopying is legal). Clients normally notify license agencies of a new address when they move or renew their license. You can explain to the client that making a copy could be helpful in preventing identity theft should another person claim to be the client. Sending letters to all contacts in the client file can be helpful. Depending on the economics involved, it may be worthwhile to hire a professional skip tracer or search organization. All the energy and money expended on these methods could probably be avoided by simply closing the file with an "implied consent" letter.

Some states have a system allowing a lawyer or executor to open a court file by filing a pleading, paying the filing fee, and then depositing the client documents with the court as exhibits that don't get returned. This system is sometimes available only for wills and trusts and other financially operative documents. Where such a system exists, it is available for all lawyers admitted to practice in a specific court. This is a system that can easily overload the court, which might have to receive many boxes of files for a single filing, and for that reason often is not advertised.

V. General Observations Concerning File Destruction

The rules for file destruction are state-specific and case-type specific. There is no general rule applicable to all jurisdictions or type of matter, nor necessarily any uniformity within a single jurisdiction.

Cases involving minors, trust account transactions, guardianships, bonded attorney performance, insolvency, bankruptcy, probate, or criminal law may have special rules.

When no specific guidance is given in the rules, a good starting point would be to determine the statute of limitations for conversion of personal property or breach of written contract. This might be the period in which a client could sue for converting his or her file. This might or might not be the same period as the rules would have provided, had there been rules for breaching your written fee agreement.

Some lawyers destroy the paper file and preserve a digital copy of the contents by scanning or other process. These lawyers take a middle approach of destroying the paper file to reduce storage costs and replace the paper file with an on-premises digital file. I see nothing wrong with converting a file from paper to digital to reduce on-premises storage costs, but it is my opinion that the file has not yet been destroyed and can still be obtained by subpoena or court order, in electronic form as well as in paper form.

There is a further problem of being able to read digital format information when the software or hardware needed to do so no longer exists. One can consider the plight of those lawyers who stored files on mag cards, 8-inch floppies, 5-inch floppies, 3-inch floppies, analog tapes, or other systems requiring programs or equipment no longer in existence to read the information electronically stored.

VI. Destroying the File

There are several ways to destroy a file, depending on the risks a lawyer wishes to take and the costs involved.

1. **Dump the file in the office trash.** This may be cheap but should never be done. The discarded file probably has lost all attorney-client privilege and becomes a finders-keepers situation. Once you put the file into a trash bin, you probably lose all rights of ownership. I recommend against doing this.
2. **Shred the file yourself.** Shredding is the most common method of proper file destruction. The U.S. Department of Defense issues standards for the size of the shredded material. You should insist on a shredder that meets these standards. The vendor of the shredder should be able to provide you with current data. <u>Get a powerful shredder that will accept and shred paper clips, cardboard, etc., to avoid spending time clearing jams in the shredder.</u> The files marked for destruction should be accumulated and all shredded at the same time by the lowest-paid person available. The shredded file(s) can then safely be put into the office trash system.

3. <u>Hire door-to-door shredders.</u> This is an <u>expensive</u> way to shred files on-site. Vendors offering this service typically operate from a truck that contains a shredder. They drive to your office and grind the files in the truck while parked outside your building. You will be invited to stand in the truck and watch your files being shredded so you can feel comfortable that they were, in fact, shredded. The shredder company may give you a certificate attesting to what was shredded.

4. <u>Sell your files to be destroyed for recycling.</u> Depending on the going prices for paper, a file storage company may buy your old files for the value of the scrap paper. Paper used in offices is generally higher quality and can bring some good money into the firm's income. The company pays you a set amount per banker's box of files and then hauls them away. The files are pulled apart on a conveyer belt to get rid of metal and other objects that are not supposed to be included in the recycled paper. The paper is then pulped into mush and added to the new paper being prepared. I personally have accompanied my files through this destruction process and feel comfortable that client confidences have not been violated. I recommend that you personally accompany some files through this system.

A. Non-Client Files

Although this chapter concerns itself primarily with the destruction of client files, there are other files, some client related and some not, that also must be destroyed.

- Financial information no longer needed should be destroyed as soon as possible. Financial information containing client identity (e.g., old client billing or time records) must be destroyed in such a way that client identity is not disclosed.
- Other financial records with expired income tax or other statute of limitations should be gotten rid of as well.
- Old bank records and canceled checks should be given special attention both to protect client identity and to prevent identity theft.
- <u>Trust account records in some jurisdictions should never be destroyed.</u>

VII. Conclusion

File destruction should begin long before file storage space becomes a problem or before a lawyer dies or a decision is made to close the office for any reason, especially retirement. Active control over one's files is sound management and a policy that controls the information coming into your firm from creation to destruction will enhance the value of your practice—and ease the inevitable transitions.

Forms, Guidelines, and Checklists

A. Implied Consent to Destruction Letter

A. Implied Consent to Destruction Letter

Dear [Client name]:

We have concluded our services in the matter of [describe matter]. All legal work has been done and all your fees and costs have been paid.

We thank you for the opportunity to have been of service: We are including a questionnaire to enable you to express your opinion of our services.

We have examined your file and we do not now have in our possession any original documents or items that belong to you. If you are aware of anything we may have that you want, please let us know immediately so that we may send it to you. We have previously sent to you [or, as appropriate, the letter can alternatively state, "We are sending under separate cover" or "We are enclosing"]: _____. [describe materials]

We have endeavored to send you copies of everything that has happened on your matter and accordingly you have a file that duplicates our file. Please note that we have renumbered your file to indicate the month and year in which it was closed and are moving the file to our closed file storage area where it may be destroyed without further notice to you. Retrieval of the closed file or its contents prior to its destruction may require delay as well as a waiting period and charges for the service.

Again, please let us know if there is anything that you want from the file. If we do not hear from you within 30 days, we shall assume you have anything you might want or need and that you understand our closing, retrieval, and destruction system.

A new file number has been assigned to this one file only. The new file number is [2007 12-12].

It would be appreciated if you would sign a copy of this letter acknowledging its receipt and your new file number of [2007 12-12].

Very truly yours,

_____
[Your name]

_____
[Client name]

Enclosure: Client satisfaction survey card
 Copy of this letter
 Self-addressed postage-paid envelope

Further Reading

Gibson, K. William. *Flying Solo: A Survival Guide for the Solo and Small Firm Lawyer,* 4e. Chicago, Il: American Bar Association Law Practice Management Section, 2005.

Pennsylvania Bar Institute. *Drafting a Document Creation, Retention & Destruction Policy for Clients and Law Firms.* Mechanicsburg, PA: Pennsylvania Bar Institute, 2007.

Solo & Small Firm Practice Retreat, Pennsylvania Bar Institute, and Pennsylvania Bar Association, Solo and Small Firm Practice Section. *Eighth Annual Solo & Small Firm Practice Retreat,* 8e. Mechanicsburg, Pennsylvania: Pennsylvania Bar Institute, 2001.

Chapter 12

Ending Client and Employee Relationships

by Harold G. Wren and James H. Wren, II

I. Introduction

There are as many reasons to close a law practice as there are persons desiring to do so. Chapter 8 provided a checklist of 68 steps to be taken to close a practice successfully. Chapters 9, 10, and 11 dealt with the problems of your business responsibilities, what to do with existing client files, and ethics and notification requirements. We now turn to the problem of ending client and employee relationships. This chapter assumes that you are a solo practitioner or the survivor of a small law firm, and that you must shut down the operations of the firm. If you are a lawyer practicing in a large firm or as a partner in an operation with as few as two principals, you are blessed with a situation where you can simply turn over your portion of the practice to others. Or, if your firm must be closed by virtue of your untimely death, your personal representative will carry out the responsibilities of closing the practice. Whatever the case may be, you or your representative will have to end relationships with the firm's clients and employees.

> ### *Key Points*
> - The solo practitioner or small firm has different relationships and possibly greater ethical responsibilities to employees than larger firms do.
> - Making an agreement whereby an "assisting lawyers" is given full power to close the law office of you, the "planning lawyer," can ease a transition.
> - Not purging files can vastly complicate a career change as well as subject you to disciplinary action.
> - If you are in a jurisdiction that does not recognize the sale of a practice, including goodwill, you will have to dispose of furniture, office equipment, law books, file cabinets, etc.
> - Several anecdotal situations provided in this chapter illustrate how the reasons behind closing a firm or leaving a practice change the nature of the exit strategy.

II. Ending Relationships with Employees

Before you can end your relationships with various employees in your law practice, it will be necessary for you to have them clear any responsibilities that they might have in connection with the closing of your practice. Consider the employees who have contributed to your successful practice over the years. Each of them will have responsibilities to be carried out before the practice is closed. Equally important, however, is the fact that you have a moral—if not legal—responsibility to make sure that each employee will be able to find a new position or retire happily. The following are some of the more important employees with whom you may have had a relationship over the years.

A. The Long-Time Secretary

It is not easy to bring to an end a long-time association with a secretary who has served you well. You should begin planning for your closing at least six months ahead of the actual time you will shut down. If your secretary is planning to retire at about the same time that you close your practice, you may coordinate your respective changes in life style. If she[1] is not yet ready to retire, you may have a moral obligation to see that she is financially secure and reasonably content with her new role. If she is older, she may have some difficulty finding a new position.

Before she leaves your employment, there are a number of areas where the secretary can help you with the closing of your practice. One important example is the handling of your active and closed files. First of all, you will close as many active files as possible. With your secretary's help, you will then write to clients with active files remaining, explaining that you can no longer represent them and that they need to retain another lawyer. Your secretary can coordinate the pickup of your files by your clients or their transfer to a new lawyer and the appropriate realeases that might accompany those tasks.

In time, you and your secretary will have dealt with the many problems involving your files, and she will have completed her many duties. Your obligation to her at this point is to make sure that she will be financially secure and reasonably content with her new status as either a retiree or as an employee in a new firm.

B. The Older Employee

Severing the employer-employee relationship with the older employee requires that you have previously taken care of such matters as Social Security and health care. If you have planned the conduct of your practice so as to care for those in your employ, a pension program to supplement their Society Security will be available to them. Assist them by making sure that an individual retirement account (IRA) has been established

---

[1] In the interest of a simpler narrative, we shall use female pronouns for all employees.

in this connection. Make sure that an appropriate healthcare program is available for anyone who leaves your employ.

C. The High-Tech Employee

One employee that has undoubtedly served you well is the electronic technician who has taken care of all your electronic equipment, including computers, i-Pods, BlackBerrys, cell phones, and the like. Such a valued employee likely will have no problem finding new employment, and you probably will not need to concern yourself with her employability. Before she departs, however, make sure that you have preserved the electronic records of your practice. These include the hard drive of your computer and back-up discs for important records. If these records are carefully stored, you may find that you can destroy some hard copy files that are no longer necessary.

D. The Paralegal

As with the high-tech employee, the departure of a paralegal may cause you some concern. Make sure that the documents she has prepared are carefully indexed and readily accessible. She, too, is probably readily employable, but you should assist her in finding a new position where her expertise can be put to good use. Make sure that any pension plan or health plan is portable so that she will continue these important benefits with her new employer.

E. The Bookkeeper

Since the bookkeeper is often in charge of the financial affairs of a small law firm or solo practice, you may find that she is of great importance in the closing of your law practice. She may be the person who is most familiar with the insurance programs of your firm. She will also determine what tax returns must be filed in connection with the closing. The bookkeeper will be familiar with all bank accounts and safe deposit boxes and will know the location of a variety of insurance policies, including malpractice, workers' compensation, automobile, medical, life, and fire and casualty. She should make a schedule of all these policies, with a description of their coverages and premiums. All insurance policies should be reviewed, and determinations made as to whether they should be continued or cancelled in light of the closing of the practice. As with your other employees, assist your bookkeeper in obtaining new employment.

F. The Associate

If you have been associated in the practice of law with another lawyer-employee and she has acquired sufficient knowledge and experience in the practice, you may find that you can successfully sell the practice to her. If you are in a jurisdiction that does not permit the sale of a practice, including goodwill, you may find that the young associate will be interested in purchasing your furniture, law books, and the like. If you find that it is not feasible to transfer the practice, you should assist the young associate in finding employment with another law firm.

G. The Investigator

Small law firms or solo practitioners may have an investigator in their employ. It may be more difficult for such an employee to find similar employment than for some of your other employees, which is why you should do all you can to assist her. Truly competent investigators are often hard to find, and you may know of another law office that could use the investigator's services.

H. Problems Common to All Your Employees

In most of the situations cited above, you should do everything you can to help the employee shift into new employment with as few problems as possible. Offer to serve as a reference as your employees find new employment and provide them your new contact information. Write letters of recommendation on their behalf and use your connections to alert them to any openings in other law firms. In addition, make sure that your employee's retirement benefits are portable. Similarly, arrange for the transfer of health benefits to the new employer. Although this may seem difficult for a small firm or solo practitioner, insurance agencies can assist you in establishing retirement and health programs.

III. Ending Relationships with Clients

Ending your relationship with clients is more difficult than ending your employee relationships.

A. Using an Assisting Lawyer

Many clients will feel uncomfortable going to another lawyer after being associated with you for a long period of years. Yet, if you are to be successful in closing your practice, you should have another lawyer stand in for you and serve your clients to the best of her ability. You may resolve this problem by making an agreement whereby an "assisting lawyer" is given full power to close the law office of you, the "planning lawyer." The Oregon State Bar has suggested a form for a contract between two such lawyers, available at Appendix 12-1, *infra*.

B. Notifying Your Clients

Chapter 10 outlined your ethical responsibilities and how you should notify your clients that you are closing your practice. Despite your efforts to cut down on the number of clients, many clients will want *your* counsel, and no one else's. Each of your clients should receive a letter in which you diplomatically make it clear that you will no longer be able to represent them. In such a letter, you might list at least three lawyers who would be willing to serve as their counsel. Inform them of any time limitations on their cases and where they may pick up their files. Give them a deadline for picking up their files, or alternatively, have them sign an authorization to release their files to a new lawyer.

Obtain permission from your clients to destroy their closed files after a substantial time period, say, 10 years.[2] You may have to keep some files (e.g., a file involving a long-term trust that may remain active for some years) that could become important sometime in the future.

Appendix 12-2 is a sample letter notifying clients that you are closing your practice. Appendix 12-3 is a sample transfer of client file authorization form, and Appendix 12-4 is a sample acknowledgement of receipt of file. Each document should be customized to your personal situation and jurisdiction.

IV. Other Specific Client Communication Issues: Real Life Examples

A. Relocating Your Practice

A common reason for closing your practice is to relocate to another jurisdiction, whether for business or for personal reasons. Diane Hornstein practiced solo for eighteen years in Connecticut. Although Hornstein had a satisfying practice in Bridgeport, she missed being with her children and grandchildren who had moved to Illinois. When her husband decided to close his dentistry practice, they decided to relocate to Buffalo Grove, Illinois.

Hornstein enjoyed her practice in Connecticut, where she shared office space with four to six other lawyers. She described her practice as client-friendly and not intimidating. Her caseload consisted of a variety of types, including personal injury, juveniles, real estate closings, and wills. Many of her clients knew the other lawyers with whom she shared office space, and she listed them as possible future counsel in her notification letter to clients.

According to Hornstein, the key to a successful closing is advance planning. She recommends that you start preparing your clients for your departure at least *one year* in advance, and that you list at least three alternative lawyers in your letter to your clients. She further recommends that you shred all files older then ten years, except for those that might raise questions in the future, such as those involving trusts or minors.

B. Representing a Deceased or Disabled Lawyer

Some of the most difficult problems arising from the closing of a practice center around the situation where you, as the personal representative or assuming lawyer, must close the practice of a deceased or disabled lawyer. Bill Shapiro faced this problem after the

---

[2] For a detailed discussion of the preservation of files, see Chapter 11.

death of his father, Isadore Shapiro, who had maintained a solo practice for more than seventy years in Newburgh, New York. Shapiro described the difficult task of tracing the beneficiaries of 400 original wills found in his father's files:

> I was able to locate the testator or establish his or her death for all but 20 of the approximately 400 wills I found among the office papers; . . . virtually all these wills were originals, not copies. . . . The few files other than wills did not pose any special problems. In addition, there were a substantial number of closed files stored in my father's house.[3]

Before his father's house was sold in July 2002, Shapiro arranged for the destruction of his father's closed files, after verifying the contents and establishing a closing date for each file. He described that work as follows:

> I created a four-part index of these files, employing the categories my father had established, namely: General Files, Estates, Negligence and Family Files. . . . The closed files, which measured some 75 shelf-feet, were then packed in 43 cartons. . . . I transported the cartons of closed files to the Hudson Baylor Corporation, a waste-recycling firm located in Newburgh, where I witnessed the secure destruction (shredding) of the files.[4]

One cannot help but admire the dedication of Shapiro, who was determined to make certain that his father's lifelong practice was brought to a proper conclusion. His experience illustrates the importance of keeping an organized filing system. Your employees can be charged with these types of tasks prior to the closing of your practice.

C. Moving from the Bar to the Bench

Eighty percent of law practice in our nation is handled by small firms or solo practitioners. When a lawyer from this group is elected or appointed to the bench, the problems regarding the treatment of clients become critical.

1. Judge Chris Graham Many lawyers aspire to become members of the judiciary, whether by way of election or by appointment. Chris Graham went down that road when he accepted a gubernatorial appointment as an administrative law judge (ALJ) in the Missouri Department of Transportation and, later, a federal ALJ in the Office of Hearings and Appeals of the Department of Defense. In his role as a federal ALJ, Judge Graham handles a variety of industrial cases arising from government contracts with defense industries. He also handles a substantial number of individuals, both military and civilian, where security clearances are involved. For example, he might have to rule whether an applicant employed by a defense contractor who has relatives in the People's Republic of China should be granted a top level security clearance. The judge's concerns today are far different from his practice in Missouri.

---

[3] Letter of William A. Shapiro, Esq. to the authors, dated January 18, 2007.
[4] Exhibit A to the Affidavit of William A. Shapiro, Esq., dated March 6, 2003, on file with the authors.

Knowing that his appointment was coming, Graham began to ratchet down his practice several months before he took office. Having practiced for 25 years with his father, he alerted his clients to his changed status and arranged for tail insurance for any errors and omissions he may have made in practice.

After Judge Graham left the practice, his father kept their general practice office open for two more years, scaling back the firm's practice. The judge's mother passed away in 1998, and his father died two years later. The closing of his father's practice was not particularly difficult, because his father had to a large extent already made arrangements with clients to seek other counsel. One result of the closing was particularly serendipitous: His father's secretary of 40 years had handled a large number of estate administrations, and the Governor appointed her Public Administrator to continue the administration of decedents' estates and the estates of the disabled.

This example illustrates how closing a practice can go smoothly with advanced planning and steadily scaling back your practice.

2. A Classic Case: Judge Hunter ("Pat") Patrick Judge Hunter ("Pat") Patrick, of Powell, Wyoming, started his law practice in 1966 and first went on the bench in 1970, in a court of limited jurisdiction, on a part-time basis. After 18 years in this role, he closed his law practice in 1988 and became a judge of the District Court, Wyoming's court of plenary jurisdiction.

Judge Patrick practiced in the small town of Powell, where everyone knew everyone. Unfortunately, the closing of his practice to go on the bench appeared in the local newspaper before he had an opportunity to notify his clients. His first step was to prepare a letter to his clients, informing them that he had been appointed to the District Court, and asking them to come to his office and pick up their files. He gave them the names of at least three lawyers, any one of whom would be capable of representing them.

The judge had a general practice, including personal injury, divorce, wills, and estate planning. He also served a number of small corporations that needed ongoing legal representation. For personal reasons, the associate in the practice with him was not interested in acquiring the practice. Many of his clients came in and took their files with them, but the judge sent out a second letter urging those who did not to come in and do so. He succeeded in getting all of the corporate record books in his clients' hands, and placed all remaining files in a banker's box marked "pending open files." He chose to shred the files of the many adoption cases he had handled, as they contained a substantial amount of confidential material. Active trusts did not present a serious problem, since nearly all of these files were taken over by successor lawyers.

Judge Patrick commented that he made a mistake in not purging some of his files while in practice. He urged that a lawyer should purge files once every five years as a matter of course.[5] Since he had not purged any of his files during his 22 years of practice, he used 60 to 70 banker's boxes for his closed files, which he placed in a rented storage unit for protection from dust, water, and the like. The judge had a card index for the files in storage, where he noted any files removed by a client or another lawyer. In one instance, he prepared wills for a couple who had moved to Texas. Some years later, after both persons had died, he received a call from a representative seeking the will of

---

[5] Some would argue that it would be more appropriate to purge client files once every ten years.

the second to die. The original was never found, but thanks to his card index, the judge located a copy, which could be used to prove a lost will. Eventually, the judge finally closed the storage unit and shredded all remaining files.

V. Closing Your Practice

The preceding chapters have outlined the details involved in the closing of a practice. In this chapter, we have considered problems involved in ending your relationships with employees and clients. A final word regarding the more significant aspects of closing a solo practice follows.

A. Physical Assets

If you are in a jurisdiction that does not recognize the sale of a practice, including goodwill, you will have to dispose of furniture, office equipment, law books, file cabinets, and the like. Judge Patrick found that he could sell the large number of file cabinets that had retained files from 22 years of practice, but other physical assets may be difficult to dispose of. Law schools are reluctant to take on additional sets of West Publishing's national reporter system due to space limitations and the additional expense of maintaining these systems. Even the disposition of computer equipment may pose problems in view of the rapid obsolescence of computers. This makes sufficient advanced planning all the more imperative.

B. Intangibles

Financial matters may present problems. Rents and employee salaries must be paid up to the date of closing. If you have been careful to keep your business and personal bank accounts separate from one another, you will have no difficulty in distinguishing items that are properly deductible from those that are not. But if you have blended these in the same bank account, you will have to analyze and distinguish those items connected with your practice from those that are not. Similarly, you should analyze all credit card accounts to differentiate personal and business items. Again, the maintenance of a separate credit card just for your law practice will make this analysis simpler.

C. Insurance

Make a schedule of all insurance policies, such as life, casualty, legal malpractice, automobile, etc. Make sure that you have adequate tail insurance to cover any claims that may be filed in the future for any errors or omissions that may have occurred while you were in practice. Contact all insurers to make sure that you have proper coverage both for the present and in the future.

D. Communications

Arrange for the stopping of all mail deliveries as of a certain date and for the forwarding of any mail thereafter to a new address. Notify clients and persons with whom you have business arrangements of your new address. Make similar arrangements for your e-mail and telephone communications.

E. Bar Relations

Notify state and local bar associations of the closing of your practice and arrange for the payment of any outstanding bar dues. Many bar associations have arrangements whereby you can obtain a substantial waiver or reduction of your bar dues upon assuming an inactive status. Make arrangements with a lawyer with whom you have a close relationship to act as an assumption attorney for matters not fully resolved at time of closing. Check with court clerks so that you will no longer be listed as attorney of record on any outstanding matters. To the extent that you are so listed, arrange with the assumption attorney for the handling of such cases.

VI. Conclusion

The character of each solo practitioner and of each small firm, as well as the specific reasons for leaving or closing a law firm, dictate the nature of ending your relationships with both employees and clients. Regarding employees, long-time loyalty should be rewarded, and long-time knowledge should also be very helpful in closing the practice. With clients, differing reasons for leaving your practice will direct how you end the relationship. Regardless, there are firm ethical guidelines for the communication of your plans, the handling of client files, and the disposition of client accounts. In addition, there are standard business steps to take to close the law firm properly.

Further Reading

English, H. "Managing Culture Shock: Dealing with the People Factor in a Merger." *Law Practice Management* v. 27, Part 4 (2001): pp. 42–48.

Solo & Small Firm Practice Retreat, Pennsylvania Bar Institute, and Pennsylvania Bar Association, Solo and Small Firm Practice Section. *Eighth Annual Solo & Small Firm Practice Retreat*, 8e. Mechanicsburg, Pennsylvania: Pennsylvania Bar Institute, 2001.

Appendices

Appendix 12-1. Agreement to Close Law Practice

Appendix 12-2. Sample "Office Closing" Letter

Appendix 12-3. Sample Transfer of Client File Form

Appendix 12-4. Sample Acknowledgment of Receipt of File

Appendix 12-1

Agreement to Close Law Practice*

Between: _____, hereinafter referred to as "Planning Attorney,"
And: _____, hereinafter referred to as "Assisting Attorney."

1. Purpose.

The purpose of this agreement is to protect the legal interests of the clients of Planning Attorney in the event Planning Attorney is unable to continue Planning Attorney's law practice due to death, disability, impairment, or incapacity.

2. Parties.

The term *Assisting Attorney* refers to the attorney designated in the caption above or the Assisting Attorney's alternate. The term *Planning Attorney* refers to the attorney designated in the caption above and the Planning Attorney's representatives, heirs, or assigns.

3. Establishing Death, Disability, Impairment, or Incapacity.

In determining whether Planning Attorney is dead, disabled, impaired, or incapacitated, Assisting Attorney may act upon such evidence as Assisting Attorney shall deem reasonably reliable, including, but not limited to, communications with Planning Attorney's family members, representative, or a written opinion of one or more medical doctors duly licensed to practice medicine. Similar evidence or medical opinions may be relied upon to establish that Planning Attorney's disability, impairment, or incapacity has terminated. Assisting Attorney is relieved from any responsibility and liability for acting in good faith upon such evidence in carrying out the provisions of this Agreement.

4. Consent to Close Practice.

Planning Attorney hereby gives consent to Assisting Attorney to take all actions necessary to close Planning Attorney's legal practice in the event that Planning Attorney

---

* Reprinted with the permission of the Oregon State Bar Professional Liability Fund. All rights reserved except that lawyers may copy and reproduce the material for their own use.

is unable to continue in the private practice of law and Planning Attorney is unable to close Planning Attorney's own practice due to death, disability, impairment, or incapacity. Planning Attorney hereby appoints Assisting Attorney as attorney-in-fact, with full power to do and accomplish all of the actions contemplated by this Agreement as fully and as completely as Planning Attorney could do personally if Planning Attorney were able. It is Planning Attorney's specific intent that this appointment of Assisting Attorney as attorney-in-fact shall become effective only upon Planning Attorney's death, disability, impairment, or incapacity. The appointment of Assisting Attorney shall not be invalidated because of Planning Attorney's death, disability, impairment, or incapacity, but instead the appointment shall fully survive such death, disability, impairment, or incapacity and shall be in full force and effect so long as it is necessary or convenient to carry out the terms of this Agreement. In the event of Planning Attorney's death, disability, impairment, or incapacity, Planning Attorney designates Assisting Attorney as signatory, or in substitution of Planning Attorney's signature, on all of Planning Attorney's law office accounts with any bank or financial institution, including, but not limited to, checking accounts, savings accounts, and trust accounts. Planning Attorney's consent includes but is not limited to:

- Entering Planning Attorney's office and using the Planning Attorney's equipment and supplies as needed to close Planning Attorney's practice;
- Opening Planning Attorney's mail and processing it;
- Taking possession and control of all property comprising Planning Attorney's law office including client files and records;
- Examining files and records of Planning Attorney's law practice and obtaining information as to any pending matters that may require attention;
- Notifying clients, potential clients, and others who appear to be clients, that Planning Attorney has given this authorization and that it is in their best interest to obtain other legal counsel:
- Copying Planning Attorney's files;
- Obtaining client consent to transfer flies and client property to new attorneys;
- Transferring client files and property to clients or their new attorneys;
- Obtaining client consent to obtain extensions of time and contacting opposing counsel and courts/administrative agencies to obtain extensions of time;
- Applying for extensions of time pending employment of other counsel by the clients;
- Filing notices, motions, and pleadings on behalf of clients where the clients' interests must be immediately protected and other legal counsel has not yet been retained;
- Contacting all appropriate persons and entities who may be affected and informing them that Planning Attorney has given this authorization;
- Arranging for transfer and storage of closed files;
- Winding down the financial affairs of Planning Attorney's practice, including providing Planning Attorney's clients with a final accounting and statement

for services rendered by Assisting Attorney, return of client funds, collection of fees on Planning Attorney's behalf or on behalf of Planning Attorney's estate, payment of business expenses, and closure of business accounts when appropriate;

- Advertising Planning Attorney's law practice or any of its assets to find a buyer for the practice; and
- Arranging for an appraisal of Planning Attorney's practice for the purpose of selling Planning Attorney's practice.
- Planning Attorney's bank or financial institution may rely on the authorizations in the Agreement unless such bank or financial institution has actual knowledge that this Agreement has been terminated or is no longer in effect.

5. Payment for Services.

Planning Attorney agrees to pay Assisting Attorney a reasonable sum for services rendered by Assisting Attorney while closing the law practice of Planning Attorney. Assisting Attorney agrees to keep accurate time records for the purpose of determining amounts due for services rendered. Assisting Attorney agrees to provide the services specified herein as an independent contractor.

6. Preserving Attorney-Client Privilege.

Assisting Attorney agrees to preserve confidences and secrets of Planning Attorney's clients and their attorney-client privilege and shall only make disclosures of information reasonably necessary to carry out the purpose of this Agreement.

7. Assisting Attorney Is Attorney for Planning Attorney (delete one of the following paragraphs as appropriate).

Assisting Attorney is the attorney for Planning Attorney. Assisting Attorney will protect the attorney-client relationship and follow the Oregon Code of Professional Responsibility. (Optional: Assisting Attorney has permission to inform the Professional Liability Fund of errors or potential errors of Planning Attorney, may inform Planning Attorney's former clients of any errors or potential errors, and instruct them to obtain independent legal advice. Assisting Attorney also has permission to inform Planning Attorney's former clients of any ethics violations committed by Planning Attorney.)

OR

7. Assisting Attorney Is Not Attorney for Planning Attorney

Assisting Attorney is not the attorney for Planning Attorney. (Optional: Assisting Attorney has permission to inform the Professional Liability Fund of errors or potential errors of Planning Attorney, may inform Planning Attorney's former clients of any errors or potential errors, and instruct them to obtain independent legal advice. Assisting Attorney also has permission to inform Planning Attorney's former clients of any ethics violations committed by Planning Attorney.)

8. Providing Legal Services.

Planning Attorney authorizes Assisting Attorney to provide legal services to Planning Attorney's former clients providing Assisting Attorney has no conflict of interest and obtains the consent of Planning Attorney's former clients to do so. Assisting Attorney has the right to enter into an attorney-client relationship with Planning Attorney's former clients and to have clients pay Assisting Attorney for his or her legal services. Assisting Attorney agrees to check for conflicts of interest, and when necessary, to refer the clients to another attorney.

9. Informing Oregon State Bar.

Assisting Attorney agrees to inform the Oregon State Bar Disciplinary Counsel where Planning Attorney's closed files will be stored and the name, address, and phone number of the contact person for retrieving those files.

10. Contacting the Professional Liability Fund.

Planning Attorney authorizes Assisting Attorney to contact the Professional Liability Fund concerning any legal malpractice claims or potential claims. (**Note to Planning Attorney: Assisting Attorney's role in contacting the Fund will be determined by Assisting Attorney's arrangement with Planning Attorney. See Section 7 of this Agreement.)

11. Providing Clients with Accounting.

Assisting Attorney agrees to provide Planning Attorney's former clients with a final accounting and statement for legal services of Planning Attorney based on the Planning Attorney's records. Assisting Attorney agrees to return client funds to Planning Attorney's former clients and to submit funds collected on behalf of Planning Attorney to Planning Attorney or Planning Attorney's estate representative.

12. Assisting Attorney Alternate (delete one of the following paragraphs as appropriate).

If Assisting Attorney is unable or unwilling to act on behalf of Planning Attorney, Planning Attorney appoints _____ as Assisting Attorney's Alternate, hereinafter known as Assisting Attorney's Alternate. Assisting Attorney's Alternate is authorized to act on behalf of Planning Attorney pursuant to this Agreement. Assisting Attorney's Alternate shall comply with the terms of this Agreement. Assisting Attorney's Alternate consents to this appointment, as shown by the signature of the Assisting Attorney's Alternate on this Agreement.

OR:

If Assisting Attorney is unable or unwilling to act on behalf of Planning Attorney, Assisting Attorney may appoint an alternate. Assisting Attorney shall enter into an agreement with any such Assisting Attorney's Alternate under which Assisting Attorney's Alternate consents to the terms and provisions of this Agreement.

13. Indemnification.

Planning Attorney agrees to indemnify Assisting Attorney against any claims, loss, or damage arising out of any act or omission by Assisting Attorney under this agreement, provided the actions or omissions of Assisting Attorney were made in good faith, were made in a manner reasonably believed to be in Planning Attorney's best interest, and occurred while Assisting Attorney was assisting Planning Attorney with the closure of Planning Attorney's office. This indemnification agreement does not extend to any acts, errors, or omissions of Assisting Attorney while rendering or failing to render professional services in Assisting Attorney's capacity as attorney for the former clients of Planning Attorney. Assisting Attorney shall be responsible for all acts and omissions of gross negligence and willful misconduct.

14. Option to Purchase Practice.

Assisting Attorney shall have the first option to purchase the practice of Planning Attorney under the terms and conditions specified by Planning Attorney or Planning Attorney's representative in accordance with the Oregon Code of Professional Responsibility and other applicable law.

15. Arranging to Sell Practice.

If Assisting Attorney opts not to purchase Planning Attorney's practice, Assisting Attorney will make all reasonable efforts to sell Planning Attorney's practice and will pay Planning Attorney or Planning Attorney's estate all monies received.

16. Fee Disputes to Be Arbitrated.

Planning Attorney and Assisting Attorney agree that all fee disputes between them will be decided by the Oregon State Bar Fee Arbitration Program.

17. Termination.

This Agreement shall terminate upon: (1) delivery of written notice of termination by Planning Attorney to Assisting Attorney during any time that Planning Attorney is not under disability, impairment, or incapacity as established under Section 3 of this Agreement; (2) delivery of written notice of termination by Planning Attorney's representative upon a showing of good cause; or (3) delivery of a written notice of termination given by Assisting Attorney to Planning Attorney, subject to any ethical obligation to continue or complete any matter undertaken by Assisting Attorney pursuant to this Agreement.

If Assisting Attorney or Assisting Attorney's Alternate for any reason terminates this agreement or is terminated, Assisting Attorney or Assisting Attorney's Alternate acting on his or her behalf shall (1) provide a full and accurate accounting of financial activities undertaken on Planning Attorney's behalf within 30 days of termination or resignation and (2) provide Planning Attorney with Planning Attorney's files, records, and funds.

_____   _____
[*Planning Attorney*]   [*Date*]

STATE OF OREGON   )
) ss.
County of _____)

This instrument was acknowledged before me on _____ (date) by _____ (name(s) of person(s)).

                                   _____
                                   NOTARY PUBLIC FOR OREGON
                                   My commission expires: _____

_____   _____
[*Assisting Attorney*]   [*Date*]

STATE OF OREGON   )
) ss.
County of _____)

This instrument was acknowledged before me on _____ (date) by _____ (name(s) of person(s)).

                                   _____
                                   NOTARY PUBLIC FOR OREGON
                                   My commission expires: _____

_____   _____
[*Assisting Attorney's Alternate*]   [*Date*]

STATE OF OREGON   )
) ss.
County of _____)

This instrument was acknowledged before me on _____ (date) by _____ (name(s) of person(s)).

                              _____
                              NOTARY PUBLIC FOR OREGON
                              My commission expires:_____

Appendix 12-2

Sample "Office Closing" Letter*

Re: [*Name of Case*]

Dear [*Name*]:

As of [*date*], I will be closing my law practice due to [*provide reason, if possible*]. I will be unable to continue representing you on your legal matters.

I recommend that you immediately hire another attorney to handle your case for you. You can select any attorney you wish, or I would be happy to provide you with a list of local attorneys who practice in the area of law relevant to your legal needs. Also, The Florida Bar provides a lawyer referral service that can be reached at 1-800-342-8011.

When you select your new attorney, please provide me with written authority to transfer your file to the new attorney. If you prefer, you may come to our office and pick up a copy of your file and deliver it to that attorney yourself.

It is imperative that you obtain a new attorney immediately. [*Insert appropriate language regarding time limitations or other critical time lines that client should be aware of.*] Please let me know the name of your new attorney, or pick up a copy of your file by [*date*].

I [*or, insert name of the attorney who will store files*] will continue to store my copy of your closed file for 10 years. After that time, I [*or, insert name of other attorney if relevant*] will destroy my copy of the file unless you notify me in writing immediately that you do not want me to follow this procedure. [*If relevant, add: If you object to (insert name of attorney who will be storing files) storing my copy of your closed file, let me know immediately and I will make alternative arrangements.*]

---

*Reprinted with permission from the Florida Bar's Law Office Management Assistance Service (LOMAS).

If you or your new attorney need a copy of the closed file, please free to contact me. I will be happy to provide you with a copy.

Within the next [*fill in the number*] weeks I will be providing you with a full accounting of your funds in my trust account and fees you currently owe me.

You will be able to reach me at the address and phone number listed on this letter until [*date*]. After that time, you or your new attorney can reach me at the following phone number and address:

_____
[*Name*]

_____
[*Address*]

_____
[*Phone*]

Remember, it is imperative to retain a new attorney immediately. This will be the only way that time limitations applicable to your case will be protected and your other legal rights preserved.

I appreciate the opportunity of providing you with legal services. Please do not hesitate to give me a call if you have any questions or concerns.

Sincerely,

[*Attorney*]

[*Firm*]

Appendix 12-3

Sample Transfer of Client File Form*

AUTHORIZATION FOR TRANSFER OF CLIENT FILE

I hereby authorize the law office of [Firm/Attorney Name] to deliver a copy of my file to my new attorney at the following address:

_____

_____

_____

_____

_____
[Client]

_____
[Date]

---

* Reprinted with permission from the Florida Bar's Law Office Management Assistance Service (LOMAS).

Appendix 12-4

Sample Acknowledgment of Receipt of File*

I hereby acknowledge that I have received a copy of my file from the law office of [name].

_____
[Name]

_____
[Date]

---

* Reprinted with permission from the Florida Bar's Law Office Management Assistance Service (LOMAS).

Index

ABA/BNA Lawyers' Manual on Professional Conduct, 15, 138n7, 141, 143n10
access to clients, 26–27. *See also* clients; goodwill
accounting firms, 6, 58, 124. *See also* certified public accountants (CPA)
accounts, settling, 83, 96, 181, 194. *See also* bank accounts; law offices, expenses of; trust accounts
active files, 86–87. *See also* files
active incomes, losses offsetting, 51
adjusted profit margins, 36. *See also* valuations
adverse interests. *See* conflicts of interest
agreements
    for closing practices, 191–197
    partnership, 43–44, 65
Altman Weil, Inc.
    Report to Legal Management, 58
    Survey of Law Firm Economics, 59
American Bar Association (ABA)
    ABA/BNA Lawyers' Manual on Professional Conduct, 15, 138n7, 141, 143n10
    Center for Professional Responsibility, 13, 135n1
    Ethics 2000 Commission (E2K), 13–14, 18, 137, 137n5
    ethics and, 19–20, 27–28, 136–139
    Formal Opinion 90-357 (1990), 19
    Formal Opinion 92-369 (1992), Disposition of Deceased Sole Practitioners' Client Files and Property, 21, 147, 165–170
    Formal Opinion 94-388 (1994), 19
    Formal Opinion 96-400 (1996), 20
    Informal Opinion 1384 (1977), Disposition of a Lawyer's Closed or Dormant Files Relating to Representation of or Services to Clients, 22, 23–24, 143, 143n10, 149, 163–164, 170
    Model Rules of Professional Conduct (See Model Rules of Professional Conduct)
    on sales of goodwill/solo practices, 2, 27–28 (See also Model Rules of Professional Conduct, Rule 1.17, Sale of a Law Practice)
anti-abuse provisions, 54–55
appraisal methods/appraisers, 7–8, 193. *See also* professionals, engaging; valuations
areas of practice, 5, 58–59, 104–105, 137, 154–155
"Are Lawyers for Sale?" (Overton), 141
Arizona State Bar Association
    Opinion 04-05 (2005), 148
    Opinion 06-01 (2006), 138–139n7, 140
Arkansas State Bar Association, Rule 1.17, 140
assets, 5, 25–27, 44, 88, 186
assisting attorneys, 191–197. *See also* assumption/temporary attorneys; attorneys-in-fact; personal representatives
associates, 181–182. *See also* staff
assumption/temporary attorneys, 10, 21–24, 84, 124, 148–149, 168–170, 183, 187. *See also* assisting attorneys; deceased lawyers; personal representatives
attorney-client privilege. *See* client confidentiality
attorneys. *See* assisting attorneys; assumption/temporary attorneys; business transaction attorneys; deceased lawyers; disabled lawyers; disbarred lawyers; missing lawyers; planning attorneys; successor lawyers/firms; suspended lawyers
attorneys-in-fact, 4–5. *See also* assisting attorneys; personal representatives
Avery, Luther, 160

Index

bank accounts, 84, 97, 131, 181, 186, 192
bar associations, 90, 98, 132, 187. *See also* American Bar Association (ABA); *specific state bar associations*
bench, assignment to, 184–186
benefits, employee, 180–182. *See also* health insurance; staff
bills, unpaid, 83, 96. *See also* settling accounts
Blackwood; Clinard v. (2001), 17
Block; Vollgraff v., 167n3
Bluebook, 54–55
bookkeepers, 124, 181. *See also* certified public accountants (CPA); staff
books, law, 5, 88, 186
brand name recognition, 62, 77–78
business cases, for proposed mergers, 62–63. *See also* mergers, law firm
businesses *vs.* practices, valuations of, 26, 31–32. *See also* valuations
business evaluators, 73. *See also* professionals, engaging; valuations
business transaction attorneys, 73. *See also* professionals, engaging
buyers. *See* purchasers

calendars, 86
California State Bar Association, Rule 2-300 (on sale of goodwill/solo practice), 2, 136n3, 157–158, 159, 160–161
Cameron, David L., "The Lazarus Effect: A Commentary on In-Kind Guaranteed Payments," 45
capital, in service firms, 44
capital gains/losses, 43, 44–45, 53–54
capitalized cash flows, 33. *See also* valuations
capitalized excess earnings, 33–34. *See also* valuations
Cavender v. US Xpress Enterprises, Inc. (2002), 16
Center for Professional Responsibility, 13, 135n1
certified public accountants (CPA), 72–73, 124. *See also* accounting firms; professionals, engaging
checklists
 closing practices, 123–133
 integration plans, 66
 law office expenses, 107
 leases/service contracts, 113
 sales of niche practices, 78–79
 scope mergers, 66
 valuations, 35, 37–40
Chinese Wall, and conflicts of interest, 17

client confidentiality. *See also* conflicts of interest
 closing practices and, 85, 86, 142
 disclosure and, 6–7
 large law firms and, 3
 lawyer's death, impact on, 9, 22, 168n8, 193
 sales of solo practices and, 2, 3, 6–7, 105, 138–139n7, 155, 161
clients
 access to, 26–27
 as commodities, 103, 136, 153
 confidentiality of (*See* client confidentiality)
 conflicts of interest between, 16–18, 19–20
 corporations as, 61
 deceased, 144, 145 (*See also* nonresponsive clients; unlocatable clients)
 electronic communication and, 84–86, 145–147, 173, 175
 identities of, 6, 176
 implied consents for file disposition, 173–174, 177
 lists of, 86–88
 locating, 174, 200 (*See also* unlocatable clients)
 nonresponsive, 8–9
 notifications of closures, 86, 88–90, 148–149, 169, 180, 182–183, 186–187, 192, 199–200
 notifications of sales, 6–7, 75, 105, 138–139, 155, 160–161
 protecting interests of, 147–149, 158, 166–168
 relationships with, 31, 179, 182–183 (*See also* closing practices; sales of niche practices; sales of solo practices)
 retaining, 29
 trust of, 26–27
 unlocatable, 87–88, 95, 105, 139, 145–147, 155, 174
 withdrawals from representing, 16–18, 20, 142 (*See also* conflicts of interest)
Clinard v. Blackwood (2001), 17
closed files, 86–87, 143–144, 163–164, 172–174. *See also* files
closing practices
 agreements, sample, 191–197
 assumption attorneys and, 21–24, 84, 124, 148–149, 168–170, 183, 187
 bank accounts and, 84, 97, 131, 181, 186, 192

calendars and, 86
client confidentiality and, 85, 86, 142
client lists and, 86–88
client notifications and, 86, 88–90, 148–149, 169, 180, 182–183, 186–187, 192, 199–200
computers and, 84–86, 88, 146, 186
disposal of tangible assets and, 5, 26, 88, 186
ethical considerations of, 135–136, 141–149
file disposition and (*See* files)
guidelines for, 141–147
insurance and, 19–127, 31, 83, 90–91, 99–100, 181, 186
inventory of contacts and, 123–133
judicial appointments and, 184–186
licensing authorities and, 84, 98–99
occupancy and, 83, 98, 124
one's own, 96 (*See also* preparedness of lawyers)
reasons for, 82, 94–95, 147–149, 183–184
responsibility for, 82–83
safekeeping property and, 97–98, 143–144, 146, 164
settling accounts and, 83, 96, 194
staff and, 83, 90–91, 99, 179, 180–182, 185
summaries of key points on, 81–82, 93–94, 186–187
taxes and, 83, 84
trust accounts and, 88, 97, 130, 176, 192, 200
collateral, 8, 76
colleagues, closing solo practices of. *See* assisting attorneys; assumption/temporary attorneys; personal representatives
comparables, as appraisal method, 8
compatibility factors, 63–64. *See also* mergers, law firm
compensation, 31, 46–47, 64. *See also* incomes
competence, of purchasers, 13, 15, 105, 137, 155. *See also* Model Rules of Professional Conduct, Rule 1.1, *Competence*
competition for business. *See* noncompete covenants
computers, 84–86, 88, 146, 175, 186. *See also* electronic information; emails; passwords
confidences, 6. *See also* client confidentiality
confidentiality. *See* client confidentiality

conflicts of interest
  assisting attorneys and, 194
  between clients, 16–18, 19–20
  opinions on, 19–20
  purchasers and, 6–7, 13, 15–16, 139
  sales of niche practices and, 75
Connecticut State Bar Association
  Opinion 05-09 (2005), 20
  Opinion 94-9 (1994), 20
consolidations, industry, 57–58. *See also* mergers, law firm
contacts
  client, 174, 200 (*See also* unlocatable clients)
  inventory of, 123–133
  referral, 31, 199
contingencies, planning for, 8, 123–133, 148–149, 166–168, 191–197
contingent fees practices, valuations of, 31
"Continuation of a Partnership: Avoiding Adverse Tax Consequences" (Kennard), 43
continuing succession, 14, 140–141
contracts, service, 83, 98, 113. *See also* maintenance contracts
corporations, 51, 59–61, 125, 161. *See also* large law firms; mergers, law firm
costs, reducing, 59–60. *See also* expenses, law office
courts
  bench, assignments to, 184–186
  noncompete covenants and, 5
  unlocatable clients and, 88, 95, 105, 139, 155, 174
covenants, noncompete, 5–6, 48–49, 72, 76
Coy, Gayle, "Permitting the Sale of a Law Practice: Furthering the Interests of Both Attorneys and Their Clients," 141
CPA (certified public accountant), 72–73, 124. *See also* accounting firms; professionals, engaging
Crawford, Barton, "The Sale of a Legal Practice in North Carolina: Goodwill and Discrimination Against the Sole Practitioner," 141
credit card accounts, 131, 186. *See also* settling accounts
cultural compatibilities, 63. *See also* mergers, law firm
Cunningham, Laura and Noel, *The Logic of Subchapter K: A Conceptual Guide to the Taxation of Partnerships*, 44

data, removing, 85, 88. *See also* computers; electronic information
debts, unpaid, 83, 96. *See also* settling accounts
deceased clients, 144, 145. *See also* nonresponsive clients; unlocatable clients
deceased lawyers. *See also* Model Rules of Professional Conduct, Rule 28, *Appointment of Counsel to Protect Clients' Interest When Respondent Is Transferred to Disability Inactive Status, Suspended, Disbarred, Disappears, or Dies* (1989)
 client management for, 9, 147–149, 166–168, 168n8, 169
 closing practices of (*See* closing practices)
 disposition of client files for (*See* files)
 ethics and, 21–23, 147–149
 hypothetical scenario on, 12
 licensing authorities and, 84, 98–99
 payments to estates of, 159
 personal representatives of, 4, 8, 84, 94–95, 183–184
 preparedness of, 8, 148–149, 166–168, 191–197
 receivers for, 22–23, 86, 168n9, 172
 selling practices of (*See* sales of solo practices)
defensive mergers, 59. *See also* mergers, law firm
deferred compensation program, 46–47
destruction of files, 85, 87, 172, 173–176, 177. *See also* files
deterrents, for lack of preparedness, 148–149, 167–168
DeWoskin, Alan, 2
 "When a Solo Takes Down the Shingle," 141
digital files. *See* computers; electronic information
Dimitriou, Dimitrios, "What Should Be Your Concerns? Purchase or Sale of a Solo Practice," 141
disabled lawyers. *See also* closing practices; Model Rules of Professional Conduct, Rule 28, *Appointment of Counsel to Protect Clients' Interest When Respondent Is Transferred to Disability Inactive Status, Suspended, Disbarred, Disappears, or Dies* (1989); sales of solo practices
 client interests, protection of, 147–149, 166–168
 liabilities of, 10
 licensing authorities and, 84, 98–99
 personal representatives of, 4, 8, 84, 94–95, 183–184
 preparedness of, 8, 191–197
 receivers for, 86, 168n9, 172
disbarred lawyers, 140–141. *See also* closing practices; Model Rules of Professional Conduct, Rule 28, *Appointment of Counsel to Protect Clients' Interest When Respondent Is Transferred to Disability Inactive Status, Suspended, Disbarred, Disappears, or Dies* (1989); sales of solo practices
disciplinary actions, for lack of preparedness, 148–149, 167–168
disclosure of client information, 6–7, 9–10. *See also* client confidentiality
disposition of files. *See* files
disqualification of counsel, 16–18, 19–20
dissolution of partnerships. *See* partnerships; retiring partners
distributive shares, 45, 48, 50
District Court for the Eastern District of Pennsylvania, on disqualification of counsel, 17–18
divorce, valuations and, 159
due diligence, 31, 34, 64–65, 76, 105, 137, 155
Dzienkowski, John S., *Legal Ethics: The Lawyer's Deskbook on Professional Responsibility,* "Sale of a Law Practice," 141

E2K (Ethics 2000 Commission), 13–14, 18, 137, 137n5
earnings multiples, 28–31, 32–34, 36. *See also* valuations
earn-out, 34
economic compatibilities, 63. *See also* mergers, law firm
economies of scale, 59–60, 63. *See also* mergers, law firm
electronic information, 84–86, 145–147, 173, 175, 181. *See also* computers; emails; passwords
emails, 89, 187. *See also* computers; electronic information
employees. *See* staff
equipment, office, 5, 88, 113, 129, 186. *See also* maintenance contracts; service contracts
equity equalization, 63–64. *See also* mergers, law firm

Index

equity/non-equity partners, 64. *See also* mergers, law firm; partnerships
errors and omissions insurance. *See* professional liability insurance; tail insurance
escrow accounts. *See* trust accounts
estate practices, valuation of, 31
ethics
    ABA on, 19–20, 27–28, 136–139 (*See also* Ethics 2000 Commission (E2K))
    closing practices and, 135–136, 141–149
    deceased/disabled lawyers and, 21–23, 147–149
    file retention/destruction and, 143–147
    hypothetical situations on, 12
    law firm mergers and, 16–21
    opinions on, 19–21, 135n1, 143
    sales of practices and, 13–16, 75, 77, 136–141
    summary of key points on, 11, 136
Ethics 2000 Commission (E2K), 13–14, 18, 137, 137n5
excess earnings, capitalized, 33–34. *See also* valuations
executors, 8. *See also* personal representatives
expenses, law office, 107. *See also* settling accounts
external transfers, valuations of, 31–34. *See also* valuations

family members, as personal representatives, 4–5. *See also* personal representatives
Federal Taxation of Partnerships and Partners (McKee, Nelson, Whitmire), 47
fees
    advanced, 9, 200 (*See also* trust accounts)
    of assisting attorneys, 193, 195
    increasing, 13–14, 105, 155, 160, 161
    owed to attorneys, 43, 51, 200
fiduciary duties, 167n3, 169n10
    files. *See also* American Bar Association (ABA), Formal Opinion 92-369 (1992), *Disposition of Deceased Sole Practitioners' Client Files and Property;* American Bar Association (ABA), Informal Opinion 1384 (1977), *Disposition of a Lawyer's Closed or Dormant Files Relating to Representation of or Services to Clients*
    defining, 90, 173
    destruction of, 87, 172, 173–176, 177

    disposition of, 86–90, 135–137, 142–147, 163–164, 183, 199
    electronic, 173, 175 (*See also* electronic information)
    guardianship of, 21–24, 149, 170, 192
    management of, 171, 180, 185
    transfer forms, 201, 203
financial statements, 73. *See also* settling accounts
Florida State Bar Association
    lawyer referral system, 199
    Opinion 81-8M (1981), 148–149, 167n4
Formal Opinions. *See* American Bar Association (ABA), *specific formal opinions*
furnishings, office, 5, 88, 186
future, planning, 8, 123–133, 148–149, 166–168, 191–197
future income, payment based on, 34. *See also* payment plans; valuations

gains, financial, 43, 44–45, 53–54
Geffen v. Moss, 158
geographic mergers, 58–59, 61. *See also* mergers, law firm
geographic sales of solo practices, 104, 154. *See also* sales of solo practices
Gideon, Kenneth W., 47
goodwill. *See also* access to clients; institutional goodwill; professional goodwill; trust, client
    sale of, 2–3, 5, 27–28, 136, 157–159 (*See also* sales of solo practices)
    valuations of, 26–27, 44, 47, 51, 159
Graham, Chris, 184–185
guidelines for closing practices, 141–147

Hazard, Geoffrey C., Jr., *The Law of Lawyering,* 141
health insurance, 31, 90–91, 180–182
Hodes, W. William, *The Law of Lawyering,* 141
Hornstein, Diane, 183
hostile takeovers, 60, 65–66. *See also* mergers, law firm
hot potato doctrine, 16–18
Hutchins, Edward J., Jr., "Why Attorneys Need Tail Insurance," 115–122

identities of clients, 6, 176
identity thefts, 174, 176

Illinois Supreme Court, Rule 776, *Appointment of Receiver in Certain Cases,* 168n9
illness, terminal, 148–149, 167n4
income approach multipliers, 32–33. *See also* valuations
incomes, 34, 51, 51n61. *See also* compensation
industry consolidations, 57–58. *See also* mergers, law firm
Informal Opinions. *See* American Bar Association (ABA), *specific informal opinions*
installment payments, 49–50, 53
institutional goodwill, 28. *See also* goodwill; professional goodwill
insurance
    closing practices and, 31, 83, 90–91, 99–100, 125–127, 181, 186
    health, 31, 90–91, 180–182
    professional liability, 76, 77, 99–100, 155–122
    tail, 31, 83, 99–100, 115–122, 186
integration plans, 65, 66. *See also* mergers, law firm
Internal Revenue Code (IRC), 42
    Section 409A, 46–47
    Section 736 (*See also* taxes, retirement and)
        anti-abuse provisions and, 54–55
        history of, 45–48
        installment payments and, 49–50, 53
        noncompete covenants and, 48–49
        passive activity losses and, 51–52
        retiring partners' options under, 43–45, 52–54
        self-employment taxes and, 48
        tenets of, 43–45
internal transfers, 28, 32. *See also* valuations
investigators, 182. *See also* staff

James v. Teleflex, Inc. (1999), 17–18
judicial appointments, 184–186
jurisdictions. *See also* states
    cessation of practice in, 3–4
    on client files, 90, 146–147, 174
    closing practices and, 86–87
    licenses to practice in, 4
    noncompete covenants and, 5–6, 49
    sales of solo practices and, 3, 13, 77, 136, 136n3, 140
    on screening, 18–19

Kennard, Alan, "Continuation of a Partnership: Avoiding Adverse Tax Consequences," 43
Krsul, John, Jr., 160

large law firms, 3, 61, 62, 158. *See also* corporations; mergers, law firm
Last Will and Testament. *See* wills
law firm management consultants, 73, 74, 75. *See also* professionals, engaging
law firms. *See* large law firms; mergers, law firm; niche practices; solo practices
Law for Dummies (Ventura), 77
law libraries, 5, 88, 90, 186
law offices
    expenses of, 107 (*See also* settling accounts)
    inventory of contacts for, 123–133
Law of Lawyering, The (Hazard and Hodes), 141
law review articles, 141
law schools, 62, 88, 186
lawyers. *See* assisting attorneys; assumption/temporary attorneys; business transaction attorneys; deceased lawyers; disabled lawyers; disbarred lawyers; missing lawyers; planning attorneys; successor lawyers/firms; suspended lawyers
"Lazarus Effect: A Commentary on In-Kind Guaranteed Payments, The" (Cameron and Postlewaite), 45
leases, 5, 83, 98, 113, 124, 129
Legal Ethics: The Lawyer's Deskbook on Professional Responsibility, "Sale of a Law Practice" (Rotunda and Dzienkowski), 141
licensing, 4, 84, 98–99, 174
Limited Liability Companies. *See* partnerships
Limited Liability Partnerships. *See* partnerships
Limited Partnerships. *See* partnerships
liquidations of partnerships. *See* partnerships; retiring partners
loans, recourse, 52
Logic of Subchapter K: A Conceptual Guide to the Taxation of Partnerships, The (Cunningham), 44
losses, financial, 43, 44–45, 51–52, 51n61, 53–54
Louisiana State Bar Association, Opinion 05-RPCC-001 (2005), 141–142

mail deliveries, 83, 88–89, 186
Maine State Bar Association
  Opinion 184 (2002), 140
  Opinion 189 (2004), 146
maintenance contracts, 132. *See also*
    occupancy; office equipment; service
    contracts
malpractice issues, 9–10, 83, 126, 194
management consultants, 73, 74, 75. *See
    also* professionals, engaging
management techniques, mergers as, 59, 60f
manufacturing firms *vs.* service firms, 28–29
Maryland Bar Journal, The, 115
Maryland State Bar Association
  Opinion 89-58 (1989), 22
  Opinion 2005-01 (2004), 137
  Rule 1.15, 98, 111
  on sale of solo practices, 94
material participation, 51–52. *See also*
    retiring partners
McKee, William S., *Federal Taxation of
    Partnerships and Partners,* 47
MDPs (Multi-Disciplinary Partnerships), 58.
    See also accounting firms
memberships, canceling, 90, 98, 187
memorial committees of bar associations,
    90, 98
mergers, law firm
  corporate mergers *vs.*, 59–61
  due diligence, 64–65
  ethics and, 16–21
  hypothetical, 12
  preparing for, 62–65, 66
  reasons for, 59–61
  sales of solo practices *vs.*, 138n7
  success of, 58
  summary of key points on, 57
missing lawyers, 4–5, 168n9, 172. *See
    also* Model Rules of Professional
    Conduct, Rule 28, *Appointment of
    Counsel to Protect Clients' Interest
    When Respondent Is Transferred to
    Disability Inactive Status, Suspended,
    Disbarred, Disappears, or Dies*
    (1989)
Missouri State Bar Association
  Informal Opinion 20010147 (undated),
    146–147
  Opinion 990050 (1999), 21
"Model Rule 1.17 and the Ethical Sale of
    Law Practices: A Critical Analysis"
    (Schoenwald), 141
Model Rules of Professional Conduct, 14, 77
  Rule 1.1, *Competence,* 15, 147, 166
  Rule 1.3, *Diligence,* 147–148, 166
  Rule 1.6, *Confidentiality of Information,*
    137–138, 138–139n7, 168n8
  Rule 1.15, *Safekeeping Property,*
    97–98, 109
  Rule 1.16, *Declining or Terminating
    Representation,* 142
  Rule 1.17, *Sale of a Law Practice*
    adoption of, 2, 136–137, 157
    amendments to, 136–137
    on competence, 15
    generally, 13, 27–28, 77, 95,
      103–106, 153–156
    intent of, 159–160
    state versions of, 139–141
  Rule 5.6(a), Restrictions on Right to
    Practice, 49
  Rule 7.1, Communications Concerning a
    Lawyer's Services, 14
  Rule 7.5, Firm Names and Letterhead, 14
  Rule 28, *Appointment of Counsel
    to Protect Clients' Interest When
    Respondent Is Transferred to
    Disability Inactive Status, Suspended,
    Disbarred, Disappears, or Dies* (1989),
    22–23, 23n5, 169n12
  state adoption of, 49n43
Moss; Geffen v., 158
Multi-Disciplinary Partnerships (MDPs), 58.
    See also accounting firms
multipliers. *See also* valuations
  of income approach, 32–33
  valuations by, 8, 28–31, 36

names of practices, 14, 62, 77–78
Nassau County (NY) Bar Association
  Opinion 92-27 (1992), 170n15
  Opinion 93-23 (1993), 144–145
negotiations, 64, 76
Nelson, William F., *Federal Taxation of
    Partnerships and Partners,* 47
Nemchek, Lee R., "Records Retention
    in the Private Legal Environment:
    Annotated Bibliography and Program
    Implementation Tools," 143n10
New York, Bar of the City of, Opinion 633
    (1943), 136
New York State Bar Association, Opinion
    623 (1991), 144
niche practices, 69–70. *See also* sales of
    niche practices
non-client files, 89–90
non-client notifications, 83, 86, 88–89,
    98–99, 123–133. *See also* leases; post
    offices; professional associations
noncompete covenants, 5–6, 48–49, 72, 76

212 Index

non-equity/equity partners, 64. *See also* partnership agreements; partnerships; retiring partners
nonlocatable clients, 87–88, 95, 105, 139, 145–147, 155, 174. *See also* nonresponsive clients
nonresponsive clients, 8–9. *See also* nonlocatable clients
normalized annual earnings, 30, 32–33
North Carolina State Bar Association, Rule 1.17, 139–140
North Dakota State Bar Association, Opinion 01-03 (2001), 147
notifications, client. *See also* non-client notifications
   closing practices and, 86, 88–90, 148–149, 169, 180, 182–183, 186–187, 192, 199–200
   sales of practices and, 6–7, 75, 105, 138–139, 155, 160–161

occupancy, 83, 98, 124. *See also* leases
office equipment, 5, 88, 113, 129, 186. *See also* maintenance contracts; service contracts
Ohio State Bar Association
   Informal Opinion 98-2 (1998), 145
   Opinion 00-02 (2000), 21–22
   Rule 1.17, 140
opening files, 171. *See also* files
open transactions, 50, 53
opinions, ethics, 19–21, 135n1, 143. *See also* American Bar Association (ABA), *specific Formal and Informal Opinions;* state bar opinions; *specific state bar opinions*
Oregon State Bar Association
   Opinion 2005-23 (2005), 142
   sample agreement to close practices, 191–197
outsourced legal work, 61. *See also* professionals, engaging
Overton, George, "Are Lawyers for Sale?", 141

paper recyclers, 87, 176. *See also* destruction of files
paralegals, 181. *See also* staff
partnership agreements, 43–44, 65
partnerships. *See also* partnership agreements; retiring partners
   corporations *vs.*, 51
   deductions for, 45, 46, 53
   description of, 42
   equity/non-equity partners in, 64
   files and dissolution of, 142, 144–145
   goodwill and, 159
   installment payments and, 49–50, 53
   retirement and, 41–42, 52–54, 144, 161
   shares, selling, 43
   valuations of, 28
Partnership Taxation (Willis, Pennell, Postlewaite), 48
parts of practice, 5, 58–59, 104–105, 137, 154–155
passive activity losses, 51–52, 51n61. *See also* losses, financial
passive incomes, 51, 51n61. *See also* incomes
passwords, 86, 89, 123. *See also* computers
past revenues, 8, 30, 36
past transactions, 32
Patrick, Hunter (Pat), 185–186
payment plans. *See also* valuations
   to deceased attorneys' estates, 159
   future income as basis of, 34
   installment, 49–50, 53
   sales of practices and, 8, 76
   structure of, 30–31
Pennell, John, *Partnership Taxation,* 48
Pennsylvania State Bar Association
   Opinion 94-51 (1994), 142
   Opinion 98-55 (1998), 21
   Rule 1.17, 140
pensions, 180–182. *See also* staff
"Permitting the Sale of a Law Practice: Furthering the Interests of Both Attorneys and Their Clients" (Coy), 141
personal representatives. *See also* assisting attorneys; executors; receivers/receivership
   client confidentiality and, 86
   contacting, 124
   of deceased clients, 144, 145
   of deceased lawyers, 4, 8, 84, 94–95, 183–184
   definition of, 4–5
   responsibilities of, 9, 82–90
   sales of solo practices by, 4
Picker International, Inc. v. Varian Associates, Inc. (1987), 16
planning, for future, 8, 123–133, 148–149, 166–168, 191–197
planning attorneys, 191–197. *See also* planning, for future
Poll, Edward
   "Selling A Law Practice: Prospects and Pitfalls," 141
   Selling Your Law Practice: The Profitable Exit Strategy, 141

Postlewaite, Philip F.
   on anti-abuse provisions, 54–55
   "Lazarus Effect: A Commentary on In-Kind Guaranteed Payments, The," 45
   Partnership Taxation, 48
post offices, 83, 88–89, 186
practice areas, 5, 58–59, 104–105, 137, 154–155
practices. *See* contingent fees practices; estate practices; large law firms; niche practices; practice areas; solo practices
preparedness of lawyers, 8, 123–133, 148–149, 166–168, 191–197
present value analysis, 29. *See also* valuations
price, sales. *See* valuations
process service company, 125
professional associations, 90, 98–99, 187. *See also* bar associations
professional goodwill, 27, 29. *See also* goodwill; institutional goodwill
professional liability insurance, 76, 77, 99–100, 115–122
professionals, engaging, 71, 72–73, 76
profit margins, adjusted, 36. *See also* valuations
property, safekeeping, 97–98, 109, 111, 143–144, 146, 164
prospectus, 74–75
protecting client interests, 147–149, 158, 166–168
purchasers. *See also* sales of niche practices; sales of solo practices; sellers
   assisting attorneys as, 195
   client confidentiality and, 138–139n7
   competence of, 13, 15, 105, 137, 155
   (See also Model Rules of Professional Conduct, Rule 1.1, *Competence)*
   conflicts of interest and, 6–7, 13, 15–16, 139
   of deceased lawyers' practices, 21–23
   increasing fees, 13–14, 105, 155, 160, 161
   of niche practices, 70–71, 74–76
   rules on, 4

receivables, unrealized, 43, 51, 200
receivers/receivership, 22–23, 86, 168n9, 172. *See also* Model Rules of Professional Conduct, Rule 28, *Appointment of Counsel to Protect Clients' Interest When Respondent Is Transferred to Disability Inactive Status, Suspended, Disbarred, Disappears, or Dies* (1989); personal representatives

"Records Retention in the Private Legal Environment: Annotated Bibliography and Program Implementation Tools" (Nemchek), 143n10
recourse loans, 52
referral contacts, 31, 199
relocating solo practices, 183
Report 8(a), 157–161
Report to Legal Management (Altman Weil, Inc.), 58
retention of files. *See* files; retention period, minimum
retention period, minimum, 183
retirement. *See also* retiring partners
   benefits, 180–182
   meaning of, 3–4
   tail insurance and, 115–122
   tax consequences of, 41–42, 48
retiring partners. *See also* partnerships; retirement
   client files and, 144
   installment payments and, 49–50, 53
   noncompete covenants and, 48–49
   passive activity losses and, 51–52, 51n61
   sales options for, 43–45, 52–54
   self-employment taxes and, 48
   sole practitioners *vs.*, 136–137, 159, 161
revenues, past, 8, 30, 36
Rhode Island State Bar Association, Opinion 94-77 (1994), 20
Rikli, Donald, 2–3
risk factors, 65
Rosenzweig, Adam H., 54–55
Rothenberg, Alan I., 160
Rotunda, Ronald D., *Legal Ethics: The Lawyer's Deskbook on Professional Responsibility,* "Sale of a Law Practice," 141
Rules of Professional Conduct. *See* Model Rules of Professional Conduct

safe deposit boxes, 97, 128, 181
safeguarding client interests, 147–149, 158, 166–168
safekeeping property, 97–98, 109, 111, 143–144, 146, 164
"Sale of a Legal Practice in North Carolina: Goodwill and Discrimination Against the Sole Practitioner, The" (Crawford), 141
sales of niche practices
   checklist for, 78–79
   due diligence, 76
   engaging professionals for, 71, 72–73, 76
   ethics and, 75, 77

sales of niche practices, *continued*
   length of time for, 72
   noncompete covenants for, 72, 76
   reasons for, 71–72
   summary of key points on, 69
   uniqueness of, 70
   valuations and, 73, 74–76
sales of partnership shares, 43. *See also* distributive shares; partnerships
sales of solo practices. *See also* Model Rules of Professional Conduct, Rule 1.17, *Sale of a Law Practice;* purchasers; sales of niche practices; sellers
   ABA on, 2, 27–28
   to assisting attorneys, 195
   client confidentiality and, 2, 3, 6–7, 105, 138–139n7, 155, 161
   client notifications and, 6–7, 75, 105, 138–139, 155, 160–161
   competence and, 13, 15, 105, 137, 155
   death of lawyers and, 94–95, 193 (*See also* closing practices)
   due diligence, 31, 34, 105, 155
   ethics and, 13–16, 136–141
   fees charged after, 13–14, 105, 155, 160, 161
   geographic considerations for, 104, 154
   history of, 1–3, 157–160
   hypothetical scenarios of, 12
   jurisdictional differences on, 3, 13, 77, 136, 136n3, 140
   licensing and, 4
   malpractice communications and, 9–10
   mergers *vs.*, 138n7
   names of practices and, 14
   payment plans and, 8, 76
   summary of key points on, 1
sanctions, for lack of preparedness, 148–149, 167–168
Sarbanes-Oxley Act, 58
scale mergers, 58, 62, 63
Schoenwald, Scott, "Model Rule 1.17 and the Ethical Sale of Law Practices: A Critical Analysis," 141
scope mergers, 58, 62–63, 66
screening, 18–19. *See also* conflicts of interest; withdrawals from client representation
secretaries, 123, 180, 185. *See also* staff
secrets, 6. *See also* client confidentiality
Sections of IRC. *See* Internal Revenue Code (IRC), *specific Sections*
self-employment taxes, 48. *See also* taxes
sellers. *See also* sales of niche practices; sales of solo practices
   categories of, 3–4
   client confidentiality and, 138–139n7

   due diligence and, 34, 76, 105, 137, 155
   of niche practices, 70–71, 74–75
"Selling A Law Practice: Prospects and Pitfalls" (Poll), 141
Selling Your Law Practice: The Profitable Exit Strategy (Poll), 141
service contracts, 83, 98, 113. *See also* maintenance contracts; office equipment
service firms, 28–29, 44
settling accounts, 83, 96, 181, 194. *See also* bank accounts; law offices, expenses of; trust accounts
Shapiro, William A., 183–184
shareholders, 28, 43. *See also* corporations; distributive shares; partnerships
Shaw, Betty, "Winding Down, Closing Up or Selling Out," 141
shredding confidential information, 85, 87, 175–176. *See also* destruction of files
software, maintaining obsolete, 146, 175. *See also* computers
sole practitioners *vs.* retiring partners, 136–137, 159, 161. *See also* solo practices
solo practices
   closing (*See* closing practices)
   relocations of, 183
   sales of (*See* sales of solo practices)
   valuations of, 7–8, 25, 26–27, 32–34
South Carolina State Bar Association
   Opinion 00-13 (2000), 21
   Opinion 03-06 (2003), 140
   Opinion 92-23 (1992), 21
spouses, 4–5, 123. *See also* personal representatives
staff, 123–124
   closing practices and, 83, 90–91, 99, 179, 180–182, 185
   confidentiality and, 9
   sales of practices and, 74
state bar opinions, 20–21, 135n1, 139–141, 143. *See also specific state bar opinions*
states, 3, 8, 14, 18–19, 49n43, 87. *See also* jurisdictions; state bar opinions; *specific states*
storage locker locations, 128. *See also* files, disposition of
subscriptions, canceling, 90
succession, continuing, 14, 140–141
success of mergers, 58. *See also* mergers, law firm
successor lawyers/firms, 89, 142, 144, 172, 174, 185
summaries of key points
   closing practices, 81–82, 93–94, 186–187

ending client/staff relationships, 179
ethics, 11, 136
file management, 171
law firm mergers, 57
sales of practices, 1, 69
tax consequences of retirement, 41–42
valuations of practices, 25
Survey of Law Firm Economics (Altman Weil, Inc.), 59
suspended lawyers, 140–141. *See also* Model Rules of Professional Conduct, Rule 28, *Appointment of Counsel to Protect Clients' Interest When Respondent Is Transferred to Disability Inactive Status, Suspended, Disbarred, Disappears, or Dies* (1989)

tail insurance, 31, 83, 99–100, 115–122, 186
tangible property, 5, 26, 88, 186
Tax Equity and Fiscal Responsibility Act (TEFRA), 46
taxes
 closing practices and, 83, 84
 filing returns, 181 (*See also* settling accounts)
 retirement and, 41–42, 48 (*See also* Internal Revenue Code (IRC), Section 736)
Teleflex, Inc.; James v. (1999), 17–18
temporary attorneys. *See* assumption/temporary attorneys
Tennessee Supreme Court, on disqualification of counsel, 17
terminal illness, 148–149, 167n4
term sheets, 65
time, length of
 for closing practices, 183 (*See also* planning, for future)
 for sale of niche practices, 72
total compensation, 31. *See also* compensation
transactions
 open, 50, 53
 past, 32
transfer rules, 5, 8–9. *See also* sales of solo practices
transfers. *See also* valuations
 external, 31–34
 internal, 28, 32
treatises, 141
trust, client, 26–27. *See also* goodwill
trust accounts, 88, 97, 109, 111, 130, 176, 192, 200
unlocatable clients, 87–88, 95, 105, 139, 145–147, 155, 174. *See also* nonresponsive clients

unrealized receivables, 43, 51, 94
US Xpress Enterprises, Inc.; Cavender v. (2002), 16

valuations
 of businesses, 26, 31–32
 checklists, 35, 37–40
 of client access and trust, 26–27
 of contingent fee practices, 31
 of external transfers, 31–34
 of goodwill, 26–27, 44, 47, 51, 159
 identifying assets in, 25–27
 multipliers for, 8, 28–31, 36
 of niche practices, 73, 74–76
 of partner/shareholder interests, 28
 of solo practices, 7–8, 25, 26–27, 32–34
 summary of key points on, 25
Varian Associates, Inc.; Picker International, Inc. v. (1987), 16
vendors, notification of closures, 83, 86, 88–89, 98–99, 123–133. *See also* leases; post offices; professional associations
Ventura, John, *Law for Dummies*, 77
Virginia State Bar Association, Opinion 1818 (2005), 146
voicemails, 89
Vollgraff v. Block, 167n3

Washington State Bar Association, on noncompete covenants, 49
"What Should Be Your Concerns? Purchase or Sale of a Solo Practice" (Dimitriou), 141
"When a Solo Takes Down the Shingle" (DeWoskin), 141
"Why Attorneys Need Tail Insurance" (Hutchins), 115–122
Whitmire, Robert L., *Federal Taxation of Partnerships and Partners*, 47
Willis, Arthur, *Partnership Taxation*, 48
wills
 access to, 125
 executors' responsibilities/authorities, 8
 retaining original, 97, 145–146, 183, 185–186
"Winding Down, Closing Up or Selling Out" (Shaw), 141
Wisconsin State Bar Association
 Opinion E-00-03 (2003), 147
 Opinion E-98-01 (1998), 145
withdrawals from client representation, 16–18, 20, 142. *See also* conflicts of interest

"STO's Practice" Notes

- Start trimming clients now — to save time later if you or pchsr or svr
- Build in a consulting aspect —
  - Write/edit Newsletter
  - Mkt/entertain clients
  - Develop 1 month mktg plan
- Audit Trust Account
- Engagement Memo to define what part of retainer is earned when
- Deal w/ Closed Files starting now
- Seeking Able, Affable, Ambitious lawyer for Association with a view towards eventual merger or sale of e.p. practice
- Ellie's retirement — & ed he helping me sell or wind down my practice
- Value & Nett worth & quality index for ea client
- Put note re succession plan into Engagement memo
- Take R Ho + Larry Benen to lunch + brainstorm

Consider becoming an in-house consultant / writer for an acctg firm or Tr. Co.
Use Cliff! Dare. Use a consultant?

Become a Practice Sale Consultant!
- Dictate office manual
- Xfer Floppies to Hard Driver
- Sell MA practice : wind down AE practice!
- Ask my key referral sources if there is a lawyer they or wd recommend for pchse of practice
- Assess cost of phasing out vs cost of just terminating (selling)
    - NC
    - Establish
    - etc etc etc